Firefox
and Thunderbird
Beyond Browsing and Email

PETER D. HIPSON

800 East 96th Street
Indianapolis, Indiana 46240

Firefox and Thunderbird: Beyond Browsing and Email

International Standard Book Number: 0-7897-3458-3

Library of Congress Catalog Card Number: 2005929932

Printed in the United States of America

First Printing: November 2005

08   07   06   05   4   3   2   1

Trademarks

All terms mentioned in this book that are known to be trademarks or service marks have been appropriately capitalized. Que Publishing cannot attest to the accuracy of this information. Use of a term in this book should not be regarded as affecting the validity of any trademark or service mark.

Warning and Disclaimer

Every effort has been made to make this book as complete and as accurate as possible, but no warranty or fitness is implied. The information provided is on an "as is" basis. The author and the publisher shall have neither liability nor responsibility to any person or entity with respect to any loss or damages arising from the information contained in this book.

Bulk Sales

Que Publishing offers excellent discounts on this book when ordered in quantity for bulk purchases or special sales. For more information, please contact

U.S. Corporate and Government Sales
1-800-382-3419
corpsales@pearsontechgroup.com

For sales outside the United States, please contact

International Sales
international@pearsoned.com

ASSOCIATE PUBLISHER
Greg Wiegand

ACQUISITIONS EDITOR
Todd Green

DEVELOPMENT EDITOR
Mark Cierzniak

MANAGING EDITOR
Charlotte Clapp

PROJECT EDITOR
Tonya Simpson

PRODUCTION EDITOR
Megan Wade

INDEXER
Aaron Black

PROOFREADER
Kyle Long

TECHNICAL EDITORS
Gunnar Jurdzik
Pearce Smithwick

PUBLISHING COORDINATOR
Sharry Lee Gregory

BOOK DESIGNER
Anne Jones

PAGE LAYOUT
Bronkella Publishing
Toi Davis

Contents at a Glance

iii

Table of Contents

About the Author

Peter D. Hipson is a teacher, author, consultant, and developer who lives and works in New Hampshire. He holds a MEng in industrial engineering and management from the Asian Institute of Technology (AIT) in Bangkok.

Peter became involved in computers in the early 1970s, when he performed work at the hardware level on mainframe computers used for inventory and management. His subsequent work with mainframes continued until the mid-1980s.

His work with microcomputers dates back to their inception in the early to mid-1970s. Achievements in the early microcomputer field include patents for development of microcomputer technology dealing with secure software techniques and advanced work in data encryption. Other work included the development of interfaces for early microcomputers allowing the then-simple computers to work with a number of devices.

His current work includes teaching undergraduate classes at Franklin Pierce College in Rindge, New Hampshire, and lecturing in the corporate environment. Other continuing work includes working as a consultant (both application development and systems administration) and writing books and articles on various microcomputer-related topics (see the following for more information on Peter's books).

One of his current projects is Safe Kids on the Internet, a program that teaches children and their parents how to use the Internet safely.

Peter developed the first PC and Windows mapping (GIS) applications. Descendants of his Windows GIS products still enjoy success in the market today, almost 15 years after initial development. Peter also developed the first non-Windows PC–based mapping program and pioneered the use of microcomputers for GIS, mapping, high-speed graphics, and geographic database techniques.

He has been a member in good standing of the Association for Computing Machinery (ACM) since 1983. He is also a member of Microsoft's Expert Zone.

When not writing or doing other work, he can be found on his Trek road bicycle riding the highways of New England and working on and playing with his Hummer. He is also a tool freak and might have more tools than anyone else.

If you have questions or comments, you can email Peter at firefox@hipson.net and he'll try to answer your questions.

Dedication

This book is dedicated to everyone at Mozilla Organization and Mozilla.org, all the people who have donated their time (and money), and to you—the Firefox and Thunderbird users.

Acknowledgments

This book was a team effort. Although my name is on the cover, this book would never have happened without the hard work of everyone on this team. A very heartfelt thanks to

Our book's acquisition editor Todd Green, whose management was invaluable. Todd always came through, seemingly working about 20 hours a day.

Mark Cierzniak, for putting up with my sometimes less-than-perfect writing. Not only did he put up with it, he also did an outstanding editing job, fixing so many things that I didn't get right the first time.

Gunnar Jurdzik and Pearce Smithwick, who made sure this book was as technically accurate as possible. Their knowledge about the products was invaluable, and it proved to be a learning experience to me as I found out things I didn't know.

Harold Davis, whose hard work served as the directing force in this book. Harold worked hard to see that the book covered the "right" mix of topics.

Matt Wagner, who looks out for me by being my agent. I owe Matt a great deal; he's the best.

Megan Wade, who did extensive editing and fixing of spelling, grammar, and other bloopers I committed.

Charlotte Clapp, who as the managing editor, kept things together.

Tonya Simpson, the project editor, who did so much to ensure that everything in the book was "right."

Aaron Black, who indexed all those words that are important.

Kyle Long, this book's proofreader, who has made sure that all the i's were dotted and the t's were crossed. And, of course, he got to find all my spelling errors, too.

Sharry Lee Gregory, who took care of the very important administrative issues.

Anne Jones, the book designer, for creating a really great-looking book.

A really big thanks to everyone at Que who helped, especially Tonya Simpson, who managed the book project. The very first book I wrote, years ago, was for Que. I feel like I've come home.

And, special thanks to Nang, my wife.

Although all these people were instrumental in making this book happen, if there is anything wrong with it, the blame is mine. All the good things belong to them!

We Want to Hear from You!

As the reader of this book, *you* are our most important critic and commentator. We value your opinion and want to know what we're doing right, what we could do better, what areas you'd like to see us publish in, and any other words of wisdom you're willing to pass our way.

As an associate publisher for Que Publishing, I welcome your comments. You can email or write me directly to let me know what you did or didn't like about this book—as well as what we can do to make our books better.

Please note that I cannot help you with technical problems related to the topic of this book. We do have a User Services group, however, where I will forward specific technical questions related to the book.

When you write, please be sure to include this book's title and author as well as your name, email address, and phone number. I will carefully review your comments and share them with the author and editors who worked on the book.

Email: feedback@quepublishing.com

Mail: Greg Wiegand
Associate Publisher
Que Publishing
800 East 96th Street
Indianapolis, IN 46240 USA

For more information about this book or another Que title, visit our website at www.quepublishing.com. Type the ISBN (excluding hyphens) or the title of a book in the Search field to find the page you're looking for.

Foreword

There was a time when the Internet was a much more enjoyable place—before all the viruses and spyware and phishing scams; before all the pop-ups and pop-unders and spam. Over the last few years, the Internet (email and the World Wide Web) has become much more capable and, no doubt, more of a necessity for all of us. Unfortunately, though, it has also become increasingly difficult and considerably more dangerous to use. It was these concerns that pushed the Firefox founders to build a new kind of web browser, one that would both protect people from the dangers of the modern Web and make all the tasks people wanted to accomplish on the Web faster and easier.

How did the Internet become so difficult and so dangerous so quickly? It's pretty simple, actually. Microsoft, having successfully cornered the web browser and email application markets, became an obvious target. And the bad guys got increasingly aggressive—first with spam and viruses that targeted Outlook and Outlook Express and then with pop-ups, pop-unders, and Internet Explorer exploits that installed all kinds of adware and spyware. The bad guys managed in just a few short years to make going online a very unpleasant experience, even for the most sophisticated users, but especially for "regular people" who just wanted to get things done on the Internet.

We designed the Firefox web browser and Thunderbird email client from the ground up with these threats in mind. With modern and always-improving security, Firefox and Thunderbird keep your computer safe from malicious adware and spyware by not loading harmful ActiveX controls in the browser and not allowing email messages to install dangerous programs. Firefox and Thunderbird protect users from Internet annoyances with a world-class pop-up blocker and intelligent and adaptive spam controls. Firefox and Thunderbird also contain a comprehensive set of privacy tools to keep your online activity your business. With an ever-vigilant community of open-source developers and security experts, Firefox and Thunderbird are continually improving on these security and privacy features to keep up with the evolving threats of today's Internet.

But Firefox and Thunderbird aren't just about taking away the pain and threats of an increasingly annoying and dangerous Internet. We built these two applications to make the things you want to do online easier. Available for Apple Macintosh, Microsoft Windows, and Linux operating systems, Firefox and Thunderbird offer simple and easy-to-use (yet very powerful) tools such as tabbed browsing, smarter find and search capabilities, and fully integrated RSS support that provide everything you need to get online and quickly get all of what you want with none of what you don't.

Thanks to the open-source community that supports Firefox and Thunderbird, and the free and open standards that form the basis of these two applications, literally hundreds of amazing extensions and plug-ins that allow you to customize Firefox and Thunderbird to exactly suit your needs are available.

We created Firefox and Thunderbird to afford users a viable and safer alternative with frequent updates directly addressing the evolution of web technology and the technology of the bad guys, as well as to give users more configuration options than those of Microsoft's Outlook and Internet Explorer. We didn't just try to fix what was broken about the Internet and those outdated browser and email applications and leave it at that. Firefox and Thunderbird are going to be around for the long haul to help ensure that the Internet continues to improve the lives of everyone and to promote choice and a better future for the Internet through a commitment to free and open standards and, most important, a strong focus and commitment to the user.

Firefox and Thunderbird: Beyond Browsing and Email will guide you through setting up Firefox and Thunderbird and provide clear and concise descriptions of all the most valuable Firefox and Thunderbird features, for both the beginner and the advanced user. It will put you back in control of your Internet experience.

—Asa Dotzler

Mozilla Community Coordinator and Cofounder of the Spread Firefox Project

September 12, 2005

Introduction

aybe you are reading this in a book store, a library, or a friend's house. Maybe this is your own copy of the book. If not, you should buy it.

Let's take a quick look at Mozilla, Firefox, and Thunderbird; the book; and what is inside for you.

The Mozilla Project

Once upon a time, a long time ago, there was an idea: "Let's connect computers together so they can share data." Shortly thereafter the first network was born.

By 1992, the number of hosts on the Internet had grown, topping one million. Just a year before this, the first web server was created. In 1993 Mosaic was created, and a year later Mosaic Communications, which would later become Netscape Communications, was born.

As the Internet became more popular, the Web (and email) became the mainstay of Internet usage. By 1995, Microsoft entered the scene with Internet Explorer, given away free with the Windows 95 Plus! pack add-on. By 1998, Netscape was losing market share, and AOL (who now owned Netscape) made what was considered by many to be a radical move: It decided to release the source code for Netscape as open source.

By 2000, Mozilla was hard at work creating and enhancing the Mozilla Suite, whose browser would eventually become Firefox. Mozilla Suite's email client was also split off to become Thunderbird.

Today, the Mozilla Organization and mozilla.org are a major force in the Internet browser and email fields. Until recently, though, Microsoft (as large companies tend to do) had ignored Mozilla, feeling that its lion's share of the browser market was safe. Today, well over 50,000,000 Internet users have taken up Firefox, making it the most viable threat to Microsoft's domination to date.

The Mozilla Suite

The Mozilla project started with Mozilla Suite, a group of programs that includes a web browser, an email and newsgroup client, an IRC chat client, and an HTML editor. The most recent release of Mozilla Suite was version 1.7.8, which was released in May 2005.

Along the way, Mozilla Suite has spawned both Firefox (the browser) and Thunderbird (the email client). Many users have found that they don't need the full suite and only want one part, or the other.

Why Firefox Now?

Why now? Why is Firefox becoming a serious contender to Microsoft's Internet Explorer?

When I first was introduced to Firefox, my thought was, "Great, another warmed-over copy of Netscape." I was happy with my browser and thought it was great. Then, slowly, things happened. Friends started to ask me, "Have you tried Firefox yet?" This was usually followed up with a comment that, once I tried it, I'd never be happy with that other browser again. I'll admit it took a lot of pushing. But when two people who never liked Netscape either suggested I try it, I knew something special was happening.

I have to be fair to everyone. Firefox is not 100% perfect. (Neither is Internet Explorer, for that matter.) It has bugs, quirks, and strange behaviors that take a bit of getting used to. But once you are started with Firefox, there is no turning back.

Will Firefox ever dominate the browser market? Truthfully, Firefox probably will not end up with 100% of the market. Internet Explorer's too entrenched, too established, and too well backed financially to fall to the wayside. But, Firefox's market share is growing at a rate that is impressive.

Today, it is estimated that there have been about 100 million downloads of Firefox. That means Firefox has more than 10% of the worldwide browser market share. As more and more people try (and accept) Firefox, the growth potential is enormous. I would not be surprised to see Firefox's share double within the next year or two. Only time will tell....

Thunderbird

Thunderbird, a very user-friendly email client program, is also gaining market share. Even a simple look shows that Thunderbird is potentially better than Outlook Express, and while there seems to be little innovation with Outlook Express, Thunderbird continues to get better everyday.

Thunderbird has not achieved the market penetration that Firefox has, which is only reasonable because it has not had the publicity Firefox has—yet. But usage of Thunderbird will grow as users of Firefox search for other great Mozilla products.

The Mozilla Open Source Community

Open Source is an idea where the source code for computer programs should be made freely available to users. Being freely available (the operative word being *free*) means products that are open source are not sold; instead they are given away.

We do, however, have to pay a price. Perhaps if we are technically competent, we might contribute to the various projects such as Firefox and Thunderbird. Or we might make a monetary contribution or help with fundraising, evangelizing, marketing, or designing icons. The Mozilla Organization does have employees who must be paid, and that funding has to come from somewhere. Think of this as a public broadcasting pledge drive: Please contribute whatever you can. It is important.

The Mozilla community is worldwide. Developers from virtually every country work on these projects. The common language is English, although some countries have organized groups with their own languages. If you are bilingual, consider working on a translation of one of the Mozilla products. Many locale-specific versions already exist, but there is always room for more.

Who Should Read This Book?

Who should read this book? Why, you should! This book is intended to help both the beginner and the more experienced Firefox and Thunderbird user. As such, you can start at the beginning of the book and work to the end, or if you are more experienced, you can jump directly into one of the later sections.

What Is in This Book?

I have arranged this book into parts and chapters. Both parts and chapters run from basic techniques to advanced topics, such as creating extensions and building Firefox or Thunderbird.

Part I, "Making Firefox Yours," is your introduction to Firefox. This part covers user-oriented topics, ranging from basic techniques, to advanced changes in Firefox's look and feel.

Chapter 1, "Hitting the Ground Running with Firefox," is an introduction to Firefox, mostly for those of us who have never used Mozilla, Firefox, or Thunderbird. This chapter takes you through downloading and installing Firefox, migrating Internet Explorer settings, and basic Firefox configuration.

Chapter 2, "The Power of Tabs and Bookmarks," tells all about tabbed browsing and bookmarks. It covers how to open tabs; close tabs; and have multiple home pages, one in each tab.

Chapter 3, "Finding Information with Firefox," details Firefox's extensive and powerful search capabilities. The Firefox Location bar and the built-in Firefox search bar are described, showing how to search for sites by name or by text contained on the site. This chapter also discusses how to store a search for later reuse and how to use bookmarks.

Chapter 4, "Managing Profiles," gives you the story on setting up and modifying a user profile. Each user can have her own profile, allowing users to have different extensions, themes, and other features (such as bookmarks).

Chapter 5, "Taking Control of Your Browser," covers the important things websites can do that affect users without their control. Firefox takes control and contains built-in tools to block pop-up ads. In addition, several important extensions are available that enhance this capability.

Part II, "Extending and Modifying Firefox," brings on more advanced Firefox techniques. It covers extensions, themes, customization, and plug-ins, as well as a number of other useful topics.

Chapter 6, "Power Firefox Tricks and Techniques," shows you how to customize Firefox to suit your own desires. You can control how Firefox looks using skins, which are called *themes* in Firefox. This chapter also covers some performance enhancements.

Chapter 7, "Themes and Plug-ins," is dedicated to themes, which control how Firefox looks to the user, and installing some of the more popular plug-ins, such as the Adobe Acrobat Reader, QuickTime, and Real Player.

Chapter 8, "Making Extensions Work for You," is an in-depth discussion of the user side of extensions. It talks about how to install an extension, some popular extensions, privacy and security issues, and search-related extensions.

Chapter 9, "Changing Preferences and Settings," shows how you can use the various built-in locations, such as about:config, about:plugins, and about:cache. These built-in locations enable you to see how Firefox is currently set up, which plug-ins are in use, what the cache status is, who helped build Firefox, and other useful information.

Part III, "Using Thunderbird," switches the focus from Firefox to Thunderbird. It starts at a basic introductory level and moves to more advanced user topics.

Chapter 10, "Hitting the Ground Running with Thunderbird," covers the basics of Thunderbird. It explains how to download, install, and configure Thunderbird for typical users. It also covers topics such as composing emails and using the spelling checker.

Chapter 11, "Organizing Email with Thunderbird," shows you how to organize, sort, filter, and otherwise process messages. You can label messages and group messages based on user-specified criteria. Also in this chapter is an introduction to the Thunderbird address book features.

Chapter 12, "Fighting Spam," discusses Thunderbird's Bayesian spam filter. Thunderbird's spam fighting technology is very advanced and is one of the best available.

Chapter 13, "Customizing Thunderbird for Power Users," covers topics such as installing themes—you can modify Thunderbird's look and feel just as you can modify Firefox's look and feel. This chapter also covers extensions and setting preferences in Thunderbird using the `about:config` extension.

Part IV, "Web Development and Firefox Extensions," covers both web development and creating Firefox extensions.

Chapter 14, "Web Development with Firefox," explains topics such as Cascading Style Sheets (which can affect the way content looks in Firefox), the JavaScript Console, and DOM (using the Document Inspector).

Chapter 15, "Creating Your Own Theme," walks you through the process of creating a simple theme for Firefox. Themes are one way you can express your personality with Firefox. Themes for Thunderbird are very similar to Firefox themes.

Chapter 16, "Writing an Extension," covers creating an extension that can be used with Firefox. Extensions are somewhat more complex than themes, but once the basics are mastered, they can be fun to write.

Part V, "The Way of Mozilla for Programmers," is a look into the inner workings of the Mozilla Organization; the tools available for supporting developers; how you build the products; and the future of Mozilla, Thunderbird, and Firefox. You can find Chapters 17–19 and the Glossary on our website at www.quepublishing.com/title/0789734583.

Chapter 17, "Mozilla's Tools for Developers," describes online tools such as Bugzilla (a bug management and tracking tool), Tinderbox (a tool giving the up-to-date status of the state of the Mozilla products), and LXR (a source code tool to search and find cross-references in the source). It also talks about Open Source and the various types of public licenses.

Chapter 18, "Browsing the Code," takes you through the process of setting up a development environment for the Mozilla products. You'll find in-depth coverage of what is needed to configure your development computer, how to get the most recent source code, and the etiquette and rules for being a contributor to the Mozilla effort.

Chapter 19, "The Future of Firefox and Thunderbird," is the final chapter. Here you will find a history of Mozilla, along with some comparisons between Firefox and Internet Explorer and a comparison between Thunderbird and the various versions of Outlook.

NOTE
A note is an idea or action that affects how things work. Information in a note would need to be considered to get the effect suggested in the book's text. Notes are necessary information, but were a note's contents ignored, nothing would be lost—you would simply not get the results you expected.

TIP
A tip is a suggestion that you will find makes using Firefox or Thunderbird easier. There is no reason to worry about a tip; they are just there to make things easier.

CAUTION
A caution is information that, if not followed, might result in incorrect operation of the product, or even loss of data. Whenever you see a caution, read and heed its advice!

From the Author

Just a few final words before starting this book: You will see many email addresses showing in the book's figures in the domain hipson.net. These addresses were created specifically for this book and were deleted when the book was finished. Don't send email to those addresses hoping to get directly to me—it won't work! Instead, you can email me at firefox@peterhipson. com (or firefox@hipson.net). I'll try to answer all emails (especially if you are nice to me). If you have suggestions about how the book could be made better, or find any mistakes, please do send them to me.

Both hipson.net and peterhipson.com are my domains. If you wish, visit them at http://www.hipson.net and http://www.peterhipson.com. All are located at my home, using an ADSL connection. The servers include five Dell PowerEdge servers, a hipson.net server, and a whole mess of workstations and notebooks. For a computer geek, it doesn't get any better than this.

We have a few conventions we are using in this book. There are notes, tips, and cautions. We've included examples of each.

Code in this book is signified using a monospaced font. Some code contains **bold**; in these you should read the text to determine what the bold means. Usually bold text is unique to a given user, so the example might need to be edited for your situation prior to being used.

MAKING FIREFOX YOURS

PART I

Hitting the Ground Running with Firefox

This chapter seems somewhat out of place with an advanced book such as this one. However, we have to start somewhere. Installing any application means that we first must have the product to install. We are going to work with several products in this book. Firefox is available from a few locations; however, I strongly recommend that you use http://www.mozilla.org/ as a starting point.

The Internet and Web have made this world of ours smaller. We, as Internet users, should try to accommodate people from various countries. Most of us speak English, but not everyone speaks it. Many other languages are spoken throughout the world.

If you want a language other than the default (English), click the hyperlink on the Mozilla site for Other Systems and Languages. This enables you to download Firefox Windows, Mac OS X, and Linux i686 versions in a number of languages. More languages are added from time to time, and if the language you are interested in is not listed, maybe you can do the translation!

> **CAUTION**
>
> Careful! Do not confuse the site www.firefox.org with Mozilla or the Firefox web browser. This site is actually the site of a web designer and is not connected with Mozilla!

> **NOTE**
>
> What should you do if the Mozilla product you are interested in does not support your language? This is where Open Source becomes valuable—you can convert (and translate) the application as needed for your language. I won't say this is easy to do, but that is how these products support languages they were not originally written for. You could see how others have done this type of translation and do yours the same way. You should use a system that enables you to transport your language modifications to newer versions of the product as they appear.

Installing Firefox

The installation of Firefox is easy. You first must download the latest version of Firefox from the Internet. Start at http://www.mozilla.org/products/firefox/ and download the product. Figure 1.1 shows the download area on the Mozilla web page. This download section has a green background. Click Free Download.

FIGURE 1.1

The Mozilla Products page for Firefox.

The download starts automatically, and you see a prompt asking whether you want to save or run the downloaded file. Select Save (saving allows you to have a copy of what is installed on your computer should you ever need to reinstall with the saved version).

> **NOTE**
> Some versions of Windows, and other operating systems, provide somewhat different prompts. Follow the prompts to save (not run) the product to a location on your hard drive.

Windows presents the Save As dialog box next. The default name is the product name (Firefox), the word Setup, and the version number:

Firefox Setup 1.5

It is best to create a folder for the Mozilla products and subfolders for each individual product. For example, in your `My Documents\My Downloads` (create it if you do not have a My Downloads folder), create a folder called Mozilla and then a subfolder called `Firefox`. With a broadband connection (DSL, cable, or T1), the download takes about 30 seconds, whereas a typical dial-up line takes about 16 minutes.

Windows

Let's do a Windows installation of both Firefox and Thunderbird. Starting with Firefox, the first step is to go to the Mozilla website. Mozilla has done a good job of designing its site, and the site can determine the operating system you're using. You can override this behavior if you want and force a download of any version for any platform of Mozilla's products. We are lucky because we can just work with Firefox's Windows release.

NOTE

To save or to open? That is the question. With downloads of executable software, Windows gives you a choice of opening or saving the file. My personal preference is to save the file in the My Downloads folder. Then if I need to reinstall it, I don't have to download the file again. Sometimes you need to fix minor glitches. When doing so, be sure you always reinstall the same version of files when making these simple fixes. (Yes, I know, you never delete or overwrite a file by mistake, but things do happen.)

MIRRORS

Mirror servers have the same content as the main server. They are kept up-to-date (usually automatically) and serve both as a backup site in case the primary site is unreachable and as a method of sharing the load.

When you connect to ftp.mozilla.org, a primary mirror is automatically selected for you. A *secondary* mirror is a site you can manually select if you experience connection or speed problems with your download.

Even though we think of the Internet as being without physical space, the Mozilla servers are located in California and nine other states. If you are located some distance from these servers, this can impact the performance of the download. Additionally, the main mirrors are often much busier than the secondary mirror servers. This can be especially problematic if you are located outside the United States.

To find, and use, a secondary mirror, go to http://www.mozilla.org/mirrors.html, find the mirror location nearest to your location, and try that mirror (just click the link below the description of the mirror location).

Under Windows, Firefox's installation program is a self-extracting compressed file. You will see some notifications about uncompressing the files; these notifications are closed when the process is complete. Once uncompressed, the installation program runs.

The first of a number of dialog boxes (windows) displayed by the Firefox setup is the welcome screen (see Figure 1.2). This screen provides information as to which version of Firefox you are installing and a suggestion that you close other Windows applications that are running. After closing any unnecessary applications, click the Next button.

DON'T CLOSE EVERYTHING

When an installation recommends closing any unnecessary running applications, this is a reference to those programs that you explicitly opened prior to beginning to install the new software. These are programs that show up on the Windows taskbar.

You should not close or shut down programs such as your antivirus, firewall, or similar programs. (These are not normally found on your taskbar.) Just close programs such as the word processor, spreadsheets, email, and browser programs.

FOR A REALLY CLEAN REINSTALLATION

If you have an earlier version of Firefox installed, it is strongly recommended that you uninstall the installed extensions and themes and any earlier version of Firefox. First, start Firefox and remove any extensions or themes you have installed. If you have not installed extensions or themes, you can skip this step.

Then open the Control Panel and select Add or Remove Programs to uninstall Firefox.

The second window shows the Firefox license agreement. You must accept this agreement to be able to install Firefox. If you decide you cannot accept this agreement, your only option is to end the installation. (You probably would not be reading this book if you didn't already realize that you would have to accept a license agreement.) Check the I Accept option button, and click Next.

FIGURE 1.2

Mozilla Firefox Setup Welcome screen—note the version number for your installation.

SPYWARE AND ADWARE

Some software installs spyware or adware at the same time the application is installed. They usually bury an acceptance of this software somewhere deep inside the license agreement. If you complain, they point to the license agreement and say that you agreed to it.

Mozilla does not install anything such as spyware or adware. In fact, it only installs what you think you are installing—Firefox. Don't take this to be a recommendation that you not read the license agreement, though; it is always important to read a contract before agreeing to it!

There are two setup types for Firefox (see Figure 1.3). The default, Standard, installs Firefox with the most common options selected. As an advanced user, select Custom instead of Standard; then click Next.

Most Windows applications install in the Program Files folder. Firefox is no exception to this rule and by default installs in the folder `\Program Files\Mozilla Firefox` (see Figure 1.4). This folder is automatically created if it does not already exist.

INSTALLING IN THE DEFAULT LOCATION

There are good reasons to install Firefox in the default location. This scheme that Windows uses for programs (the Program Files folder) enables you to quickly find a program you have installed. Additionally, if you used another location, you would have to remember that it is the active Firefox folder.

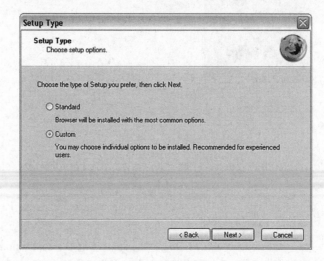

FIGURE 1.3

As an advanced user, you can do a custom installation that enables you to specify developer support.

Because you selected Custom options (refer to Figure 1.3), the Firefox installation program displays the Select Components dialog box (see Figure 1.5). There are (at this time) three options:

- **Developer Tools**—Select Developer Tools to modify Firefox. If you do not need these tools, they will be unobtrusive.

- **Website reporter**—You can report broken websites with Firefox 1.5's broken website reporter feature.

- **Quality Feedback Agent**—This option is more for Mozilla than for you. Mozilla uses this feature to get feedback about usage and performance whenever Firefox crashes. The information returned is anonymous and cannot be linked to a user, and the Quality Feedback Agent asks permission before sending anything to Mozilla.

FIGURE 1.4

It is recommended that you keep the default installation location.

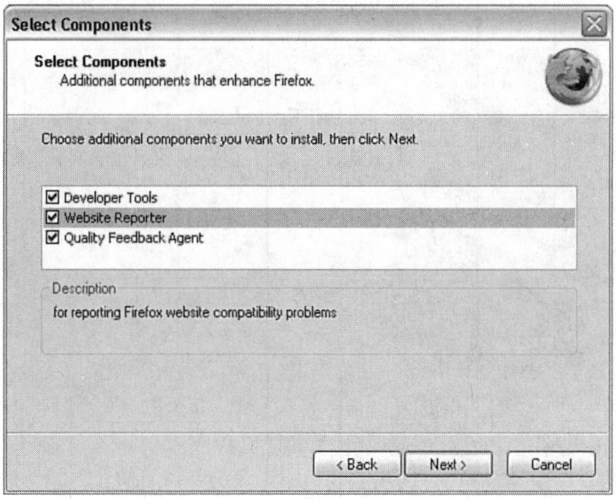

FIGURE 1.5

Custom options are important, so be sure Developer Tools and Website Reporter are selected. The Quality Feedback Agent won't hurt if it is installed. Other options or components might be added to Firefox as the product develops. If this is the case, simply use your best judgment as to whether to install them.

When Firefox installs, it offers to create shortcuts on the desktop, Start menu, and Quick Launch bar (usually at the left end of the taskbar). Unlike Mozilla Suite or Netscape 7.x, there is no Quick Start (Turbo Launch) for Firefox.

At this stage, Firefox is ready to install (yes, all the previous work was just in preparation for the actual install). The dialog box shows which options, components, and locations you have selected. Click Next to begin the actual installation.

When the installation has completed, Firefox's installation program displays options in a window similar to Figure 1.6.

It won't hurt to use Mozilla's web page for Firefox as your home page (the alternative is the Firefox Google search page). Later, you can change it to a different location. The other option, Launch Mozilla Firefox Now, starts Firefox when the installation program exits. By choosing to launch Firefox you take care of the final configuration of Firefox.

Whenever you click a web hyperlink, the default browser is launched. Your default browser is most likely Internet Explorer, which is not what we want. Fortunately, when you launch Firefox, the browser displays a dialog box that enables you to specify that Firefox will be the default browser. Click Yes in this box and check the Always Perform This Check When Starting Firefox box (see Figure 1.7). If Internet Explorer ever changes your default browser, Firefox prompts you to change it back to Firefox.

FIGURE 1.6

You should launch Firefox when the installation completes.

FIGURE 1.7

The message box and the option to make Firefox the default browser: Click Yes.

After you get past the default browser check, Firefox is up and running. If Firefox fails to run, your user profile might have become corrupted. Start Firefox by clicking the Start button, selecting Run, and typing the command **Firefox -profilemanager**. Then try creating a new profile. (Any extensions and themes you have installed will have to be reinstalled if you create a new profile.)

Firefox also might ask whether you want to import settings from Internet Explorer. Generally this is a good idea because it reduces the time needed to set up Firefox the way you like it. If Firefox does not prompt you to import settings, after it starts, click Files, Import from Firefox's main menu.

You should download the file from Mozilla again and try reinstalling Firefox. If this fails a second time, consider the possibility that your Windows installation has been damaged in some way. (This is rare, but it is possible that some other program has changed something in the Windows configuration, causing Firefox to fail.)

Linux

First, there are a number of versions of Linux. They are generally standardized, but you will find differences between the various versions. I currently use a version of Linux from Novell that is also known as SUSE Linux. (SUSE was acquired by Novell a few years ago.)

> **NOTE**
> Suse, SuSE, SuSe, SUSE, and other permutations of the name are common. They are all the same product.

What you see after installing Linux depends on which user interface you choose at setup/installation time. Other versions of Linux offer other user interfaces (virtually all are based on the same basic concepts and code but are customized or enhanced by the publisher).

Throughout this book, I will be using Novell SUSE Linux. If your version of Linux is from another source, you will probably see some slight differences between my screen shots and what your screen looks like. But don't worry—you're smart, you'll figure it out.

First, go to the Mozilla home page (see Figure 1.8). Mozilla.org is smart enough to check which operating system you are using and adjust accordingly. If, for some reason, you don't get the Linux version of the Mozilla home page, you can still navigate to an acceptable download page by clicking Other Systems and Languages located at the bottom of the green Free Download part of Mozilla's home page. (There are many routes to the Firefox main download page with all versions and languages.) Download Firefox for Linux.

FIGURE 1.8

Mozilla's home page shows the default download for Linux.

WHICH CAME FIRST—THE CHICKEN OR THE EGG?

You have to have a web browser to download a web browser—or at least some way to transfer files. With Novell Linux, Firefox is installed by default, so you do have a web browser. Perhaps with other versions of Linux you won't have a usable browser (if such a thing is possible!).

There is a fix: You can use FTP to download your browser. In fact, you can download everything you could want, including source. To use FTP to download the software, start at ftp.mozilla.org/pub/mozilla.org/firefox/releases. From there, you can navigate to the folder with the most recent version of Firefox (historical copies of earlier versions of Firefox are here as well). A little common sense tells us that the file is in the folder linux-i686. Also located here is the source for Firefox. At 31MB in size, this is a download you should undertake only if you have a fast Internet connection. With a T1 connection, the source downloads in about 5 minutes, whereas a 56K modem connection running at full speed takes several hours.

If, for some reason, you can't download Firefox, the final alternative is to order a CD version of the program. However, this is not free: The CD costs $6.95, and a CD and guidebook together cost $13.95. Figuring in the cost of shipping (about $5) brings the total to about $20 for U.S. residents (international shipping costs a bit more). However, you will be helping to supporting Mozilla....

Continuing with the web-based download, you must next select the file you want. A window pops up and asks whether you want to open the file or save it (see Figure 1.9). As always, I suggest that you save the file to your download folder (or whatever folder you want).

FIGURE 1.9

When downloading, it is best to save to disk rather than opening the file.

The download manager shows the progress of the download (see Figure 1.10). The download manager also lists other recently downloaded files if the Clean Up button has not been recently clicked.

When the download completes, your My Downloads folder opens. Most file compressions are done using GZip. The file-roller utility is used to open and then decompress your Firefox file. This utility looks similar to that shown in Figure 1.11.

Simply click Extract and file-roller displays the Extract window. You'll extract all the files (see All Files in the lower left of Figure 1.12) and choose to re-create folders (to the right of Files). This ensures that the folder structure remains intact. When you're happy with the options and the location to which you are extracting, click the Extract button.

TIP

file-roller enables you to create a container folder to hold the files you extract. Name and place this folder so that you will be able to find it at a later time. I place application installation programs and folders as subfolders in my bin folder. You can choose another location, although I recommend you be consistent about your choices.

After file-roller completes its job, the folder you extracted to is opened. It should contain a subfolder named `firefox-installer`. Open the `firefox-installer` folder and you'll see eight items, including an executable (see the icon in Figure 1.13).

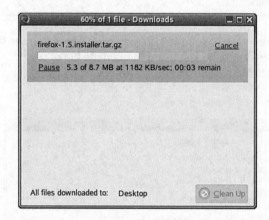

FIGURE 1.10

With a high-speed Internet connection, download progresses quickly.

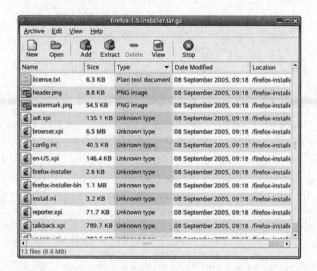

FIGURE 1.11

Using file-roller enables you to open the compressed file and decompress the contents while restoring the original file and folder structure.

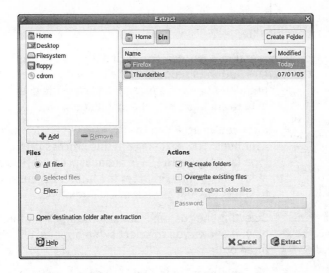

FIGURE 1.12

Extracting to a new location enables you to continue with the Firefox installation.

FIGURE 1.13

Run the firefox-installer program in the top row, the third icon on the right in this example.

Installing Firefox is as simple as running the firefox-installer program! The installer begins and presents a welcome screen. This screen is relatively standardized for each platform on which Firefox is installable. The only important thing to do is to confirm that the installer will install the correct version of Firefox. The version is shown in the line directly below the title.

When you are sure the version is correct (that is, it matches the version that was downloaded), click the Forward button to proceed to the next step in the installation. Many of today's programs present a license the user must accept to be able to continue with the installation.

> **CAUTION**
>
> I strongly recommend reading all license agreements presented by programs you are installing, and be sure to abide by the terms of the license agreement. Even though it is unlikely that any software maker would sue a single user for violating the license agreement, it has happened several times that I know of! Accepting the license is a contract, and once you click Accept (or otherwise indicate your acceptance of the license), you are bound by that license.

After you've accepted the license, the Firefox installation program continues. The next stage in this process is to choose the setup type (see Figure 1.14). We are advanced users and will be doing many things with Firefox in the future. Because of this, it is best to select Custom as your installation type.

Selecting the custom installation causes another window to display; it allows you to select setup options. With Firefox there are three options:

- **Developer Tools**—this option is important to anyone who will be doing development on Firefox. This is the case for us, so we make sure that this option is selected.

- **Website reporter**—When you find a website that doesn't display or work correctly in Firefox, you can automatically generate a report that will be sent to Mozilla with information about that website.

- **Quality Feedback Agent**—this installs an add-on component that is able to give Mozilla information about how Firefox is running. This feedback is anonymous, and I recommend selecting it. This will allow Mozilla to improve Firefox and fix problems that users find.

Again, after you have set the options, just click Forward (see Figure 1.15).

After you have selected your options and moved forward, the final installation occurs. The default (and unchangeable) location to install Firefox is the same folder from which you launched the Firefox installation program. (Now you see why I put it in the Bin folder.) Confirm that your options are correct and make a mental note of where Firefox is being installed; then click the Install button.

After the installation is complete, the installer checks to see whether the newly installed version of Firefox is the default browser. Generally it is not (although an earlier version of Firefox might be the default browser). A default browser message box displays, allowing you to set Firefox as the default browser. Another option in this message box allows you to have this test performed each time Firefox starts. Unless you will not be using this browser installation, select Yes. (You might not want this because you might be installing to do a few temporary tests of some feature or change you have made.)

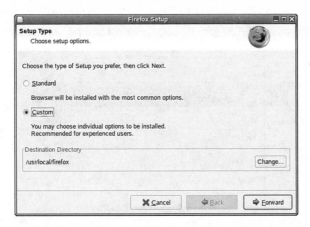

FIGURE 1.14

Select the custom installation option.

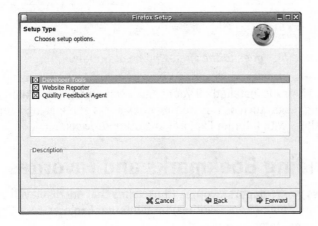

FIGURE 1.15

Select (turn on) Developer Tools, Website Reporter, and Quality Feedback Agent when you install Firefox.

Finally, Firefox starts, taking you to Firefox Google, the default start page (see Figure 1.16). Of course you can change the default page if you would like.

FIGURE 1.16

Firefox is running, and first goes to the Firefox home at Google.

At this time, Firefox is installed on your Linux computer. It's now time to do a final few housekeeping tasks, such as transferring bookmarks and making Firefox work well (as well as possible) with Internet Explorer and other browsers.

Understanding Bookmarks and Favorites

Firefox allows you to import favorites (those sites that are displayed when you click the Internet Explorer menu item Favorites) from Internet Explorer. Let's first look at how Internet Explorer stores your favorites.

Internet Explorer's Favorites

Windows has the capability to store more than files and folders on the disk. One non-conventional object stored in a folder is a link (which Windows usually calls a *shortcut*). Windows has a location named My Documents where the user's personal documents and information are stored.

A link is one of the following:

- **A pointer to a file or folder**—The link might have its own icon, or it might be customized. Changes you can make include changing the target executable or location, changing the icon, setting some relatively unimportant (in the context of this book) advanced options, and enabling security and compatibility.

> **NOTE** Internet Explorer calls them *favorites*, but Firefox calls them *bookmarks*. Regardless of the name, and how they are stored or saved, they are the method by which you open web pages without typing the entire URL.

- **A web URL**—Web URLs are stored or saved as shortcuts or link objects. A URL shortcut allows modification of the actual URL and the displayed icon. As with file or folder shortcuts, security is also available as an option in the Properties window.

- **A special shortcut**—There are some special shortcuts that exist. Basically, they take a program's globally unique ID (GUID) as their target name. Windows then looks up the GUID in the Registry and launches the correct application. By default, some of the shortcuts on the Start menu (such as Control Panel) are of this type.

Also, an important part of Windows XP's multiuser capabilities is a folder in the root of the C: drive, called Documents and Settings. Contained in the Documents and Settings folder are subfolders for each user and two special folders:

- **All Users**—This folder contains items that are common to all logged-on users. When an application is installed that is going to be available to all users, it places a shortcut to its executable in the All Users folder's Start menu. In fact, All Users contains most of the folders that all other users have, and Windows simply merges (so to speak—they don't actually mix) your folder in Documents and Settings and the All Users folder.

- **Default User**—This folder contains data for any users who are not logged on. (If this seems impossible, remember that it is technically possible to use Windows without logging on.) Most installations of Windows have relatively empty Default User folders.

Each user's files and personal "stuff" is contained in her folder that is contained in the Documents and Settings folder. Say the current user has the user ID Smith. Her files are therefore in Documents and Settings\Smith. Smith's folder contains a number of subfolders, some that are visible and some that are hidden. The visible subfolders include (but are not limited to) My Documents (although it might be called Smiths Documents), Desktop, Start Menu, and Favorites.

The Favorites subfolder is used by Internet Explorer (and perhaps other programs that use favorites) to hold the user's favorite locations. (Firefox uses bookmarks for the same purpose.) The Favorites folder contains shortcut URLs that are used in Internet Explorer's Favorites feature. The shortcuts and subfolders in Favorites are easily backed up and copied to other users.

TIP The Application Data folder is a hidden folder. To see this file in Windows Explorer, you need to turn on the display of hidden files. To turn on viewing of hidden folders and files, select Tools, Folder Options in Windows Explorer; then click the View tab and, under Advanced Settings, click Show Hidden Files and Folders.

TIP With Internet Explorer, you can back up favorites with any backup tool, copying the backup to a disk (or CD-R) or some other safe location. In Firefox you back up your bookmarks by starting Firefox's Manage Bookmarks; then in the Bookmarks Manager, select File, Export. Firefox then writes a copy of bookmarks.html to the location you specify.

Firefox's Bookmarks

Firefox is very different from Internet Explorer. Firefox has its own way of doing things, and that includes bookmarks. Firefox's bookmarks do store the same type of information as Internet Explorer's favorites, however.

Why doesn't Firefox use URL shortcuts? Because Firefox is a multiple-platform program that runs on different hardware and operating systems. Not all operating systems allow for Windows's URL shortcuts.

Firefox stores your bookmarks in an HTML page, and this web page is stored in your Documents and Settings subfolder:

C:Documents and Settings*UserID*\Application Data\\Mozilla\Firefox\Profiles*identifier*\bookmarks.html

In the previous location, *UserID* and *identifier* are unique to the user. *UserID* is the logon name for that user (see the previous for how Documents and Settings is set up). *identifier* is a unique name, consisting of two parts—the first part is a set of random numbers and letters followed by a dot and the word *default*. For example, on one of my computers this location is 08ka9s3i.default. Those eight random characters are one of the ways that Firefox keeps your user profiles secure.

You can open the bookmarks.html file that is in your profile using any compatible editor. But I don't advise this! Leave this file alone, at least until you are more experienced. Instead, let Firefox maintain this file.

Transferring Internet Explorer's Favorites to Firefox

There are two paths to importing Internet Explorer's bookmarks into Firefox.

The first method is to select File, Import from Firefox's menu. This starts the Import Wizard; you then need only follow its prompts. By default, the Import Wizard imports everything it can from Internet Explorer. If you want to import only Internet Explorer's favorites into Firefox's bookmarks, uncheck the other items.

The second way to import Internet Explorer favorites is to follow the steps in the following section, "Synchronizing with Internet Explorer." Mozilla Suite/Netscape 7.x users can use the following technique to import data into their bookmarks:

1. In Firefox, select Manage Bookmarks under Bookmarks in Firefox's menu. This displays the Bookmarks Manager window Figure 1.17.

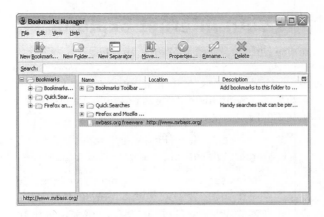

FIGURE 1.17

The full-featured Bookmarks Manager uses multiple panes to show bookmark information.

2. In the Bookmarks Manager, select File, Import. This displays the Import Wizard window (see Figure 1.18).

FIGURE 1.18

The Import Wizard lets you choose where to import data from.

3. After selecting Microsoft Internet Explorer, click Next. The Import Wizard looks in the location for the current user's Internet Explorer favorites and imports them. When importing from Internet Explorer, a new bookmark folder is created with the name `From Internet Explorer`. When the import has completed, click Finish and the import is done. Inspect the imported favorites in Bookmark Manager to ensure that all the desired objects have been imported.

27

Synchronizing with Internet Explorer

You can synchronize with Internet Explorer at any time. You might do this because you are using both browsers, or perhaps you want to import more than just Internet Explorer's favorites. Firefox allows importing options, cookies, history, and passwords as well. (Notice, I'm not saying the reverse is possible—there is no way to import these items back into Internet Explorer!)

> **NOTE**
> Firefox imported from Internet Explorer, Netscape, Mozilla, and Opera at the time this book was written, but additional import support will be added in future releases. Not all the choices are available on all platforms.

In Firefox, select File, Import from the menu. This launches the Import Wizard, which guides you through the import process.

Firefox supports importing only from installed browsers. If you are trying to import from a browser that is not installed on your computer, you might be out of luck. (If your browser is not supported, there is nothing preventing you from writing your own Import Wizard to import from a different browser.)

The first window of the Import Wizard specifies from where you are importing. For Internet Explorer users, the choice is Internet Explorer, which is selected by default. Click Next.

Import Wizard displays a second window, allowing you to specify what you want to import (see Figure 1.19).

FIGURE 1.19

The Import Wizard imports more than bookmarks; any combination can be chosen.

You can select, or not select, each of these options. This enables you to synchronize with certain aspects of another browser and to not synchronize with others. (Items in the Import list in Figure 1.19 can vary from browser to browser and platform to platform.)

SECURITY ALERT!

Firefox can import passwords from Internet Explorer; therefore, it knows the location and format of Internet Explorer's saved password cache.

Because Firefox source is available to one and all, someone could write a program or routine capable of reading Internet Explorer's saved passwords.

Panicked yet? Actually, you should have panicked a long time ago because browser-stored passwords have never been secure! There are many freely available password browsers, dumpers, and utilities on the Internet. The only browser that is password-secure by default is Opera, and it can be compromised easily enough. *Never* use the save password feature on a public accessible computer or on a notebook because it can be stolen, and never use that feature on any computer you don't have full-time control of!

What to do, then? First, in Internet Explorer (or any other browser that has saved passwords), clear your saved password cache. Then turn off password saving. The website http://www.americanfunds.com/help/auto-complete.htm has an excellent discussion of disabling and clearing password caching.

Another option is to use Firefox's master password. This option forces Firefox to encrypt the saved passwords, thus increasing their security.

After you have selected those items to import, click Next. The Import Wizard displays the Import Complete window (see Figure 1.20). Review the list of successful imports, and then click Finish.

FIGURE 1.20

The Import Manager shows what was successfully imported.

Making Firefox the Default Browser

During installation you can tell Firefox to check whether it is the default browser and, if it is not, to set itself as the default browser. What you don't see is that Firefox and Internet Explorer can duel over who is the default browser!

This happens whenever you check Always Perform This Check When Starting Firefox in Firefox and select Tools, Internet Options, Internet Explorer Should Check to See Whether It Is the Default Browser in Internet Explorer.

With both selected, whenever the nondefault browser starts, it checks and prompts you to change the default to itself. Because both Internet Explorer and Firefox are checking, they can switch back and forth between both.

Is this good? Sometimes it is—for example, if one browser isn't working properly, you might need to rely on the other to surf the Web until you fix the broken one. However, I find that unchecking the option in both browsers, or at least in Internet Explorer, is best. (No matter which browser is set as the default, the other can still be used.)

Installation and Configuration Secrets for Power Users

- A smart user backs up her profile. This can be done by simply copying the profile or, even better, using the MozBackup program.

- Keeping a copy of the installation package on your computer makes reinstalling Firefox much easier.

- There is no reason not to be able to use both Firefox and Internet Explorer together. Even though only one can be the default browser, the other is still usable.

- All your personal settings are stored in the Firefox profile. If the profile becomes corrupted, it can cause Firefox to fail to run.

- The Firefox Profile Manager enables you to create new profiles.

- Under Windows XP and Windows 2000, each user has her own profile. This allows customization of Firefox on shared computers. Firefox always loads the correct profile for the user.

The Power of Tabs and Bookmarks

Firefox opens the door to some very useful functionality. Tabs allow multiple documents (web pages, for example) in a single Firefox session. Using these tabs is much faster than trying to switch between multiple browser sessions.

Bookmarks enable frequently accessed pages to be quickly selected. Similar to Internet Explorer's Favorites, the Firefox bookmarks are somewhat more powerful and useful.

This chapter covers using both Firefox's built-in tab support and Tabbrowser Extensions. In the sections that follow, if Firefox supports a functionality without Tabbrowser Extensions, the differences are also described.

Using Tabs to Manage Pages

You can open multiple websites in Firefox using tabs, as shown in Figure 2.1.

Firefox's tabs are relatively simple and, as such, are easy for new users to understand. They are a major step forward in usability. With Firefox's tabs, you can control the behavior of tabs when a new page is opened and use some simple management options.

To improve on Firefox's tabs, you can install tab feature extensions that enable you to do more with them. The many tab feature extensions include

- **Tabbrowser Preferences**—This extension, written by Bradley Chapman, extends the Firefox tab feature. Its enhancements are relatively simple, and the product is stable and easy to use. This add-on lets users customize Firefox's tabs using a new section named Tabbed Browsing in the Firefox Options dialog box. Tabbrowser Preferences essentially adds more control and customization to tabs, without adding a lot of functionality. Tabbrowser Preferences can be downloaded from http://216.55.161.203/theonekea/tabprefs/.

Three tabs open in one Firefox window

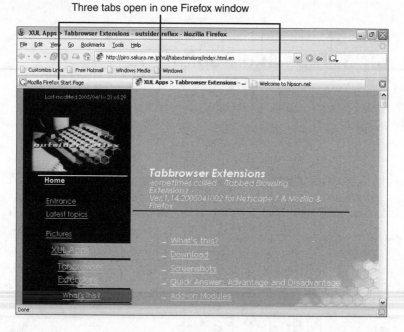

FIGURE 2.1

Firefox with three open tabs.

- **Tabbrowser Extensions**—Many features make this add-on excellent for both beginning and experienced users. The configuration for Tabbrowser Extensions enables
  you to specify whether you want features that are intended for experienced users or
  for novice users. Some of the features Tabbrowser Extensions offers include a throbber for each tab, a close box in each tab, and tab grouping using colors. Tabbrowser
  Extensions is a much more extensive add-on compared to Tabbrowser Preferences
  because it adds substantial functionality to the Firefox tabs.

  Other interesting features of Tabbrowser Extensions include the capability to switch
  tabs by hovering the mouse pointer over a tab, tab coloring, and the ability to
  reopen a tab that had been closed. This program can be downloaded from
  http://piro.sakura.ne.jp/xul/tabextensions/index.html.en.

Shown in Figure 2.2 is Firefox with Tabbrowser Extensions loaded and active. Notice
that the tabs now have a close button in the upper right of each tab. One click to close
is all you need! Other features that are not apparent in this figure include the throbber
capability, which shows when a page is being loaded, and the load progress. Also visible in Figure 2.2 is the Tab menu item that Tabbrowser Extensions adds to Firefox.

Notice close button in tabs

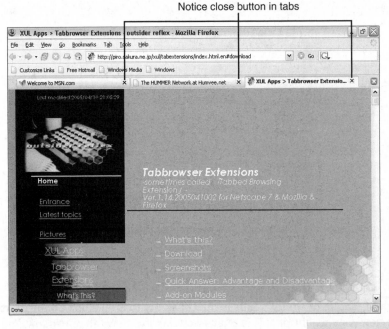

FIGURE 2.2

Firefox with Tabbrowser Extensions installed and active has a new menu selection: Tab.

Installing Firefox extensions is generally easy. All extensions are managed with the Extensions Manager, which is displayed when you select Tools, Extensions in the menu. The Extensions Manager is shown in Figure 2.3. If you download the extension, it loads automatically. However, Firefox must be restarted for the extension to become active and available to the user.

In the Extensions Manager is a list of all the installed extensions—the information includes the name, version information, and a short description. The Extensions Manager has three buttons at the bottom: Uninstall, Update, and Options (not all three can be active at the same time, however!). Additionally, a link next to the Options button displays Mozilla's Firefox Extensions page.

When an extension is loaded, clicking Options enables you to set options for the extension.

CAUTION

Firefox allows extensions to be installed only from approved sites. This helps protect you from rogue extensions. You can't automatically install an extension from a site that is not in the approved sites list. To add a site to the approved list, open the Options dialog box, click the Web Features button, and click the Allowed Sites button next to Allow Web Sites to Install Software. Add those sites you trust to this list. You can force Firefox to download any extension by right-clicking the extension and selecting Save Link As. Then you can install an extension by dragging its XPI file (that you have saved on your computer) and dropping it onto the Extensions Manager dialog box.

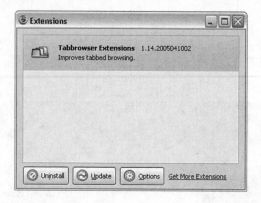

FIGURE 2.3

The Extensions Manager is where you add, remove, and configure Firefox extensions.

Opening a New Tab

One great feature of Firefox's tabs is the capability to drop a link on the toolbar's new tab or new window buttons. This opens that link in a new tab or window. You also can add a new tab by selecting File, Open Tab in Firefox's menu. However, there is an easier way to add a new tab—by customizing the toolbar.

Right-click Firefox's menu and select Customize from the pop-up context menu. Customize allows you to add and modify the toolbars used by Firefox. The Customize Toolbar window is shown in Figure 2.4.

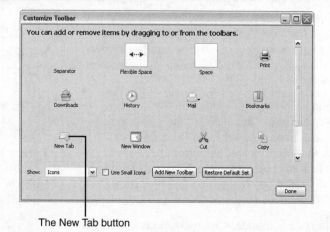

The New Tab button

FIGURE 2.4

The Customize Toolbar window enables you to add and remove toolbar buttons.

Customizing lets you add and remove buttons from existing toolbars. You can also create a new toolbar if you want. Creating a new toolbar is your choice, but I recommend you add a new tab button to the Navigation toolbar.

After the Customize Toolbar window has opened (refer to Figure 2.4), you have a choice of a few buttons you can add to toolbars. (Sadly, you can only add them once....) Like many Windows programs, toolbars are customized by dragging a tool to the desired location on the toolbar.

> **NOTE** Firefox comes with two toolbars by default: Navigation and Bookmarks. Toolbar extensions also can be added to Firefox. One that looks interesting is a Google search toolbar. (Why is this included if Google search is built in? Because users want more power!)

Opening a Link in a Tab

To open a link in a Firefox tab, click the tab and make it active. Then in the Location bar where the current website address is displayed, type a new website address and press Enter. Firefox opens that page in the active tab.

> **TIP** There are a few other ways to add a new tab:
> - Select File, New Tab in Firefox's menu
> - Double-click the tab bar where no tab is present
> - Press Ctrl+T
> - Right-click a tab and select New Tab

Changing Tabbrowser Extensions Configuration Options

After they're installed, Tabbrowser Extensions' preferences can be changed to suit your liking. Click Tab in the menu and, at the bottom of the drop-down menu, click Tabbrowser Extensions Preferences. The Preferences of Tabbrowser Extensions window displays. In this window you can set a number of parameters.

This window is arranged with extension preferences on the left side and settings for the particular option on the right side.

For the initial display (the highest level of options, Tabbrowser Extensions), you have options to save and reload. This is helpful if you want to export your settings to another copy of Firefox.

Tabbrowser Extensions has about 165 configurable options. These options cover a wide range of functionality. Table 2.1 lists the options, types of value, and typical setting values. I have not attempted to indicate a default value for any options because the defaults change depending on whether you are a novice, professional, or default user.

> **TIP** Each time you change to a different tab, Firefox updates the Location bar to reflect the URL for the page being displayed. Middle-clicking a link opens it in a new tab and loads the link in the background. By default, the new link opens in the foreground, but Firefox can also be set to load links in the background by unchecking Select New Tabs Opened from Links. This can be more convenient, especially when browsing eBay or Google search result pages because you can keep browsing the results page while the selected links load in new tabs in the background.

Chapter 2	The Power of Tabs and Bookmarks

JAVASCRIPT OPTIONS

The option settings are saved in a JavaScript file. They can be viewed using Notepad or another text editor. Of course, if you really must modify them outside of Tabbrowser Extensions, remember to keep a backup copy just in case. In a worst-case scenario, you would have to select Load Preset Settings in the Preferences window—losing all your original option settings.

TABLE 2.1 CONFIGURING TABBROWSER EXTENSIONS OPTIONS

Option Category	Option Subcategory	General Description
General		Options that affect the general operation of Tabbrowser Extensions and Firefox, such as the use and closing of windows.
	New Tab	Sets what is displayed when a page is opened and the location for new tabs.
	Close Tab	Specifies what happens when a tab is closed.
	Close Window	Specifies what will be done when a window is closed, such as closing all tabs or just the current tab.
	Undo	Tabbrowser Extensions enables you to undo a tab close action. You can specify the cache size for undo of tabs that have been closed.
Use Tab		With this set of options, you control how tabs are used. You can specify actions for both newly created tabs and existing tabs.
	Links	When the browser opens links found on a page, you can force these links to open in a new tab, an existing tab, or a background tab. You can also specify the additions to the browser's context menu here.
	External Links	When opening links in external (other than the browser) applications, you can specify whether the link is to open in the current tab, a new tab, or no control. You also can specify that the browser remain in the background (not get Windows focus) when an external link is opened.
	Pop-ups	When a page's script opens a pop-up, you can specify whether you want to open it in a new tab, new background tab, or new window.
	Bookmarks	When you open a bookmarked page, you can choose to have it opened in the current tab, a new tab, or a new background tab.

TABLE 2.1   CONTINUED

Option Category	Option Subcategory	General Description
	History	If Go, Back, or Forward is selected, you can specify that the link is opened in the current tab, a new tab, or a background tab.
	Location bar	The Location bar (found on the Navigation toolbar) can be configured to open links in the current tab, a new tab, or a new background tab.
	Web Search	When doing a web search, the search results need to go somewhere. You can configure the search results to go to the current tab, a new tab, or a new background tab.
	View Source	Sometimes you want to look at a page's source HTML. Maybe you want to see how a feature or effect was created. Other times, you might want to find out information that is not displayed. You can configure Firefox to display the viewed source in a new window, a new tab, or a new background tab.
Appearance		The main Appearance option is to turn the display of the Tab menu on and off.
	Tab	Remember those close buttons on the tabs shown in Figure 2.2? This option lets you have the close button on all tabs, the current tab, or the selected tab. As well, you can configure the width of tabs and the display of the tab meter that shows the progress of page loads.
	Tab bar	The tab bar is, by default, on the top of the display area. You can choose to have it on the bottom, have it on either side, or to hide it. When there are too many tabs to display them all, you can choose to scroll or use multiple rows of tabs.
	Tab menu	This controls the context menu displayed when the user right-clicks the tab bar. Figure 2.5 shows this context menu. Currently not shown in the figure are seven selections that are turned off.
	Context menu	A few additional menu items can be configured in this submenu.
Gestures		You can define the scroll wheel, button actions, and pointing effects relating to the tabs with this selection.
Features		This includes a number of features, such as locking, blocking, plug-ins, JavaScript, frames, and autoloading.

TABLE 2.1   CONTINUED

Option Category	Option Subcategory	General Description
TabGroups		Tabs can be grouped. That way, tabs that are related (such as a number of pages from a website) can be managed as a group. Tab groups are shown by colors by default.
Startup		When Firefox starts, it usually just loads the defined home page. With Tabbrowser Extensions, you can choose to restore the last tab session. This is handy if you have a continuing project and need to have certain pages opened repeatedly.
Misc		With this option group, you can choose a different appearance when Firefox is running on Mac OS X. You can also choose to save or restore blank tabs and automatically reload restored session tabs.
Modules		Management of installed modules can be performed here.

Pop-up context menu ——

FIGURE 2.5

Manage and use the tabs with the context menu. There is a lot of functionality here!

Now, let's move on to using tabs and Tabbrowser Extensions.

Navigating Between Tabs

Tabbrowser Extensions gives you power. When you start with Firefox without Tabbrowser Extensions, you have simple tabbing, where you can create tabs and navigate between tabs using mouse clicks. You can also switch between tabs using Ctrl+Tab.

With Tabbrowser Extensions installed, you can change your tab navigation and make multiple pages much easier to use. Let's look at some of the options Tabbrowser Extensions gives you.

Navigation between tabs is controlled by some of the options that were described previously in Table 2.1. Switching between tabs can be accomplished either by hovering over the tab or by clicking. This option is set in the Gestures options, shown in Figure 2.6.

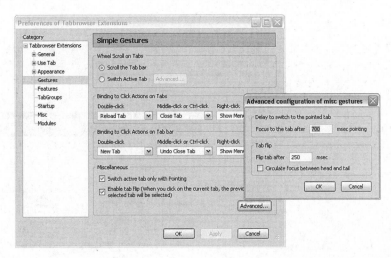

FIGURE 2.6

Tab navigation is controlled in the Miscellaneous section. There is also an Advanced button to display additional settings.

If the Switch Active Tab Only with Pointing box is checked, hovering the mouse over a tab causes the tab to become the active tab automatically. You won't have to click. This is most useful when you need to quickly switch between two pages to check information.

Click the Advanced button to set the focus change delay. The default is 100 milliseconds. (That's just 1/10 of a second.) This delay enables you to pass over a tab—for instance, to move the mouse to the menu or toolbar from the main browser

> **CAUTION**
>
> Some users find this behavior to be unsettling! It does lead one to believe that the computer is doing something it was not asked to do! However, I recommend you give it a chance—it will grow on you!

window—without a tab change. I've found that 100 milliseconds is a bit fast for my liking and usually set it to a slightly higher number. Experiment with numbers between 50 and 1,000 (make changes by about 50 milliseconds at a time) and see what you like.

Automatic switching works well when you configure the tabs to be on the left (see Figure 2.7) or right of the browser window. There is less tendency to accidentally switch between tabs because you don't have to pass over the tab bar when going to the menu or toolbars.

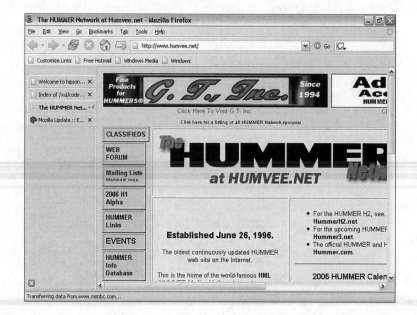

FIGURE 2.7

With the tabs moved to the left side, the hover-to-switch feature works nicely.

Rearranging Tabs

There are several ways to rearrange your tabs. One is mouse centric, whereas the other is based on the keyboard.

Rearranging Tabs with the Mouse

To rearrange tabs, you use a common drag-and-drop technique. Click the tab to be moved, and drag it to the new location on the tab bar.

While the drag is in progress, Firefox indicates the new location with a down-pointing arrow that shows the new location. Figure 2.8 shows a tab being dragged on the tab bar (the down-pointing arrow is not visible in this figure, although it appears directly above the space between the two tabs where the mouse cursor is). Notice the drag cursor position showing where the dragged tab will be dropped.

FIGURE 2.8

Firefox allows easy drag and drop reordering of tabs.

Rearranging Tabs with the Keyboard

When you're using Tabbrowser Extensions and you have your hands on the keyboard, you can move the currently active tab to a new location. This is not as powerful as the drag-and-drop method shown previously because you can move only the current tab, but it is still useful.

TIP

When using the keyboard to move tabs, the browser window must be active. If the Location bar or Search bar is active, these two keyboard shortcuts act on these items and not on the tabs.

To move a tab to the left for the top and bottom tab bars, press Ctrl+Shift+Page Up. To move a tab to the right for the top and bottom tab bars, press Ctrl+Shift+Page Down.

To move a tab up for the left and right tab bars, press Ctrl+Shift+Page Up. To move a tab down for the left and right tab bars, press Ctrl+Shift+Page Down.

I am not sure that these keyboard shortcuts are remembered by anyone, but they are there if needed.

Opening Multiple Bookmarks in Tabs

Bookmarks enable you to save page locations you might want to revisit at a later time. I have several hundred bookmarked pages, although I suspect some are no longer valid.

The last item on each bookmark menu is Open in Tabs. Click this and Firefox opens all the bookmarks, each in its own tab. See Figure 2.9 for an example.

When you use Tabbrowser Extensions, you add many enhanced features to the bookmarks and Live Bookmarks. Live Bookmarks are bookmarks that point to the Really Simple Syndication (RSS) content capability of Firefox. The following section, "Using Live Bookmarks and Bookmarks in Firefox," covers Live Bookmarks and RSS more fully.

Creating and Using TabGroups

Firefox supports tab groups as part of the bookmarks functionality. For example, you might create a Bookmark folder called My Automobile Sites. Creating this Bookmark folder is easy: You just select Bookmarks, Manage Bookmarks. The Bookmark Manager window is displayed, and toolbar buttons are available to create a new bookmark, new folder, or separator. In addition, a Move Bookmark button enables the rearranging of bookmarks and there are Properties, Rename, and Delete buttons.

TIP

With tabs, your home page can be home *pages*. You can tell Firefox to open several different sites as your home page. For example, you could have a site with news, a search page, and perhaps your personal web page.

After a bookmark folder has been created, simply add bookmarks to the folder. (I recommend keeping the number of bookmarks in a folder that will be opened as a group to a manageable number—say, fewer than five.)

After adding bookmarks to the bookmark folder, you can go to the Bookmarks menu and select the folder. The bookmark folder contents are displayed, along with an additional item at the end named Open in Tabs. When you select Open in Tabs, all the bookmarks are opened in tabs, and these tabs are managed as a TabGroup. TabGroups are easy to spot because Firefox colors the groups tabs uniquely (see Figure 2.9).

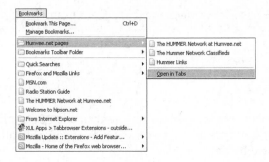

FIGURE 2.9

Open Bookmarks and navigate to any bookmark folder. Note the Open in Tabs at the end of the list of pages.

What constitutes a group of bookmarks is solely up to you, but most of us group by topic or theme.

Using Live Bookmarks and Bookmarks in Firefox

Just like Internet Explorer's Favorites, Firefox supports a method to save page locations for those sites you want to visit on a regular—or even an irregular—basis. Bookmarks, and Live Bookmarks, can be added, deleted, and managed easily in Firefox.

Live Bookmarks, Live Bookmark Articles, and Bookmarks

For those who are Internet Explorer users, *Live Bookmarks*, *RSS*, *RDF*, and even *XML* are foreign terms. Many have heard of XML, but few have experienced it, and RSS and RDF are new to many.

Bookmarks are similar to Live Bookmarks except that they are static. They represent a single web page, and when that web page changes, the bookmark is not updated. A Live Bookmark takes the form of a folder.

RSS is a protocol used by websites to serve dynamic content. When the content changes, an RSS client (Firefox, for example) can discover these changes automatically and take appropriate action. RSS feeds are usable for any content that changes from time to time. News feeds, blogs, and even this book's revisions and updates can use RSS.

To the user, all this means that some have constantly changing content, so static bookmarks would quickly become outdated. These websites instead can use RSS to publish pages that are linked through Live Bookmarks—content need not be part of the base page, either.

The acronym RSS has many different meanings; for example, *RSS* is known as

- Rich site summary

- Really simple syndication

- RDF site summary

This list is not intended to imply there is more than one RSS standard. In fact, RSS has seven formats (technical descriptions of how RSS works), with no promise of compatibility between the different formats.

RDF stands for resource description framework, and *XML* stands for Extensible Markup Language.

Let's link some of these terms together. First, a Live Bookmark is a special type of bookmark to a site that has an RSS feed.

As an example, MSNBC's page at http://www.msnbc.com is a page that has an RSS feed and supports Live Bookmarks. We know this because the right end of the location bar (located in the middle of the navigation toolbar) shows either an orange button (see Figure 2.10) or a lightning symbol.

Other sites might not support RSS feeds...yet! It is coming for many sites. The same site might have a standard bookmark for the page itself and a Live Bookmark for the RSS content.

No matter what symbol is displayed, clicking this button shows that you can subscribe to MSNBC - Top Stories, MSNBC - Most Viewed, or any other RSS feed the page offers. RSS feeds change frequently, so it pays to check from time to time to see whether there are any new RSS feeds on your favorite sites. When you select an RSS feed to which you want to subscribe, Firefox creates a pseudo folder in Bookmarks. That bookmark folder, when expanded, lists the content as a number of bookmarked pages the site offers. For example, I subscribed to Mozilla's Live Bookmark Mozilla Announcements. In my bookmarks a folder is created named MSNBC - Today's News. If I open that Live Bookmark folder, I see a number of news items. From time to time, these items change, but I don't have to update my bookmarks to reflect these changes—it is all automatic.

> **NOTE**
> A Live Bookmark is the pseudo folder created when you add a Live Bookmark to your bookmarks list. A Live Bookmark Article is the actual page found inside a Live Bookmark pseudo folder you open.

From our standpoint, Live Bookmarks can be treated as bookmarks. If you click a Live Bookmark, the page indicated is displayed. You don't have to worry about the fact that these Live Bookmarks will be automatically updated as necessary.

Live Bookmark button

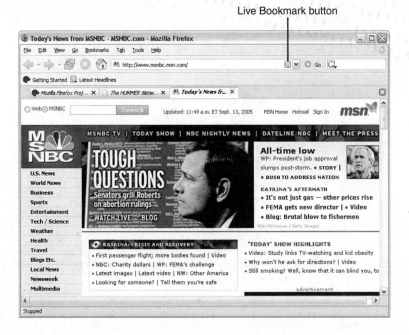

FIGURE 2.10

Today the MSNBC website has many Live Bookmarks. Also notice that the far right of Firefox's location bar has the Live Bookmarks indicator/button.

Configuring Live Bookmarks and Bookmarks in Tabbrowser

To configure the Tabbrowser Extensions bookmark options, again you use your Preferences for Tabbrowser Extensions window.

In the Category list on the left of the Preferences of Tabbrowser Extensions window, expand Use Tab and then click Bookmarks. This opens Advanced Bookmarks on the right (see Figure 2.11). You can set options for both Bookmarks and Live Bookmarks.

NOTE There are two ways to display the Tabbrowser Extensions window. One way is to select Tools, Extensions, Tabbrowser Extensions and click Options. The other way is to select Tab, Tabbrowser Extensions Preferences in the menu. This second way is slightly faster.

FIGURE 2.11

You can set how both bookmarks and Live Bookmarks are handled in tabs.

In the section titled Bookmarks Loading, you can set whether a bookmarked page is loaded in the current tab, a new tab, or a new tab in the background. As well, you can click the Advanced button to display the Advance Preferences of Bookmarks window (see Figure 2.12).

Configuration of middle-clicking or Ctrl-clicking enables you to either do nothing or open a bookmark. You can also choose to recursively open bookmarks if you desire by middle-clicking or Ctrl-clicking. Be sure that you understand what will happen when this option is enabled—you can open multiple tabs.

A context menu is displayed whenever you right-click an item in the Bookmarks list. This context menu is customizable as well.

When a bookmark is opened, you can choose to have either the bookmark name or the page's title as the tab label. I personally like the bookmark name because some pages do not have sensible titles.

You can also save the tab status when saving a bookmark.

Two tabs enable you to configure the handling of Live Bookmarks. You can choose to open a Live Bookmark in the current tab, a new tab, a new background tab, or you can open all items as a bookmark group. This refers to Live Bookmarks only (again, Live Bookmarks are the folder and Live Bookmark Articles are the pages in a Live Bookmark folder).

FIGURE 2.12

The Advance Preferences of Bookmarks window enables you to further customize how book-marks are handled.

You can choose to open a Live Bookmark article the same way as a normal bookmark is opened, in the current tab, in a new tab, or in a new background tab.

Working with Multiple Home Pages in Tabs

With tabs, you can have as many home pages as you want. Practically speaking, it is probably a good idea to limit the number of home pages to something manageable (in my case, I have three).

To set multiple home pages, first open each of the pages that make up your set of home pages in tabs. For example, you might open http://www.hipson.net, http://www.mozilla.org, and http://www.google.com. This gives you three tabs, one for each of these pages.

Next select Tools, Options in Firefox's menu. In the General section at the top of the window, you can set the location or locations of the home pages you want to use (see Figure 2.13). Simply click the Use Current Pages button; whatever pages are currently displayed in the tabs become your home pages.

Now whenever you click the home page button, the pages you set will be displayed.

> **NOTE**
> When you have multiple home pages opened, Firefox does not look at which pages are already opened in tabs. Instead, it creates new tabs for each of the pages defined in your set of home pages.

FIGURE 2.13

To use multiple home pages, open each in a tab and click Use Current Pages.

Tabbing and Bookmark Secrets for Power Users

Here are a few ideas from the experts:

- Use multiple home pages. This is a great technique because it seems that no one home page covers everything.

- You can easily open a new tab by double-clicking in the tab bar or pressing Ctrl-T. You can close an unneeded tab by clicking the close button at the end of the tab bar or pressing the middle mouse button.

- New links can be opened by default in new tabs or by reusing the current tab.

- A new tab doesn't have to be in the foreground. A tab can be created, and loaded, while it is in the background.

- Tabs are easy to manage. You can reorder your tabs using the keyboard or mouse.

- Live Bookmarks and Live Bookmark Articles enable bookmarks in Firefox to respond to dynamic content.

- Bookmark and use http://mozillazine.org! This site requires a free logon to post in the forums and is worth the effort.

- Consider limiting the number of bookmarks in a bookmark folder to a reasonable number. I use five as my ideal maximum, but that is often exceeded.

- TabGroups enable you to group, or organize, tabs by subject or content.

Finding Information with Firefox

In this chapter we will work with Firefox's search and find components. The World Wide Web is vast and complex with literally billions of web pages to choose from, but sophisticated search engines such as Google are making it easier to organize and find content of interest.

Firefox Search Engines

The following is a listing of popular search engines. For each of these sites, I did a search for my name (Peter Hipson):

- **Google (http://www.google.com)**—Google is a search engine that is very effective and easy to use. Unlike some search engines, Google doesn't offer a lot of fluff such as advertising, news, and such; instead it has a simple user interface that allows for searches—and that's about all. Google is supported mostly by paid advertising, which is presented with the search results. My name search returned just over 800 hits.

- **Yahoo! (http://www.yahoo.com)**—Using Yahoo! opens a wide vista of features and functionalities. This site provides searching and more. With Yahoo!, you'll sees news, advertising, email, and many other features that Yahoo! hopes adds value to the user experience and promotes return usage. My name search returned about 1,700 hits.

- **MSN (http://www.msn.com)**—Microsoft created an online service called MSN (Microsoft Network) as a precursor to its foray into the world of the Internet. As strange as it seems, Microsoft almost missed the Internet boat, only jumping onboard at the last minute! MSN offers news and many other services that make it a favorite home page for many Internet users. MSN's search-only URL is at http://search.msn.com. My name search returned just under 5,000 hits.

- **AOL (http://www.aol.com)**—It seems that people either love or hate AOL. I tried an AOL search and got...only about 50 pages of hits. My name search didn't even find my own website in the first page! AOL's search is linked to Google.

- **Excite Network (http://www.excite.com)**—Excite looks a lot like other multifunctionality search sites, in that it offers news, sports, and other features. My name search returned only 72 hits.

- **AskJeeves (http://www.ask.com)**—Like Google, Ask Jeeves is primarily a search site and provides little other material. My name search returned more than 3,900 matches.

- **InfoSpace (http://www.infospace.com)**—InfoSpace specializes in searches for people and companies. It's your best bet for searching telephone records and other public record caches.

- **AltaVista (http://www.altavista.com)**—Like Google and Ask Jeeves, AltaVista is mostly a search site, with little news or other information. AltaVista's a well-respected site, though, and its searches work well. My name search returned about 1,600 hits.

- **AllTheWeb (http://www.alltheweb.com)**—With a look and feel similar to Google and Ask Jeeves, AllTheWeb is a basic search site. My name search returned about 1,400 records.

- **HotBot (http://www.hotbot.com)**—Another search-only site, HotBot uses either Google or Ask Jeeves to perform its searches.

- **Lycos (http://www.lycos.com)**—Similar to HotBot, Lycos uses another search site (AskJeeves) to do its work. Although AskJeeves returned thousands of matches on my name, Lycos only gave me a little over 100.

- **Netscape (http://www.netscape.com)**—These people don't give up, you have to say that! Netscape took a beating from Microsoft in the browser wars but managed to bounce back as a search engine and an ISP. Netscape uses Google to do its searches, and my name search returned an unknown number of results.

- **Teoma (http://www.teoma.com)**—This is another search-only site, without news or other nonrelated features. Teoma returned about 4,000 hits on my name search.

Of all these search engines, is one the best? Well, the answer to this is that it depends on what you are looking for. With my name search, most hits were book related. However, I've done other things.

Using the Location Bar

Firefox's Location bar, located in the middle of the navigation toolbar, is where you type the URL of the website you want to visit. At the far right of the Location bar is the Live Bookmark indicator/button. (This button is only displayed for pages that support RSS feeds.) I'm lazy, and many others are, too. Firefox thus figured out that users like to do as little as possible, especially when it comes to typing URLs.

The Location bar enables you to type fully formed URLs. That's expected. However, Firefox also allows you to type partial URLs and tries to send you to the right website anyway.

For example, in Firefox's Location bar I typed `Jupiter`. There is a Jupiter.com (and they make some interesting products), and there's probably also a Jupiter.net and Jupiter.org. But without more information, Firefox treated this as a search and took me to http://www.solarviews.com/eng/jupiter.htm.

Using the Search Bar

The Search bar is also located on the navigation toolbar. Google seems to be the search engine of choice for many Firefox users, and by default it is the search engine used by Firefox. However, you are not restricted to Google, or any other specific search engine, and switching search engines involves a quick click on the Search bar icon.

A default installation of Firefox includes definitions for Google, Yahoo!, Amazon.com, Creative Commons, Dictionary.com, and eBay. You may add search engines to this list as well (see Figure 3.1). The default search engines in Firefox are

- **Amazon.com**—You might wonder why some of these are considered search engines. For example, Amazon is a bookseller. Searching on Amazon enables you to find books and other products it sells that match your search criteria. A good extension for Amazon is called MAB. With this extension, you get a greatly improved search capability.

- **Answers.com**—A search engine similar to Google. Answers.com has a toolbar for Firefox, and there is a supporting utility named 1-Click to allow the user to get information by pressing Alt and clicking text.

- **Creative Commons**—This is an innovative, nonprofit, alternative to traditional copyrights and can be found at http://creativecommons.org. Anything written, created (as in an artistic creation), and so on is protected automatically by a copyright. The author need do nothing and is always protected by international convention. This is an *implied* copyright, which allows the holder to enjoin (or prohibit) an infringer from using the copyrighted work. The holder cannot, however, recover damages with an implicit copyright. An artist (author, performer, and so forth) can also apply for an *explicit* copyright, which allows the holder to recover damages from an infringer in addition to preventing an infringer from copying his work.

- **eBay.com**—eBay is the largest, best-known online auction site on the Internet. (eBay says it's not an auction house, but a place where people can auction items.) If you want to buy something, new, used, or whatever, you can probably find it on eBay. Of course, if you're selling something, eBay offers an international audience of millions of potential buyers.

Chapter 3	Finding Information with Firefox

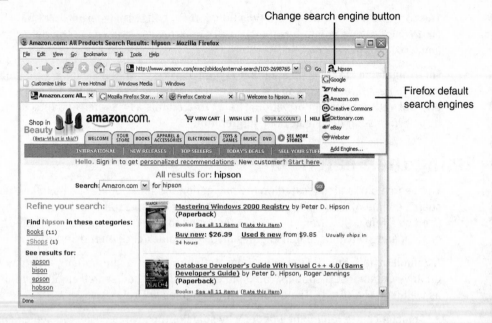

Change search engine button

Firefox default
search engines

FIGURE 3.1

For many users, Firefox's default group of search engines, displayed when you click the Change Engine button, is sufficient.

Firefox saves a history of searches, which can be cleared in the Saved Forms tab in the Privacy section of the Options dialog box. In addition, Firefox has a feature called Sanitize that clears certain information, such as history, forms, cache, and so on, when Firefox closes. Sanitize is available as a command in the Tools menu, in addition to being called when Firefox exits.

Adding Search Engines to the Search Bar

You are not limited to these search engines. You can add search engines to Firefox if you want. In Figure 3.1, you saw the built-in search engines preinstalled in Firefox. When you click the icon on the left of the Search bar, a drop-down lists the currently installed search engines. At the bottom of the list of installed search engines is an item named Add Engines.

Clicking Add Engines displays the web page shown in Figure 3.2. This page lists another eight search engines. At the bottom of that list is another link to find even more search engines.

Installing one of these search engines requires that you click the appropriate link. A prompting dialog box asks whether you want to add the selected search engine to the search bar. Click OK to add it; then check your installed search engines and the new one will be added to the list.

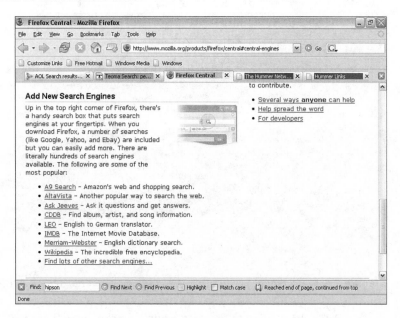

FIGURE 3.2

To add more search engines, go to Mozilla's web page.

Mozilla's top search engines to add on include

- Wikipedia (www.wikipedia.org)

- Dictionary.com (www.dictionary.com)

- IMDb (www.imdb.com)

- Astalavista (www.astalavista.com)

- Altavista (www.altavista.com)

- LEO (search.leo.org)

- MSN (www.msn.com)

As Figure 3.3 shows, literally hundreds of search engines are available. Clicking a category displays a list of search engines—for example, clicking Classified(10) displays a list of 10 search engines you can install. You can then install as many of these as you want.

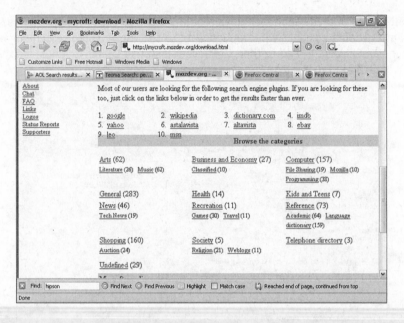

FIGURE 3.3

Each of the categories is followed with a number, the count of available search engines.

TIP

Although they're easily added to Firefox, search engines are a bit more difficult to remove. To remove a search engine, go to Firefox's installation folder and open the subfolder named searchplugins (for example, in Windows you would open C:\Program Files\Mozilla Firefox\searchplugins). The searchplugins folder has two files for each search engine you have installed: the engine (.src) and an icon file (.png or .gif). Delete both files for the search engine you want to remove.

In addition to the search engine technology, there are some useful search extensions for Firefox. If you navigate to Mozilla's Firefox extensions page and click Search in the extensions categories, you are presented with these extensions.

Switching Search Engines

Firefox enables you to easily switch between search engines. For example, when first installed, Firefox uses Google to execute searches when the Search bar is used. To switch search engines, click the change search engine button at the left end of the Search bar (see Figure 3.4). This icon has a down arrow symbol to signify that this is a drop-down control.

When the Change Search Engine button is clicked, you can select any of the search engines listed (see Figure 3.4). (If the search engine you want is not listed, refer to the previous section.) Clicking a search engine makes it the new default for searches.

Change search engine button

Click a search engine to
make it the default

FIGURE 3.4

Drop down the search engine selector and pick your default search engine.

Working with Firefox's Keywords System

Firefox offers many unique tools and techniques. This is a direct result of a product that is not only driven by the users, but developed by them as well. One very powerful system in Firefox is the keywords capability.

With keywords, you can type a keyword in the Location bar and Firefox goes to the desired site and uses that site's search to find the search terms. Configuring keywords is not difficult, but it's not well documented. Let's go through an example, step by step. Go to a site that has a search box. This site could be a search engine or any site that has an internal search capability.

Start with adding a keyword:

1. Navigate to the desired page (it must have a search edit box).

2. Right-click the search edit box on the page (see Figure 3.5). Don't try to right-click Firefox's Search bar.

3. In the Add Bookmark window, type a name for this bookmark and a keyword (see Figure 3.6). When done, click OK.

4. Use the keyword. In the Location bar, shown in Figure 3.7, type the keyword and a search term. The search term can be anything the site expects you to use.

> **NOTE**
> Keywords are not case sensitive, but you can define both upper- and lowercase keywords using the same characters. For example, you can create two keywords: HID and hid. I try to avoid confusion by always keeping my keywords lowercase—it is easier to type and being consistent helps me avoid any conflicts.

Chapter 3	Finding Information with Firefox

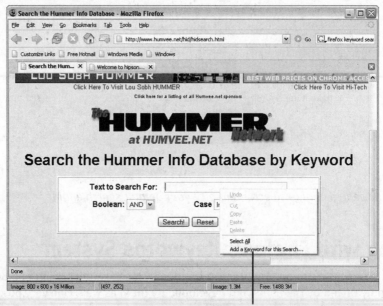

Add a bookmark to automate site-specific searches

FIGURE 3.5

At any site that has one, right-click the search box and select Add a Keyword for This Search.

Name

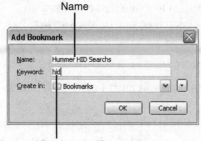

Create a keyword for site-specific searches

FIGURE 3.6

A search bookmark differs from a regular bookmark, in that it lets you specify a key in addition to the name.

Type the keyword and a search term (one or more words)

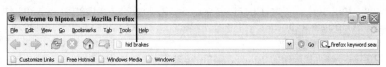

FIGURE 3.7

In Firefox's Location bar (not the Search bar!), type the keyword and search word.

5. If all goes well, you should be taken to the site's search results (see Figure 3.8).

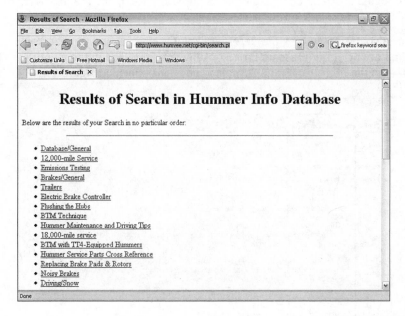

FIGURE 3.8

Press Enter after typing a keyword and search term in the Location bar. Firefox goes to the site and tells the site to search.

Now, if that isn't the coolest trick, then nothing is.

> **TIP**
>
> This cannot be done when selecting Bookmarks, Add Bookmark. Firefox does not know where the search terms should be placed, so you must right-click the site's search edit box.

Working with the Find Bar

Let's face it, some web pages are so long that locating the term or word you are interested in on the page is like finding a needle in a haystack. Internet Explorer sports that painful, crude find text capability that is only slightly better than Notepad's truly horrid find. Savvy Internet Explorer users have used Google's toolbar to enhance finding items. With Google's toolbar, you get a place to enter your search terms, a search button, and (on the right end) a set of dynamic search buttons—one for each term you type into the search terms box. You can search for one set of terms and type something else into the search terms box without doing a new Google search and have those dynamic buttons redefined.

Firefox does not have an official Google toolbar. Google is working on it, so there might be a Google-supplied Google toolbar by the time you read this. A Googlebar extension is available, though. It's not developed by Google, but it's a very good implementation. This Googlebar extension doesn't have a pop-up blocker, however, because this functionality already exists in Firefox.

Firefox also has something that Internet Explorer lacks: a find toolbar. You can display the Find bar by either pressing Ctrl+F or selecting Edit, Find in the menu. The Find bar is located on the bottom of Firefox's main window, as shown in Figure 3.9.

The first Find: text is highlighted

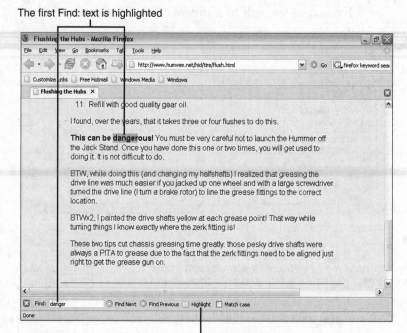

Click Highlight to highlight all occurrences.

FIGURE 3.9

The Find bar lets you search for words on the current page. It can also highlight the term searched for.

Using the Find bar's Find area, you can type a word(s). As you type, Firefox searches for what you type, finding and highlighting the first occurrence. As you type more letters, the search moves to the next match. For example, I typed h and Firefox found the first h it encountered. Then, I added another letter, making it hu, and Firefox found the first occurrence of these two letters. Adding more letters makes the search more precise.

If, at some point, you type something that is not on the current page, Firefox highlights what you are typing in red and at the right end of the Find bar displays the message Phrase not found to tell you that the word is not on the page.

Storing Searches

Sometimes after you perform a search, it would be nice to save the search results. There are many reasons for doing this, but for the sake of argument, let's say you just finished a complex search and were then called away from your computer.

Using Firefox's bookmarks, you can save a search by selecting Bookmarks, Bookmark This Page in Firefox's menu. You are prompted for a name for the bookmark; you can either use the default (the search engine name with the search terms appended) or give the search a more meaningful name.

Figure 3.10 shows a Google search and the Add Bookmark window. The name, Google Search: hena-c shepard, is the default name for the search.

TIP

Firefox's Find bar can highlight all occurrences of the find text in the document if you click the Highlight All button.

NOTE

The Firefox Find bar—or, as it's sometimes called, the *Find toolbar*—has a number of controls. From the left they include an area in which to type characters to look for, a Find Next button, a Find Previous button, a Highlight All button, a Match Case button, and a message area. Firefox always highlights the first occurrence of the term typed. Clicking the Highlight button tells Firefox to highlight all occurrences of the search term found on the page. Pressing F3 or clicking Find Next takes you to the next occurrence of the find text.

Each time you click this bookmark, the search will be repeated

FIGURE 3.10

First, search with Google; then when the results are displayed, add a bookmark for the search.

Navigating the History

Each user has a history. Firefox keeps track of your history, where you've been, what you've done.

When you need it, Firefox puts the history in a window on the left side. It is able to display either history or bookmarks in what it calls a *sidebar*. This history list is well organized and useful in helping you return to a website or URL you looked at previously. For example, Figure 3.11 shows the history for my past browsing.

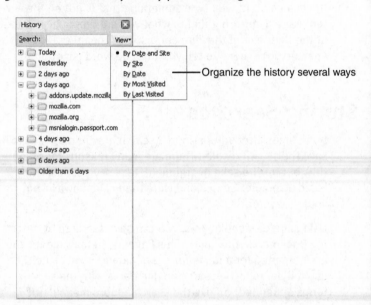

FIGURE 3.11

Your Firefox history is organized by date and site by default.

Configuring History

Along with the default date and site organization, you can select options to order your history by Site, Date, Most Visited, or Last Visited.

Date organization is arranged by days (Today, Yesterday, 6 Days Ago, and Older than 6 Days). History older than nine days is deleted by default, but you can set this in Tools, Options, Privacy tab (see Figure 3.12).

FIGURE 3.12

You can configure how long to keep items in your history list, but the default is nine days.

Downloaded History

In addition to your history of pages visited, Firefox also maintains a history of files downloaded. Each time you download a file, Firefox gives you the option of either opening the file or saving it. Some file types, however, must be saved; in this case, the Open option is disabled.

You can see which files have been downloaded by Firefox by selecting Tools, Downloads in Firefox's menu. The Download Manager also displays when a download is in progress. You can also simply press Ctrl+J to display the Download Manager.

Firefox's Options dialog box has a tab under Privacy named Download History. You can choose how Firefox removes items from the Download Manager's list: Select Manually, Upon Successful Download, or When Firefox Exits. My preference is manually, the default action.

CAUTION

Don't confuse deleting a download from the Download Manager's list with the Remove option. Deleting the file from the Download Manager leaves the file in the download location. Clicking Remove removes the file from the list and deletes it.

TIP

The Download Manager's Clean Up button, shown in Figure 3.13, deletes download entries from the list. It does not delete these files from your drive! You must do this manually by clicking Remove for each file you want deleted.

FIGURE 3.13

Click Clean Up to clear the history.

Downloads, by default, are placed on your desktop by Firefox. I don't like this convention—things on my desktop should be of a more permanent nature. I do have a location for downloads, though—a subfolder in the My Documents folder, called My Downloads. Under My Downloads I have created folders to allow me to easily organize my downloads.

The default download folder can be set in Firefox's Options dialog box by setting the Downloads setting. You can specify a folder location or have Firefox prompt you for a location for each download by selecting Ask Me Where to Save Every File.

I've found that some downloaded files have sensible filenames but that some do not. By creating subfolders in My Downloads, you can easily determine what any cryptically named files are for.

Sadly, Firefox doesn't allow you to dynamically create or specify locations for a given download. This can be one of the things about Firefox that you fix when you start customizing.

Searching Secrets for Power Users

Here are a few ideas from the experts:

- Use more than one search engine. Each search engine specializes in its own way and can return vastly different results.

- For common searches, save the search as a bookmark. This saves having to type the search terms.

- Site-based searches can be done quickly from the Location bar. Just type a term and press Enter. Firefox tries to find the site that most closely matches the term.

- With Firefox, you can have more than one favorite search engine. Just add more search engines to the Search bar.

- Switching search engines is easily done using the Search Engine drop-down button on the Search bar. Display the list and click the desired search engine.

- Keywords enable Firefox users to create searches for sites that have a search capability but are not search sites.

- The Find bar enables you to search the current page for a term. The search starts as soon as you begin to type the search term. Optionally, you can highlight all occurrences of the term.

- Firefox's History sidebar enables you to return to a site that you recently visited. Sites can be organized by date, name, and popularity.

- Firefox keeps a history of all files it has downloaded. This history can be cleared as desired. Select the download in the Download Manager and press Delete. An option exists that tells the Download Manager to remove a download from the list after a successful download.

Managing Profiles

Profiles are used by Firefox to store data that is specific to a user. You can save and restore profiles, share profiles with other users, and customize your profiles both by using Firefox and by carefully editing (perhaps using WordPad) the files that make up your profile.

When Firefox loads, it first loads all the default preferences. It then loads the preferences stored in `prefs.js`. Finally, it loads the preferences stored in `user.js`. Any setting in `prefs.js` overrides the default value, whereas any setting in user.js overrides both the default value and the setting in prefs.js (if one exists). Any change made using `about:config` updates `prefs.js`; if there is an entry for the preference in `user.js`, this change is ignored in favor of the `user.js` setting. Just remember the precedence order: Firefox defaults load first, `prefs.js` loads second, and `user.js` (if present) loads last.

Locating Your Profile

Each user typically has a personal profile located in a predefined location, depending on the operating system. The following list shows the profile settings for a number of operating system platforms:

- **Windows XP/2000**—Profile files are typically located in the folder `%AppData%\Mozilla\Firefox\Profiles\ xxxxxxxx.default\`. With Windows Explorer, go to `C:\Documents and Settings\[User Name]\ Application Data\Mozilla\Firefox\Profiles\`, where `[User Name]` is the user whose profile you are navigating to. (Note that `Application Data` is normally a hidden file, so you must turn on the hidden file display to see it.)

- **Windows 95, 98, and Me**—The profile files are often located in `C:\WINDOWS\Application Data\Mozilla\Firefox\ Profiles\xxxxxxxx.default\`. Because these versions of Windows do not properly support multiple users, only one profile is stored.

NOTE The characters xxxxxxxx in the previous profile names represent a string of random characters (numbers and letters). This serves a dual purpose. First, it ensures that the profile for one installation does not overwrite another profile. Second, it helps protect the profile from attacks or exploitation by rogue applications. When Firefox is installed, it creates an initial profile with an extension of .default. When you create new profiles, the extension for your new profile will be the same as the profile name and not default.

NOTE When you have a user.js file and you set a preference in it, this preference can be migrated to prefs.js by Firefox.

NOTE The file extension .js is defined as JavaScript. JavaScript files are edited, by default, using Notepad. The default execution (open) is wscript.exe (the Windows scripting host), or the equivalent in other operating systems. There is also a file type .jse, for JavaScript Encoded files. However, Firefox does not use .jse files.

- **Linux**—Look for the folder path ~/.mozilla/firefox/ xxxxxxxx.default/.
- **Mac OS X**—Look for the folder path ~/Library/Application Support/Firefox/Profiles/xxxxxxxx.default/.

A default installation of Firefox has more than 100 files in the profile location. Most can be safely ignored; some, however, are important to us.

Configuration File: user.js

The main profile configuration file is called user.js. This file contains various preferences the user can set. A *preference* is a Firefox option. For example, the color of a hyperlink in a web page can be set with the preference browser.anchor_color.

Firefox only reads user.js and never writes to it. (When Firefox writes preference changes, they are written to prefs.js.)

The user.js file, by default, is not created by the Firefox installation process; you need to create it using Notepad or some other suitable text editor. I recommend avoiding word processing editors (such as Word) because they can leave undesirable characters and formatting in the file.

Preferences stored in user.js are loaded whenever Firefox is started. If user.js is modified while Firefox is running, the changes take place the next time Firefox is restarted.

All the parameters you can configure in user.js can also be set by typing about:config in Firefox's Location bar. This displays the Firefox configuration page.

Creating a user.js File in Windows

You should already know how to create a file in your operating system. However, if you are unsure of how to create and edit text files, try the following steps. Although they're written for Windows XP users, Linux and OS/X users would follow almost identical steps. Instead of using Notepad, though, they would use whatever text editor they are most familiar with:

1. Open a command prompt window. (Click Start and select All Programs, Accessories, Command Prompt.)

2. Using the command prompt, change to the Application Data folder by typing the command **CD %APPDATA%** at the command prompt. Do not forget the closing percent sign!

3. Navigate to the Firefox configuration folders using a series of CD (CHDIR) commands: **CD MOZILLA, CD FIREFOX, CD PROFILES, CD xxxxxxxx.DEFAULT.** (Remember that xxxxxxxx will be a string of eight random letters and numbers.)

4. Type **notepad user.js**. If a user.js file already exists, it opens in Notepad. If the user.js file does not exist, Notepad asks whether you want to create it. Confirm that you want to create user.js.

5. Edit your user.js file, changing or setting whatever preferences you want to change. When you're done, save the file if you have made changes you want to keep. You can also discard your changes by exiting Notepad without saving.

> **TIP**
>
> In any .js (Java Script) file, comments can be included using the Java comment syntax: /* starts a multiline comment and */ ends the multiline comment. For a single-line comment, prefix the comment with //.
> Here's an example:
>
> ```
> /* Everything in user.js
>    overrides prefs.js! */
> ```
>
> This line inserts a comment in the file, which Firefox ignores. Comments are useful as reminders of why (or perhaps how) you made a given change. I recommend that each line you add to your user.js include a corresponding comment line that specifies why you added the line and what the default value was.

Customizing Firefox's Look and Feel with userChrome.css

Just like .js is a JavaScript file, .css indicates a Cascading Style Sheet (CSS). The userChrome.css file is used to customize how Firefox's user interface looks. As with user.js, userChrome.css does not exist by default. However, a sample userChrome file (userChrome-example.css) is supplied with Firefox. You can rename and edit this sample file to make it the starting point for your own userChrome.css file.

The userChrome.css and userContent.css files contain CSS rules to describe how things should appear. Chapter 15, "Creating Your Own Theme," goes into more detail about Cascading Style Sheets. Additionally, if you want to become a CSS expert, visit the W3C website (http://www.w3c.org) and read the specifications for CSS.

The sample userChrome.css file has only a few sample settings. But many more settings are possible in userChrome.css.

Customizing How Content Is Displayed with userContent.css

To modify the default display of web content, use the userContent.css file. The layout and syntax of userContent.css is identical to userChrome.css, as discussed previously.

As you might expect, a useful extension for Firefox is available that edits the userChrome.css, userContent.css, user.js, and prefs.js files. This editor, named ChromEdit, is a simple text tool with tabs for each of these four configuration tools.

> **CAUTION**
>
> Prior to making wholesale changes to prefs.js or any other Firefox configuration file, you should make a backup copy. Doing this enables you to recover if you change something that prevents Firefox from running.

Keep in mind that, if prefs.js is edited and saved using ChromEdit, Firefox overwrites any edits you saved.

The ChromEdit utility can be installed from http://www.extensionsmirror.nl/index.php?showtopic=21 (see Figure 4.1). Once installed, a new menu item—Edit User Files—is installed in the Tools menu.

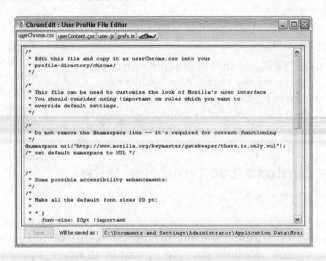

FIGURE 4.1

The ChromEdit editor window with the profile files opened.

Using about:config

When Firefox loads, it first loads all the default preferences. It then loads the preferences stored in prefs.js. Finally, it loads the preferences stored in user.js. Any setting in prefs.js overrides the default value. Any setting in user.js overrides both the default value and the setting in prefs.js—if one exists. Any change made using about:config updates prefs.js—if there is an entry for the preference in user.js, this change is ignored in favor of the user.js setting. Just remember the precedence order: Firefox defaults load first, prefs.js loads second, and user.js (if present) loads last.

The preferences in about:config are essentially ported from Mozilla. Many have not been implemented in Firefox, and there might be no plans to actually implement them.

If you find that changing one of these items does not have an effect, or the effect observed was not the one expected, this is why.

To change items in about:config, simply double-click the line to change. If it is a Boolean (true or false) value, it toggles. If a value (integer or string) is needed, an Enter Value window is displayed. String values can have any valid characters as their content, but integer values must contain a signed, 32-bit number, in the range of −2147483648 to 2147483647.

Also part of about:config is a filter entry box (see Figure 4.2). Entering characters in the filter box causes about:config to display only those preferences whose names (or some part of their names) match the filter characters.

The user changed this preference

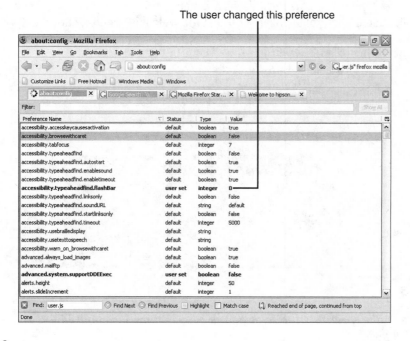

FIGURE 4.2

Firefox's about:config *sets everything that can be set in* user.js.

All preferences that are changed from their default values by the user (both in about:config and using Firefox's various customization features) are highlighted in bold and their statuses read user set. When the status reads default, this indicates that the preference is still at the default state or value.

All preferences that are set in about:config are saved in prefs.js (the preferences file). Do not manually edit prefs.js while Firefox is running because when Firefox exits, it overwrites anything you have changed manually!

> **TIP**
>
> When comparing `prefs.js` with the list of settings in `about:config`, you can see that only those items that have a status of `user set` are listed. Anything that has a status of `default` is not included in `prefs.js`. This keeps the `prefs.js` file as compact as possible.

If necessary, a preference can be reset by right-clicking it and selecting Reset from the pop-up menu.

Creating Profiles with the Profile Wizard

Earlier in the chapter, you learned how to copy a profile manually. This is a technique you'd typically use to either restore or use an existing profile.

Firefox also enables you to create profiles using the Profile Wizard. This wizard steps through the process of creating a new profile. Use of the Profile Wizard starts at the Welcome window, shown in Figure 4.3.

FIGURE 4.3

The Create Profile Wizard startup screen gives good information about why you'd want to create a new profile.

The next step (actually the important step) is to name your new profile and optionally to choose a different folder for the new profile. As Figure 4.4 shows, the new profile name is Default User and the folder name is `twvlzn16.Default User`. If you click the Choose Folder button, you could choose a different location for this profile (perhaps a network share, for example).

FIGURE 4.4

You need to supply a profile name (or accept what Firefox suggests) and a folder for the profile.

The final step is to click `Finish`. At this point, Firefox creates your profile, populating the profile's folder with the necessary files.

You have just created a new profile!

> **NOTE**
> A default profile that has not been used consists of only a handful of files occupying perhaps 25KB of disk space.

Backing Up a Profile

A user profile consists of the contents of folder `xxxxxxxx.default` (and all its subfolders, as well). A backup of this folder can serve as a method to save your profile.

Another backup technique is to use the MozBackup utility from http://mozbackup.jasnapaka.com/. This utility is freeware and works not only with Firefox, but also with Thunderbird, Mozilla, and Netscape.

> **TIP**
> The total size of the profile can exceed 5MB. However, by using a compressed folder for the destination, you can reduce the size of these files to a more manageable 1.3MB. (These sizes are typical but not absolute.)

Restoring a Profile

Generally, a profile restoration consists of restoring the profile folder. If you are restoring a profile that didn't exist in this particular installation of Firefox, you might need to add the profile to the `profiles.ini` file, found in the `%appdata%\mozilla\firefox` folder.

A profile in this file has the following five lines (a blank line separates each profile entry):

```
[Profile1]
Name=New
IsRelative=1
Path=Profiles/2qn5r34n.New
Default=1
```

The first line, (in this example it's [Profile1]) contains a number indicating the number of the profile. Numbering starts at 0 and continues up, incremented by one for each profile.

The second line is the name of the profile. This name is typically the same as the profile's folder name.

The third line (IsRelative=1) indicates whether the path in the following line is relative to the profiles.ini file, or absolute. If IsRelative is set to zero, be sure to include the full path name, including drive letter, for this profile.

The fourth line is the path and folder name for this profile. Because IsRelative is one, this path is relative to the folder that profiles.ini is in.

The fifth line, Default=1, indicates that Profile1 is the default profile when starting Firefox.

Let's say you want to restore your profile. You can follow these steps:

1. First, restore the profile's folder. This creates a subfolder with the xxxxxxxx.default filename. Let's, for the sake of argument, say the name is abcdefgh.default.

2. Next, if Firefox is open, close it!

3. Using Notepad, or whatever text editor you want, edit the profiles.ini file. This file is located in Application Data\Mozilla\Firefox.

4. Locate the section named [profile0] and change the path line to reflect the profile you just restored. (Alternatively, you could rename the restored profile's folder to the name contained in this line.) Figure 4.5 shows the profiles.ini file as it appears by default. Your profiles.ini file will look almost the same if you have not already modified it.

5. Save profiles.ini to its original location.

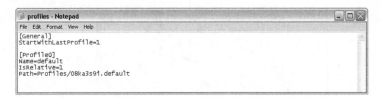

FIGURE 4.5

Notepad is used to edit a default profiles.ini *file.*

Using Multiple Profiles

Mozilla enables you to have more than one profile. When Firefox starts, the first thing it does is load profiles.ini (see Figure 4.6). If profiles.ini contains more than one profile, Firefox prompts the user to find which profile to use.

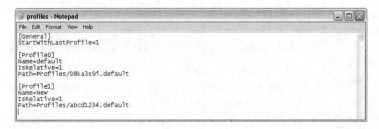

FIGURE 4.6

Notepad enables you to manually add a profile to the profiles.ini *file.*

When Firefox prompts for the profile to use, the Choose User Profile window (shown in Figure 4.7) appears, allowing you to

- Select any of the available profiles. You can choose which profile you want to use for this session of Firefox.

- Create a profile, which enables you to create a new profile using the Create Profile Wizard.

- Rename a profile, which enables you to rename the currently selected profile. If no profile is selected, this button does nothing.

- Delete a profile, which enables you to delete a profile you no longer need.

TIP

If you disabled the Choose User Profile dialog box in the Profile Manager, you can enable it by doing the following:

1. First, close all your Mozilla programs (Firefox and Thunderbird, for example).
2. Next, click the Start menu's Run option.
3. In the Run window's Open box, type **Firefox -p** or **Firefox -ProfileManager**. This forces Firefox to display the Profile Manager.

Now you can switch profiles if you like.

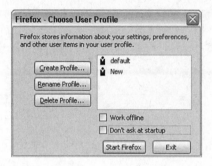

FIGURE 4.7

When Firefox finds more than one profile, it prompts for which one to use.

> **TIP**
> On your desktop you can create icons to start Firefox with each of your profiles. Simply create a shortcut to Firefox, using the command option **-p Profile Name**. This tells Firefox to start and use the named profile.

In the Choose User Profile window, you also can choose to work offline and to prevent the Choose User Profile dialog box from displaying during future starts of Firefox.

Importing Profile Information

The easiest way to import profile information is to copy the entire profile. Sometimes, though, that is not what you want—perhaps you want only part of the profile or want to withhold parts (such as cached user IDs and passwords). You can successfully copy certain files from one profile to another. These files include

- `bookmarks.html`—This file contains all your bookmarks.

- `cookies.txt`—All cookies are stored in this file. Manage your cookies by selecting Tools, Options, Privacy, Cookies (expand), View Cookies.

> **NOTE**
> If, at any time, Firefox fails to load correctly or looks strange, try deleting the `XUL.mfl` file. This file is automatically re-created the next time Firefox starts.

- `hostperm.1`—Originally called `cookieperm.txt`, this file contains information about a site's cookie saving privileges.

- `key3.db`—Firefox stores site logon information in this file.

- `user.js`—This contains your user configuration.

- `prefs.js`—This contains initial configuration information.

- `XUL.mfl`—This file is the cache for both chrome and JavaScript (it's called `XUL.mfasl` in Linux and OS/X).

- `chrome/userContent.css`—This contains your content display configuration.

- `chrome/userChrome.css`—Your browser display configuration is kept here.

There might be other significant files in the profile in addition to these examples.

Sharing a Profile

Profile sharing has only limited support at this time. Firefox can share some files in a profile with Netscape (versions 7.x) and the Mozilla suite, and you can share files between Linux and Windows.

An interesting site regarding sharing between Linux and Windows is http://sillydog.org/netscape/kb/linuxwindows.html. If you are running both platforms, I recommend you visit this site.

Profile Secrets for Power Users

Here are a few ideas from the experts:

- Firefox keeps user profiles in a specific location. Each user has her own profile location in Windows 2000 and Windows XP, although users can choose to share profiles.

- The `prefs.js` file is used to hold preferences that override Firefox's factory defaults.

- The `user.js` file contains preferences that override both Firefox's factory defaults and any preferences set in `prefs.js`.

- `userChrome.css` lets the user customize how Firefox looks. Much of the way Firefox looks can be customized in this file. You could create your own mini-theme using just `userChrome.css`.

- `userContent.css` establishes the basic look for a web page. All formatting in the web page overrides this file's defaults.

- Mozilla uses profiles to contain information specific to a user. Profiles can be shared and backed up or restored as necessary.

- Users can have as many profiles as they want. The Profile Manager enables users to switch profiles when starting Firefox.

- A profile can easily be cloned by copying the profile folder to a new name and editing the `profiles.ini` file to include this newly created copy of the profile.

- If you delete the Mozilla Firefox folder in the program files folder without uninstalling Firefox, and then you reinstall Firefox, the new installation will use the existing profiles and settings.

- Uninstalling Firefox does not remove profiles or profile information. If you want to uninstall Firefox and get rid of everything, you must manually delete the profiles.

- When you upgrade Firefox, you should first remove all the extensions and themes. Sometimes an upgrade of Firefox is not compatible with some existing themes and extensions.

- There is limited sharing of profiles between Firefox and Netscape 7.x. Profiles can be shared across platforms (such as Linux and Windows) if the user desires.

Taking Control of Your Browser

All right, everyone keep their hands off the browser and no-one gets hurt!" How many times did you hear a browser tell you that? Does that browser really know what is good for you?

You probably have had the feeling that somehow you were secondary to things such as control, privacy, and security. Sometimes lack of control occurs because the browser makers want to keep the large players happy. This can translate into minimal pop-up blocking and minimal protection for the user. Privacy has taken a back seat many times, as people are asked to register before being allowed to use a website. And in too many instances user information is accessible to many others besides the true owner of the information—a clear case of compromised security.

Do you want others to know which websites you visit? When you visit a mortgage site, you automatically become prospect material for mortgage promoters. Or maybe you visit sites that are more socially fringe than the big name sites. Maybe you visit sites that are politically oriented. You quickly see the need for privacy.

Many operating systems allow for file- and folder-level security. Many users are either ignorant about this or just not inclined to properly set up security. Sure, file and folder security takes some effort, but it is necessary—especially when some systems are designed to disable security by default.

With Firefox, you can protect yourself from many of these privacy and security hazards.

Understanding Web Security Issues

In Firefox, security starts in the Tools, Options menu selection. This displays the Options window, where you can click the Privacy option (see Figure 5.1).

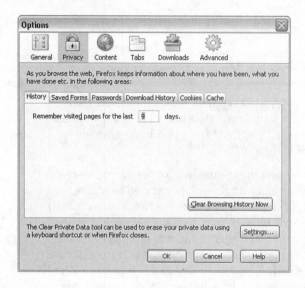

FIGURE 5.1

The Options window has six main areas: General, Privacy, Content, Tabs, Downloads, and Advanced. You are working with Privacy in this chapter.

Under Privacy are six tabs:

- **History**—Here you set the number of days to remember history. The default is nine days; most people use 7–14 days.

- **Saved Forms**—Saving form information can be turned off if you want. This is useful when visiting websites where you have to type sensitive information such as account numbers, addresses, telephone numbers, and so on.

- **Passwords**—Many websites require that you type usernames and/or passwords. This can be tedious. With this option, the saving of passwords can be turned off. You have the option to set a master password, so that a saved password is not used unless the user knows the master password. When Firefox is configured with a master password, the password cache is encrypted to prevent others from finding the passwords. Master passwords are discussed later in this chapter, in the section "Password-Protecting Firefox."

- **Download History**—Firefox keeps a history of downloads, allowing you to see which files have been recently retrieved from the Internet. The download history can be cleared when Firefox exits, when a download is successful, or manually. One of these three options must be set.

- **Cookies**—Cookies can be allowed, or not. You might choose to restrict them to the originating website only. A keep-until date can be set, such as until the cookie expires, until Firefox closes, or by prompt. Additionally, you can allow or disallow sites to use cookies. Finally, cookies can be viewed, although in many cases the contents of cookies are nonsensical.

  Cookies, if kept, are retained until the expiration (which can be many years) or until Firefox is closed, or you can have Firefox query you each time on whether to keep the cookie.

  In the Stored Cookies dialog box, cookies can be removed and you can tell Firefox not to store cookies for any site whose cookie you have removed (the site will be black-listed with regard to cookie storage).

  Keep in mind, however, that some sites use cookies for logon information, and you might not be able to log on to these sites if cookies are disabled.

- **Cache**—The browser's cache is a collection of web pages and other objects (such as images) that are saved to your drive. When the browser retrieves a web page, it can determine whether the content of the page has changed since the last visit. For example, if you use your Forward or Back button and the content has not changed, the browser might be able to load the page or objects from the cache to improve performance.

> **NOTE**
>
> Many computer users have fallen victim when they left sensitive information on a computer they didn't have control of. Whether a work computer or a home computer that other people have access to, it is important to control what is written to the computer's disk. One Massachusetts community had a computer recycling program. Companies and individuals who had old, unwanted computers could drop them in a pile at a drop-off site, and anyone who wanted a computer or accessory could take it. When several computer security experts checked, virtually every hard disk had easily recoverable, sensitive information on it!
> Remember: Files deleted from a disk can be recovered in almost all cases. Deleting deletes nothing!

For each of these Privacy dialog box areas, there is a button to clear existing information. Additionally, at the bottom is a Clear All button that clears all the privacy information, which is the same as if you had clicked Clear in each category.

Websites Written for Internet Explorer

Most Firefox users are converts from Internet Explorer. Most users naturally start with the Windows-based default browser and then find they want something else. Differences do exist between Internet Explorer and Firefox that are sometimes significant and sometimes just terminology.

We discussed terminology differences in the Introduction. Now we'll discuss what happens when you visit sites that have been written either expressly for Internet Explorer or that are different when viewed using Firefox.

Virtually all sites can be viewed using Firefox, even if they were originally written or optimized for Internet Explorer. Even Microsoft recognizes that Firefox exists, as shown in Figure 5.2.

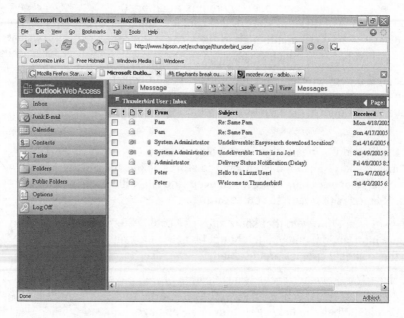

FIGURE 5.2

Firefox works well with Microsoft Exchange Server's web interface.

NOTE
This chapter assumes Internet Explorer version 6.x. This is the version of Internet Explorer that is supplied with Windows XP. There are rumors at the time of this writing that Microsoft will be offering a new version of Internet Explorer (Version 7.x) in mid or late 2005.

Hard as it is to believe, some sites are organized for, are designed for, or attempt to utilize features that are specific to a certain browser. (I won't single out Internet Explorer, but as the most commonly used browser, all web developers are aware of its capabilities.)

And some sites work better with Firefox than with other browsers. For example, Google now supports a feature called prefetching, which enables Firefox to prefetch the first item in the search results before you attempt to use it. (More information on Google's prefetching can be found at http://www.google.com/webmasters/faq.html#prefetching.)

Some features Internet Explorer supports are supported differently in Firefox. This is not to say that Mozilla got it wrong or that Microsoft did—rather, it just means they're different.

Most sites that are browser dependent work in any browser. The differences occur in the appearance, look and feel, and so forth. For a classic example, look at a typical Microsoft Knowledge Base article, at `http://support.microsoft.com/?kbid=177078`. In Internet Explorer the frame on the right side of the page, which contains translations, related support, support options, and other features, remains fixed at the side of the browser window. If the browser window is made smaller, the main frame is narrowed leaving space for the right frame. In Firefox, though, the frame on the right can (and often will) be located off the browser window. You then must scroll to see the entire page because Firefox cannot (or does not) adjust the width of the center frame that contains the actual article.

Some websites ask readers to vote on an issue. Firefox users have noted that their vote transactions do not complete sometimes. A few sites allow nothing but Internet Explorer to be used. An example of this is the HP Instant Support Professional Edition Tool site. This tool supports Internet Explorer but specifically does not support Firefox.

Because Firefox does not support ActiveX, any site that relies on this Microsoft technology will not work correctly, if at all. An ActiveX plug-in exists for some versions of Firefox. Search the web for "Mozilla ActiveX project".

What do you do if the page won't work in Firefox? Well, one good thing about Firefox is that you can switch between Firefox and Internet Explorer. Although a dedicated Firefox user would abhor the thought that another browser (especially that one!) might be used, sometimes it is inevitable.

Blocking Pop-ups

Pop-ups are ads that are displayed in their own browser windows. There are two classes of pop-up ads: a *pop-up*, which displays on top of everything and has focus, and a *pop-under*, which is placed behind the browser, lurking and waiting for you to find it later. The logic behind pop-under ads is that you might not know from which site they originated. In this chapter we'll refer to both as *pop-up ads*, even though some are pop-unders.

Another related technique is called a *pop-over*. These ads are displayed using JavaScript and are part of the web page (no separate browser window). Pop-overs are usually animated, covering the content you want to see.

For the longest time, pop-up ads were not blocked by Internet Explorer. Only after third parties started offering pop-up blockers did Microsoft realize that it had to do something. (And, yes, Firefox did figure into that as well!)

Probably the best known pop-up blocker is the Google toolbar for Internet Explorer. This add-on to Internet Explorer has proven immensely popular. My Google toolbar pop-up blocker has blocked about 1,400 ads since it started counting! That is a lot of ads that I don't have to be bothered with.

Two technologies are used to create pop-up ads. The first, and most easily blocked, is to use HTML to create a new browser window. The other technology is to create a pop-up using something such as JavaScript or Flash. These pop-ups are more difficult to stop because, once started, they do their dirty work without any further interaction with the browser!

Some websites attempt to use pop-ups to interact with the user, such as to get a username and password. This is certainly not the best way to interact with users. I still remember one site where I sat for almost a minute wondering why nothing was happening, only to realize the site had tried to pop up a new window. Microsoft's Exchange Server web interface uses pop-ups, and that requires the user to enable pop-ups for that site.

Blocking Banner Ads

What is a banner ad? A *banner ad* runs along the top of a web page and is a hyperlink—as are most other embedded ads. Typically, a banner ad is 468 pixels wide by 60 pixels high (this allows them to fit on smaller browser windows, for example).

You can limit banner ads in several ways. If you control your own proxy server, you can configure it to block certain sites. When an attempt to access these sites is made, the proxy server simply discards the request. Another technique, for those not using a proxy server, is to configure your firewall to block certain sites. Most firewalls allow this type of configuration.

A *write-up*, or script to configure your proxy server, can be found at http://www.schooner.com/~loverso/no-ads/.

An example of a banner ad is shown in Figure 5.3. This example is only a demonstration, but it does reflect what a banner ad looks like.

Are banner ads more annoying than other inline ads? I don't think so—they are all annoying. But, there is hope because you can block ads like these with Adblock! Read on....

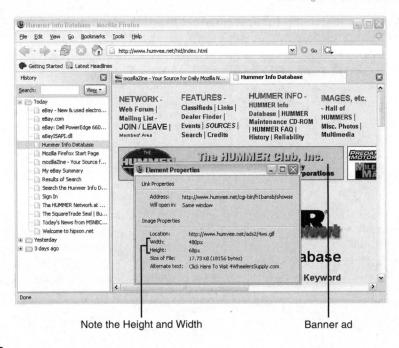

Note the Height and Width   Banner ad

FIGURE 5.3

A sample banner ad, along with the image's properties. Placement is typically at the top or bottom of a page.

Blocking Ads with Adblock

Many advertisements can be blocked in Firefox by using an extension named Adblock. Adblock lets you create, import, and export filter lists to block content.

Installing Adblock is relatively easy: Start at http://adblock.mozdev.org/ and read about the Adblock project. On the navigation bar at the top of the page click Install (see Figure 5.4). This option takes you to the Adblock installation page.

When you're at the installation page, install the latest build. (Most likely the latest build is the only build available.)

Click Install

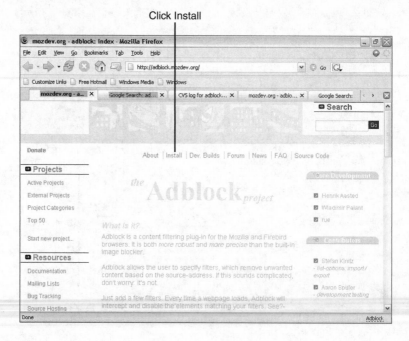

FIGURE 5.4

The Mozilla Adblock home page (http://adblock.mozdev.org) is the Adblock home page. Note the navigation bar at the top.

> **TIP**
>
> By default, Firefox is configured to block installation of software or extensions except those on the approved list. If this blocks your installation of Adblock, an error status bar appears below the Firefox toolbar (or the tab bar if you have a tab bar displayed). By default, the various Mozilla sites are preapproved.

Adblock is an easy extension to use. You configure Adblock by selecting Tools, Adblock in Firefox. This displays a second level of menu selections:

- **List All Blockable Elements**—This option scans the currently displayed page and lists all the elements that can be blocked. You can also reach this list by clicking Adblock at the right end of the status bar.

- **Overlay Flash (for left-click)**—This allows context clicking Flash objects.

- **Preferences**—As with all extensions, Adblock has a Preferences window. This window is covered next.

Figure 5.5 shows the Adblock Preferences window. This window enables you to create new filters by typing them in the New Filter box and clicking Add.

These filters were imported from a list found on the Internet

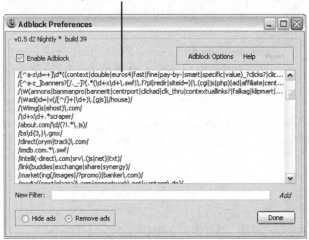

FIGURE 5.5

In Adblock's Preferences window, you can set options and create new filters.

In addition to allowing you to create new filters, the Adblock Preferences window also lets you set Adblock options and display help (this actually comprises two links—one to the Adblock home page and a second link to a page that describes regular expressions).

The Adblock options you can configure include

- **Obj-Tabs**—Obj-Tabs are small tabs displayed on content that Adblock is capable of blocking. If you click this tab, the content is automatically added to your filter list.

- **Collapse Blocked Elements**—When content is blocked, you can collapse (remove) the space that was used by that content. Some pages look better with this option utilized.

- **Check Parent Links**—This option causes Adblock to block not only the ad server, but also the site to which the ad is pointing. It's a bit radical, but for some users the target is as bad as the advertising pusher.

- **Site Blocking**—If this option is set, Adblock blocks the site; otherwise, it displays the site but not the blocked content.

- **Keep List Sorted**—The Adblock filters list can be sorted to allow easier management. In addition, you can sort the list by exporting it and sorting with a sort utility. Once sorted, the filter list must have [Adblock] as its first line.

- **Import Filters**—Even though users can create their own filters, they also can import filters from other sources (such as from the Internet) into Adblock.

NOTE

There is nothing to prevent you, or anyone else, from creating all the necessary filters. But, an old rule of computing says, "Don't reinvent the wheel!" This means that, if filters already exist that work well, then use these instead of writing your own. One site that has Adblock filters that are updated every few days is at http://www.geocities.com/pierceive/adblock/.

- **Export Filters**—A wise user will export and save his customized filters to a safe location. This allows recovery if the installation of Firefox is lost as well as sharing.

- **Remove All Filters**—Sometimes things just get too messed up to continue. We've all done it—made some rules and later found that one (we don't know which) was causing a problem. With this option, you can remove all the filters.

- **Deinstall**—It is always a good idea to remove all the installed extensions before upgrading your version of Firefox. As well, if you find that Firefox becomes unstable, try removing extensions. The Deinstall option is available in case you need to remove Adblock.

Importing, Exporting, and Removing Filters

Adblock allows you to import, export, and remove filters. This capability is the heart and soul of Adblock's functionality. Sites that serve advertisements change frequently, old sites disappear, and new sites pop up with startling regularity.

As well, sometimes it is best to just start with a clean slate. You can remove all existing filters if necessary.

Importing Filters

Importing filters lets you load filters you have created and exported (see the next section, "Exporting Filters," for details on exporting filters). A Google search shows many sites that list available filters.

Don't ignore filter lists that originate from outside your country. A filter list from Germany can work just as well as one from the United States—usually. The best advice here is to try it and see if you like it.

Importing is done from Adblock's Preferences window. Click Adblock Options, and select Import Filters from the menu displayed. This opens the Select a File window, which is the Windows Open File window, renamed. Select your text-based filter file. This file must have an extension of .txt; if it doesn't, enter a filename of *.* to see all files available in the target folder. After a file has been selected, a Confirm window asks you whether you want to overwrite the current list of filters or append to the end of the list.

RECOVERING FROM AN IMPORT DISASTER

"Oops, I made a mistake." How many times has this thought run through your mind just after confirming a choice? In importing, after you select a file to import, you have only two options: replace or append. You might append many filters to the end of your list, or you might accidentally lose the filters you created on your own.

All is not lost, though. There are two recovery tricks. First, when you are in the Adblock Preferences window, click the Close button in the title bar. This closes the window without updating the list of preferences.

Another recovery is to open a Windows Explorer window, navigate to your profile, and copy the `prefs.js` file to a backup location (refer to Chapter 4, "Managing Profiles," to find where your profile is located.) Then close Firefox and copy that saved backup copy of `prefs.js` back to the Firefox profile location. (Firefox rewrites `prefs.js` when it exits, so until then the original file is still on your drive.)

Of course, this is a good place to point out that before modifying anything, you should back up your profile!

The filter file format is a simple text file. However, Notepad will not effectively edit this file because the lack of carriage returns in the file causes Notepad difficulty. Instead of Notepad, edit this file with WordPad, and you should be set!

The first line (and only mandatory line) contains

`[Adblock]`

Each subsequent line contains one filter per line. The filters can be URLs, with an allowed * as a wildcard character. Also allowed are GREP, such as regular expressions. In Adblock regular expressions begin and end with a forward slash (/).

> **NOTE**
> *Regular expressions* are strings that contain a complex wildcard syntax to allow matching multiple strings. If you want to learn all about regular expressions, many sites on the Internet can help you. One that I can recommend is http://www. regular-expressions.info/ reference.html. Anyone familiar with GREP utilities should understand regular expressions.

Exporting Filters

Adblock lets you export their filters. When exporting, Adblock prompts for a filename to save to. I recommend supplying both a filename and an extension of `.txt`—which is not supplied by default. An exported filter set can be directly imported into Adblock as desired.

Exporting filters provides a great way to both back up and share your filters.

Removing Filters

Adblock's Remove All Filters option enables you to clear all filter definitions, which is useful if you want to start from scratch. If you will be loading new filters, you don't need to remove the existing filters. Rather, simply click OK in the Confirm dialog box.

Adblock Preferences

Adblock stores filters and Adblock option settings in `prefs.js`. There are a number of lines in this file for Adblock, as the following code shows:

```
user_pref("adblock.enabled", true);
user_pref("adblock.fastcollapse", false);
user_pref("adblock.frameobjects", true);
user_pref("adblock.hide", false);
user_pref("adblock.linkcheck", false);
user_pref("adblock.pageblock", false);
user_pref("adblock.patterns", "ads.com adserv.com advertise.com");
```

Settings are saved for a number of Adblock options, including the following. (Please note that not all versions of Adblock support all the options listed here.)

- `enabled`—This Boolean setting turns Adblock on and off. Its values allowed are `true` and `false`.

- `fastcollapse`—This Boolean setting turns on fast collapsing of frames and content to areas where advertising was removed.

- `frameobjects`—This Boolean object is used to control whether objects are framed.

- `hide`—This Boolean object controls whether objects are hidden (which does not alter the page layout) or removed (which collapses or changes the layout of the page).

> **CAUTION**
>
> You could put Adblock settings in `user.js`. However, doing so has no effect. Adblock checks for settings only in `prefs.js`, and not in `user.js`.

- `linkcheck`—This Boolean object controls whether Adblock will check the links in JavaScript for spaces.

- `pageblock`—This Boolean object controls whether Adblock will block pages.

- `patterns`—This string object contains the patterns (filters) the user has defined.

Software Installations from Non-Mozilla Sites

The best source of Firefox extensions is Mozilla. Its website, at https://addons.update. mozilla.org/extensions/, lists popular extensions and optionally all available extensions.

Sometimes, however, you might want to install an extension that is not available on the Mozilla website. Before Firefox allows these to be installed, you need to approve, or allow, Firefox to do the installation. Allowing Firefox is done on a site-by-site basis (see Figure 5.6), as well as globally. Conservative users should simply uncheck Allow Web Sites to Install Software, whereas more advanced or trusting users should check the Allowed Sites list to control which sites may (or may not, if they are not in the list!) install software.

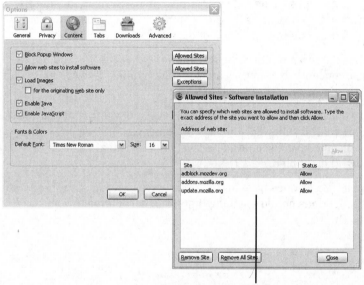

These sites are allowed to install software

FIGURE 5.6

Under Options, Content, you specify who is allowed to install software.

In my allowed sites, I have three that are Mozilla.org sites.

In addition to extensions, Firefox also supports plug-ins. The most popular plug-ins include Adobe Reader, Java Plug-in, Macromedia Flash Player, QuickTime, RealPlayer, and Windows Media Player. In addition to these, there are more than 50 additional plug-ins that work with Firefox.

Controlling JavaScript

Is JavaScript bad or good? And what's the difference between Java and JavaScript?

Java is a programming language that is platform independent and usually interpreted. It is primarily used to build HTML pages, allowing the developer to create platform-independent pages. Java programs are often called *applets*. To run Java applets, Java must be installed.

JavaScript is a scripting language that is also primarily used to build HTML pages. It is used to make the pages more dynamic, or interactive. Despite the similar names, JavaScript is separate from Java and does not require Java to be run.

So, are they the same or not? The true answer is a vague yes and no. Yes, they have the same basic concepts, but no they are separate entities. One can exist without the other.

In Firefox you can control whether to allow Java and whether to allow JavaScript. Either can be allowed or disallowed. The Java option does not have any options other than to enable or disable Java. Both Java and JavaScript can create a security risk (although it may be slight) if enabled.

JavaScript in Firefox does have options, as shown in Figure 5.7. These options ensure that JavaScript does not do anything that is not acceptable to you.

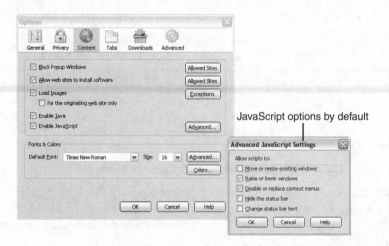

FIGURE 5.7

With JavaScript, you can set options to control how much freedom you will allow it to have.

These options include

- **Move or Resize Existing Windows**—Allowed by default, JavaScript will be able to move and resize screens it is using.

- **Raise or Lower Windows**—This refers to giving a window JavaScript focus, making it the topmost, current window. I find this behavior most annoying because I don't like software controlling what I am doing and when I do it. When I need the window, I have a mouse, and I know how to use it.

- **Disable or Replace Context Menus**—Context menus are displayed when you right-click an object or content. This is a useful feature. Context menus are unobtrusive and provide a great shortcut to the main menu. (That's why they are often called *shortcut* menus.)

- **Hide the Status Bar**—The Firefox status bar is normally at the bottom of the screen. It is used to display information about the current page, such as the destination of hyperlinks. This permission is not set by default.

- **Change Status Bar Text**—Generally, Firefox manages what is displayed in the status bar. However, JavaScript can change that display if you allow it. Sometimes this feature is used to trick a user into believing that a hyperlink points to a location other than what it really points to. This permission is not set by default.

Using BugMeNot for Anonymous Registration

Many websites, especially newspaper sites, require registration to read an article. Often they ask for your name, age, gender, and other personal information. They then send a confirmation email that is used to log on to the site. This means you must give them an email address that at least works for a short time.

To avoid this registration hassle, Firefox has an extension called BugMeNot, which consists of a large database saved at bugmenot.com (BugMeNot has moved from bugmenot.mozdev.org to http://www.bugmenot.com.)

After installing BugMeNot, go to a website that requires registration. In the box where you enter your username, right-click and select BugMeNot from the context menu. The BugMeNot extension queries the database at BugMeNot.com and enters a username and password. All that is left for you to do is press Enter or click Logon—or whatever the site expects you to do.

| Chapter 5 | Taking Control of Your Browser |

Just How Much Information Is Okay?

Not everyone likes BugMeNot. Some sites feel it is their right to demand personal information, email addresses, and whatever else they want before allowing you access. Some of us don't agree, and virtually no one gives valid information to these sites. The whole concept of registering for a free site doesn't work. Remember: We are not talking about sites that want money to browse; all they want is your email address and some personal information.

However, some sites are firing back. If they find that a given username and password are in the BugMeNot database, they delete it.

BugMeNot can hold many usernames and passwords for any one site. Selecting one at random enables you to retry the database if the first supplied username and password don't work. (At one site I tried, it took me about six tries before I got one, but it was still much faster than registering!)

A typical website registration is shown in Figure 5.8. In this example, the website asks for the user's age, gender, address, phone number, and income. I don't know about you, but to me that is outrageous!

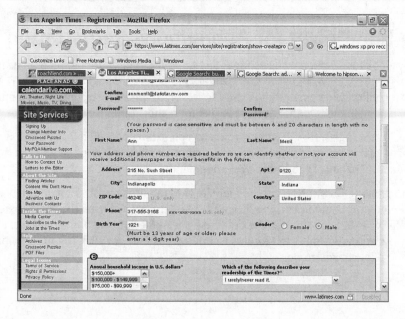

Figure 5.8

Just look what this website is asking for. Isn't this a bit personal? After all, we haven't even had our first date yet.

All in all, BugMeNot is an effective and useful tool. It is often faster than doing an "official" registration.

Understanding Cookies and Firefox Cookie Controls

There are many preconceived notions about what a website cookie is and how it can be used. Some of these ideas are not terribly factual. Let's set down a few truths first.

Cookies are not evil.

Second, cookies can be read only by the domain that saved them.

Third, cookies contain only information that you provide (either directly or indirectly).

Fourth, all cookies contain information that the server *already* has.

Fifth, the server could store this information on its local storage and you'd never know.

Cookies are capable of tracking usage over multiple sessions and sessions to computers that are behind a NAT firewall. In the latter case, many computers might visit a site and cookies can help that site keep track of the visits.

Now ask yourself this question about cookies: Would you rather this information be stored on the server's computer or yours? I'll go with mine, thank you—at least then I can delete the cookies when I want.

First, any information stored in a cookie could just as easily be stored on the web server's end. That's right, any website could store exactly the same information about you at its end instead of your end. So, then, why use cookies? Why not just put the information on the server? Cookies allow two things that a server-side solution doesn't: speed (big websites have thousands of visitors every day and millions of unique visitors over time) and storage space. If the server were to save information about millions of users, the storage requirements might begin to add up. We aren't talking just hard disk space, but backup, integrity, management, and other storage issues. Finally, cookies enable a website to store information that allows the site to determine that it is probably you it's seeing and not someone else.

Why do people object to cookies? The issue is usually that they don't like sites to store information about them on their drive. More generally, they don't want the site saving information about them at all! But remember that the site already has the information it puts in the cookie.

Also, people object to cookies because they don't want that information on their computer to be available to others. From outside (the Internet, for example), cookies are safe because only the creating website can open its cookies. As well, most sites encrypt cookie information to prevent issues of remote and local users obtaining the information and being able to utilize it.

Cookies are here to stay, and they serve a useful purpose. I've been at this Internet game for a long time and have yet to see one documented case in which cookies were improperly used.

Firefox lets you control cookies. For example, the Options Manager has settings for cookies in its Privacy section. The Firefox cookie settings include

- Allowing or disallowing sites to store cookies. If you disallow cookies, no site can store a cookie on your computer.

- If you choose to allow sites to store cookies, you can choose to allow only the originating website.

- You can choose to have cookies deleted upon expiration or upon closing Firefox, or you can choose to be prompted for deletion.

- You can choose to either allow or block specific sites from using cookies, either permanently or just for the session.

- Cookies stored on your computer can be viewed. While viewing cookies, you can delete either just the currently viewed cookie or all cookies.

Password-Protecting Firefox

Firefox supports caching of passwords, just as most other browsers do. By doing this, you usually only have to enter your username and password one time because Firefox saves this information to the password cache. The next time the site asks for identification, Firefox supplies the cached username and password information.

My password list, which I maintain in an encrypted file on my desktop, contains more than 100 usernames and passwords and almost 500 lines of identification information! It is huge.

Generally, Internet Explorer manages my passwords for those machines on which I use Internet Explorer. The same is true for my Firefox systems: I let Firefox manage my username and password information.

Still, though, I must keep a record of these vital passwords and other bits and pieces of information. You should never rely on your browser's password cache. However, Firefox does give you the ability to back up your cache of passwords. They are in the `signons.txt` and `key3.db` files. Save both to a safe location.

`signons.txt` is a text file, viewable in Notepad, although the sign-on names and passwords are encrypted to keep them safe.

When used with the master password option, `signons.txt` has encrypted usernames and passwords, and this information should not be indiscriminately distributed!

Windows XP users should consider applying security policies to all files in their profiles. If someone guesses your master password, all your passwords will be available to him!

To set security, right-click the profile folder, display its properties, and click the Security tab. Make sure that only you (and the administrator and system groups) has access to these files. In the Advanced settings, make sure that Replace Permissions Entries is checked so that all subfolders and files have these security settings applied.

With Firefox, you can set a master password. This password means you have to remember only one password, rather than hundreds (see Figure 5.9). (Hundreds? Well, it is recommended that you use unique passwords for each site that requires a password....) With the master password, Firefox prompts you for this master password as necessary and then uses this master password to encrypt your password cache files.

FIGURE 5.9

Firefox's password saving is rather advanced and manageable. You can clear, view, and set a master password.

After you click View Saved Passwords, Firefox displays the Password Manager (see Figure 5.10). To see the saved passwords, you need to respond with the correct master password, if you set one.

Each time you enter a site that requires a password, Firefox first checks the Password Manager. If a username and password are stored for the URL, Firefox uses them. If no username or password is stored for the URL, Firefox prompts you for both. If you have selected Remember Passwords (refer to Figure 5.9), an active check box appears, instructing Firefox to save this username and password.

Password not displayed by default

FIGURE 5.10

The password manager shows the URL, username, and (optionally) the password used.

Sometimes you might wonder where all this magical information is stored. Firefox stores security- and privacy-related information specific to a user's profile in the following locations:

- `bookmarks.html`—Your bookmarks (favorite sites) are stored in this file. The file is a basic HTML file.

- `formhistory.dat`—Information regarding any web forms you filled out is stored in this file.

- `history.dat`—A record of each URL you visit is saved in this file.

- `cert8.db`—This file is the client certificate database.

- `signons.txt`—This is a text file containing username and password information. The actual usernames and passwords are encrypted in this file.

- `key3.db`—This is an additional file that is used with `signons.txt` to manage usernames and passwords.

- `secmod.db`—The file used by the security module. Information in this file includes certificates.

- `cookies.txt`—Your cookies are stored in this file. Even though it's a text file, you can use the Cookie Manager to delete entries.

Determining the Real Location of Sites

Two options in JavaScript—Hide the Status Bar and Change Status Bar Text—are important in keeping the bad guys from sending you to where the sun don't shine.

These options deal with the status bar. The status bar contains a text display area that usually displays the URL of the hyperlink over which the mouse is currently hovering. This is useful because you often find that you would like to know where you are going first, before you click. (Yes, even viewing the "wrong" website can cause problems!)

An example of such malicious behavior is shown in the following segment of HTML and JavaScript:

```
<HTML>

<!-- Example of JavaScript writing to the status text output area. -->
<HEAD><TITLE>Where do you go with these two links?</TITLE></HEAD>

<body>
<br>
<center><h2> Example of JavaScript writing to the status text output
area. </H2></center>

<UL> <br><br>

<font face="Verdana" size="2">
<LI>
   Here is a real URL:  <a href="http://www.hipson.net">www.quepublish-
ing.com</a>
   that will take you to www.hipson.net. Even if Javascript's Change
status bar text
   is turned off, you still have the correct display in the status
bar.<br> </li>
</LI>
<br>

   <a href="http://www.hipson.net"
     onMouseOver="window.status='http://www.quepublishing.com';return
true;"
     onMouseOut="window.status=' '; return true;">
     www.quepublishing.com</a>

<BR><BR><br>
<LI>
   But, this url won't give us what you expect. With Change status bar
text turned
   off, you see nothing in the status bar. (Try this one with Internet
Explorer, too)
<br><br>
```

```
    Next turn on Change status bar text in Firefox, and again hover over
the URL
    and see what the status bar says. With Change status bar text on,
you think you see
    a hyperlink to our publisher's page. Regardless, what really happens
is that this
    link will take you <b>to my home page www.hipson.net</b>

</body>
</HTML>
```

If you type this short piece of code into a text file, naming it `JavaScript.html`, and then load it into your browser, you will see nothing for the URL in the status bar. That is, the status bar will not change as it would over a hyperlink. Too lazy to type? Go to http://www.hipson.net/javascript.html. After the page loads, select View, Page Source in Firefox's menu.

Many attempts to hide the true URL are phishing attacks. *Phishing* is the improper gathering of information—including account numbers, passwords, usernames, credit card numbers, and so on. These attacks are becoming more and more sophisticated as time goes on. The bad guys try something, and the good guys find a way to stop or reveal them. It then becomes a vicious circle of good versus evil. Thunderbird's anti-phishing feature is described in the Thunderbird sections dealing with privacy.

Using Firefox's Clear Private Data Feature

New in Firefox 1.5 is a useful feature named Clear Private Data. This function is controlled from the Firefox Options dialog box's Privacy tab. Clicking the Settings button at the bottom of the Privacy tab displays the Clear Private Data dialog box.

Contained in this dialog box are check boxes to define what data you want cleared:

- **Browsing History**—The history cache is a record of which websites you visited.

- **Saved Form Information**—Forms you have filled in while browsing are cached to allow Firefox to reenter information when revisiting the site. This data can contain sensitive data such as IDs, passwords, or financial information.

- **Saved Passwords**—Firefox saves passwords by default (you can turn it off either on a site-by-site basis or globally).

- **Download History**—Files you have explicitly downloaded are retained by the Download Manager until you clear them by clicking the Clear button.

- **Cookies**—Cookies are created by websites to store information about you and your usage of the site.

- **Cache**—Firefox caches (saves a local copy of) content you have viewed.

- **Authenticated Sessions**—Sessions you have had to authenticate are stored by Firefox for later reuse.

Each of these collections of private data can be set so it is cleared when Firefox exits. Another option is to have Firefox, when it closes, prompt you as to whether this data should be cleared.

Most users who are on private computers (usually at home) do not clear this data; after all, it is saved for a reason—improved performance. However, users who are using public (or semipublic such as a work computer) normally do not want this data to be saved between sessions because this might allow someone else to have access to their private data.

In an emergency, you can force a clearing of your private data by selecting Tools, Clear Private Data from Firefox's menu. Do remember, though, that once cleared, this data cannot be recovered by ordinary means—there is no undo!

Taking Control Secrets for Power Users

Here are a few ideas from the experts:

- Profiles are used by Firefox to store data that is specific to an individual user.

- If you think you might want to share a profile between a Windows computer and a Linux computer, you can go to http://sillydog.org/netscape/kb/linuxwindows.html, which will give you the details. If you are running both platforms, I recommend you visit this site.

- Web security is important. You must protect yourself, your family members, and your property from attacks. Firefox has some innovative security features, such as allowing you to configure various security settings.

- Some sites are written for Internet Explorer exclusively, but virtually all sites display acceptably in Firefox.

- Pop-ups, pop-unders, and pop-overs are all annoying ways to try to sneak advertising onto your computer.

- Adblock enables you to import, export, and remove filters for advertising content suppliers.

- Try to get your extensions from the official Mozilla website (Mozilla.org), but some interesting extensions are located at other sites, too.

- You can choose to allow or prohibit software installations based on URLs using the Web Features section of Firefox's Options dialog box.

- Both Java and JavaScript can be used to make web pages more effective and usable. However, they both can cause risks.

- If registering and providing personal information bugs you, use BugMeNot—an extension for Firefox that allows you to register anonymously.

- Cookies are often misunderstood and maligned. Actually, cookies are not the Darth Vader of the Web!

- Firefox's master password lets it encrypt stored passwords and allows users to have to remember only one (master) password.

- "Determining the Real Location of Sites" is an excellent discussion of how websites and HTML email mask the true destination of a hyperlink. You can find it at http://www.michaelhorowitz.com/linksthatlie.html, a very interesting site.

Extending and Modifying Firefox

Part II

Power Firefox Tricks and Techniques

All right, everyone keep their hands off the computer and no one gets hurt!" How many times have you felt that the program's developers don't want you to do any customization? How many times has a program been great, except for those two or three things that make it more difficult for you? Have you wondered if it might be possible to improve the performance of an application? Well, this chapter is for you: It is time to learn to spiff up and add nitrous to Firefox!

Finding Your Configuration Files

Two types of configuration files, user profile configuration files and Firefox configuration files, are found in the Firefox installation folder located in `C:\Program Files\Mozilla Firefox`.

In Windows, Firefox is installed in the folder designated by the environment variable `%programfiles%`. When the *Firefox installation folder* or the *installation folder* is mentioned, you are being referred to `C:\Program Files\Mozilla Firefox`. Throughout this chapter, it is assumed that your programs are installed in this particular folder. If yours is different, substitute your folder location as appropriate.

Found in the Firefox installation folder is a number of subfolders and files that Firefox uses. Three of these are significant:

- `Defaults.ini and components.ini`—These files are used to configure Firefox. They contain only a minimal amount of information indicating to Firefox that there are no extra configuration files.

- **Defaults**—A folder that holds default configuration information.

Specific configuration files in different operating systems are discussed next.

NOTE User profile files may be found in different locations based on which version of Windows is being used. Most users today are using Windows XP, although there are some Windows 2000, Windows 98, and Windows Me installations. There are few, if any, Windows 95 installations using Firefox.

NOTE To access hidden folders, do the following:
In Explorer, select Tools, Folder Options in the menu. Click the View tab, and check Show Hidden Files and Folders under the Hidden Files and Folders category. Also check Display the Contents of System Folders if you want.
In a command prompt (cmd.exe), use the dir command's option /ah (show hidden files) to display all hidden folders and files. A command prompt command works with hidden folders and files even if you can't see them. (That is, if you type cd "Application Data", the current folder is Application Data, even if Application Data is hidden.)
You can also turn off the hidden attribute for hidden folders and files. This is legitimate, although not really recommended.

Windows XP and 2000

Both Windows XP and Windows 2000 use a similar hierarchy to manage documents for multiple users. Each user has a set of folders located in the folder `C:\Documents and Settings`. Under this folder is a folder specific to each user (named with the user's logon name), another folder used to create a new user's profile when users log on for the first time (named Default User), and a folder shared by all logged on users (named All Users). The user's profile location is referred to as *user profile folder*.

Neither the Default User folder nor the All Users folder has a My Documents folder, but both are configured with an Application Data folder. You can place configurations for Firefox in the Application Data folders. I recommend that the Default User folder have a standardized copy of the Firefox configuration and profile folders. This folder could be copied to the All Users folder, too; however, this is probably not necessary or desirable.

The default profile information for a user is contained in the user's Documents and Settings folder, under `Application Data\Mozilla\Firefox\Profiles\xxxxxxxx.default\` (xxxxxxxx is a string of random numbers and letters). Figure 6.1 shows the directory hierarchy for a typical Firefox profile installation. In this figure the default profile is named `xrjy2cro.default`. Either a command prompt or Explorer may be used to view these files. Be aware that the Application Data folder is a hidden folder.

Windows 95, 98, and Millennium

On the earlier 16/32 bit versions of Windows (such as Windows 95, Windows 98, and Windows Me), there is no true support for multiple users. All users share the same configuration, desktop, My Documents, and other user objects.

In these operating systems, the path to the profile is `C:\WINDOWS\Application Data\Mozilla\Firefox\Profiles\xxxxxxxx.default\` (assuming that Windows is installed in the `C:WINDOWS` folder). xxxxxxxx is a string of random numbers and letters. The previous note on hidden files might be applicable in some installations.

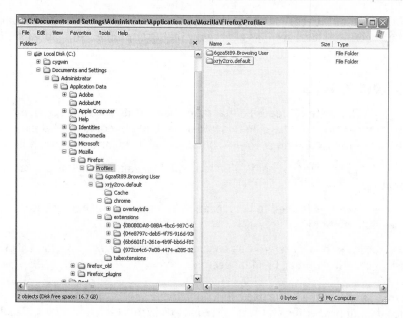

FIGURE 6.1

The location for a typical default profile is shown for the user named Administrator.

Mac

On Mac OS X (which is the only Macintosh operating system supported by current Mozilla and Firefox versions) the path to a user's profile is frequently `~/Library/ Application Support/Firefox/Profiles/xxxxxxxx.default/` (xxxxxxxx is a string of random numbers and letters). The profile holds similar files as a Windows installation of Firefox.

Linux

For most Linux installations, user profiles are stored in `~/.mozilla/firefox/ xxxxxxxx.default/` for most installations. (xxxxxxxx is a string of random numbers and letters.) The profile holds similar files as a Windows installation of Firefox.

Firefox Global Preferences and Properties

Firefox is the ultimate in flexible programs. It is possible to almost completely reconfigure Firefox for users specifically (actually user profiles; a user might have several Firefox configurations). Firefox is also able to set preferences for all users, globally.

Settings in either the local or global location produce the same effects. Global settings affect all users and local settings affect only that user profile. With global settings, it is also possible to change settings that would be applied to a newly created user profile.

Global Preferences

Firefox (and Thunderbird) reads configuration files located in *installation folder*/defaults/pref/*.js. In this folder are a number of files. The exact files might vary from version to version of Firefox, but a typical installation has the following files:

- firefox.js is a file that holds preferences in the same format as prefs.js and user.js.

- firefox-l10n.js is used to hold location information (such as country and language information).

- inspector.js holds preferences specific to Firefox's DOM inspector. This tool may be launched from Tools, DOM Inspector.

Firefox.js serves the same basic functionality as prefs.js in the user profile—it defines default properties and settings. Changes in this file are global and can affect all Firefox users on the computer.

That said, there is no reason not to alter firefox.js, assuming that you want all users to have a given preference by default. (They can override your settings in firefox.js in their prefs.js or user.js files anyway.)

A global configuration example might be an organization that is distributing Firefox to many employees or members. A company logo might be included, network settings might be preconfigured, and Firefox's chrome (the look and feel) can be altered for all copies. Of course, after a user installs Firefox, he would be able to customize it himself, too.

Global Properties

Preferences are a single setting that tells Firefox how to work. Properties are more complex objects, such as how a font looks (color, size, style, and so on).

Following is a list of the global property locations found in a typical Firefox installation:

- C:\Program Files\Mozilla Firefox

- C:\Program Files\Mozilla Firefox\res\

- C:\Program Files\Mozilla Firefox\res\entityTables\

- C:\Program Files\Mozilla Firefox\res\fonts\

The following file types might be found in these folders, although some folders differ in the types of files they contain. There might be other file types in addition to these listed:

- **CSS**—Cascading style sheets define how pages and other objects look.

- **GIF**—Graphic images, such as buttons, are stored in GIF files. (Any supported graphics format for these types of objects is acceptable, so it is possible that there will be JPG, .BMP, or other graphic formats as well.)

- **Properties**—Various Firefox properties are described in properties files. These are not formatted the same way that a JavaScript or cascading style sheet file is formatted. Rather they use # to designate comment lines, and data consists of parameter=value lines. A few lines from a .properties file are shown in Listing 6.1.

Listing 6.1 contains a short segment of the file `charsetalias.properties`. The first three lines are comments and the final three lines are parameter=value data lines. For example, these three lines define how Firefox will handle the ISO-859 character set. There are four ways that the character set might be designated (latin1, latin2, iso_8859-1, and iso8859-1) and they are all mapped to ISO-8859-1.

The entire file consists of about 500 lines of comment and data lines.

LISTING 6.1   A SHORT SEGMENT OF A FIREFOX PROPERTIES FILE

```
##
## Aliases for ISO-8859-1
##
latin1=ISO-8859-1
iso_8859-1=ISO-8859-1
iso8859-1=ISO-8859-1
```

If you are working in a language other than the default and find that some characters are not properly mapped to the correct character set, one place to look would be in `charsetaliax.properties`.

Defaults.ini **and** Components.ini

In addition to the previously mentioned configuration files, Firefox 1.x and Thunderbird 1.x both read additional configuration files found in user `profile\defaults.ini` and *installation folder*`\defaults.ini`.

The format of each of these files is identical. `Defaults.ini` describes additional files that might be loaded to set default values. This allows adding additional default initial settings. `Components.ini` allows for additional component files to be read.

The format of these two files is

```
[extra files]
count=n
filename to load
```

> **NOTE**
>
> Both defaults.ini and components.ini might also be found in the user's profile. If they are found in the user's profile, they are also read and processed by Firefox. Anything found in the user's profile overrides the global installation folder values.

[extra files] describes the purpose of this .ini file. Count=n, where n is an integer equal to or greater than zero, indicates the count of files to be loaded from the list that follows. Filename to load is the name of a configuration file that is to be loaded.

An example of defaults.ini (taken from one of my Firefox installations):

```
[Extra Files]
Count=1
File0=extensions/{6b6601f1-361e-4b9f-bb6d-
➥f8305000e4f6}/defaults/preferences
```

This says that there is a set of default preferences located in extensions\ {6b6601f1-361e-4b9f-bb6d-f8305000e4f6}. That strange set of characters in the braces is the GUID for the GoogleBar extension. Inside the extension's folder is a subfolder called defaults, which has a subfolder named preferences. Defaults are the values that would be used for a new profile's default preferences for the GoogleBar extension. These preferences are stored in a file named googlebar.js.

Changing the preferences for the GoogleBar extension requires that you extract the googlebar.js file from the extension's XPI file, modify it, and then put the modified file back into GoogleBar's XPI file. Then you could distribute this modified extension's XPI file to other users in your organization and they would then have the default preferences you have set.

Creating and Editing user.js

By default, Firefox does not have a user.js file. This file must be created by the user. There is neither a way to create the user.js file from Firefox, nor does Firefox update a user.js file. The user.js file is really the final say for preferences; it is processed last and its contents override prefs.js. (Firefox does update prefs.js based on the contents of user.js.) Because Firefox automatically updates and modifies prefs.js, Mozilla recommends (and I concur) that you not modify prefs.js. Instead it suggests adding those preferences you wish to set or modify in user.js.

There are two ways to create your user.js file. The first way, and perhaps the easiest, is to simply use a basic text-based editor (such as Window's notepad program).

The second way is to copy the file prefs.js to your user.js. (Just don't rename it, you must copy!) Change whatever items in your new user.js file as necessary, and delete any extraneous lines to clean up the file. When modifying user.js, use care to observe the syntax of the file, and add any comments necessary so that should you later go back to the file, you will be able to remember why you made a certain change.

The `user.js` file is covered in Chapter 4, "Managing Profiles."

An excellent reference for preferences that are set in `prefs.js` and `user.js` may be found at http://preferential.mozdev.org/preferences.html. This web page documents virtually every settable preference for Firefox. (However, additional extensions and plug-ins might have settings that will not be documented at this location.)

Cascading Style Sheets: A Primer

Web developers use Cascading Style Sheets to define style for their web pages. Firefox allows the user to create Cascading Style Sheets to override a web developer's settings and change the way Firefox displays web content.

What are Cascading Style Sheets (CSS)? Breaking this term into two parts, they are style sheets, which are readable and editable descriptions of how something looks. In Firefox, style sheets might change or set the look of the Firefox user interface, and set default and overriding appearance specifications for a displayed document.

> **NOTE**
>
> It is a really good idea to read and understand the CSS Level 1 and CSS Level 2 specifications that are found at W3.org. The web pages www.w3.org/TR/REC-CSS1-961217.html#css1-properties (for Level 1) and www.w3.org/TR/REC-CSS2/ (for Level 2) contain virtually all the information needed to write Cascading Style Sheet code.

Cascading is the concept that there might be many levels of style sheets and it governs how they are applied. You might have a style sheet that defines how the overall document appears. Then sections of the document might have additional style sheets that override the document's style sheet for that particular section. Hence, the term *cascading style sheets*.

A cascading style sheet consists of sets of rules describing a particular property and its attributes. The following HTML line consists of the HTML tag <blink>, some text, and the closing tag. Add this line to a HTML page and the text blinks.

```
<blink>like this</blink>
```

In this example, the text *like this* blinks in a browser window. (The fact is, it won't blink in Internet Explorer because Internet Explorer doesn't support the HTML tag <blink>!)

However, should this tag appear on a web document, Firefox blinks the text. And some of us find that blinking to be really, really annoying! With a cascading style sheet, you can configure how the <blink> HTML tag is handled (whether it will blink).

For example, your cascading style sheet might contain

```
blink { text-decoration: none !important; }
```

This rule modifies how the `<blink>` tag is handled. This is called a *cascading style sheet rule*. A rule typically consists of two parts: the selector and the declaration. Another way of expressing the syntax of a cascading style sheet rule is

```
rule {selector : value ! important ; }
/* In the syntax description above, items in italics
   are optional and need not be included if not desired.
   As well, the space before the colon, and the space after the
   exclamation are usually omitted. */
```

In your style sheet, the rule's selector is the word `blink`, the first word in the rule.

Following the rule is an opening brace `{`. Following the brace is the declaration. Your declaration consists of a keyword, `text-decoration:`; a setting, `none`; and an `!important`. Technically, the exclamation point is not part of the keyword `important`, but many people omit the space, making it appear as a single word or identifier. A space following the exclamation point is optional. The rule ends with a closing brace, `}`, which is not optional.

You can see that the `<blink>` tag's action is being changed. By setting `text-decoration:` to `none`, you are saying that you don't want any blinking. The next part, `!important`, tells Firefox that this rule takes precedence over any other rule for this selector and declaration. That way, should the writer of the HTML page tried to reset `<blink>` back on to a blinking state, you can stop her. If you leave off `!important`, the web page's cascading style sheets could turn blinking back on.

Cascading style sheets may have comments, provided they are enclosed in '`/*`' and '`*/`' pairs:

```
/* We force the <blink> tag to not do anything! */
```

A comment before a rule telling the rule's intention is a very good idea. I also recommend that if the declaration's setting values are not obvious, they be documented as well.

Rules may include as many declarations as desired. There is no limit. Each declaration must consist of an attribute that may be set for a given object. An example of a more complex rule is

```
blink{
    text-decoration: none ! important;
    color: red ! important;
    background: blue ! important;
}
```

In this example, you turn off blinking, but set the background color to blue and the text color to red (the worst possible combination of colors a page can have!)

Editing userChrome.css

The userChrome.css file is used to control what Firefox looks like. Hundreds of possible settings can be placed in this file, all of which contribute to the look and feel of Firefox.

Mozilla provides you with an example file (userChrome-example.css) you can use as the basis for your userChrome.css. To do this, copy the example file provided to a new file named userChrome.css. This file may then be edited in your favorite text-based editor (either Notepad or WordPad work fine for this task).

Most Firefox users don't realize just how customizable the user interface is. With userChrome.css it is possible to define the appearance of the following items. The list is not an exhaustive list of everything that can be set. Rather, it is intended to be representative of what can be customized in Firefox.

As an example, menus in Firefox (and in any program, really) consist of some of the following objects:

- menubar—The menubar is the top level of menu items.
- menupopup—The menupopup consists of the drop-down menus that display when a menubar item is selected (clicked).
- popup—The popup menus are those menus that are displayed when the user right-clicks.

You are able to set many aspects of what you see in each of the menu categories. For example:

- border—The number of pixels in the border of the object.
- padding—The number of pixels of padding between items in the object.
- background-color—The color of the background, expressed as a six character (three byte) red/green/blue hexadecimal number or as a predefined color attribute.
- margin—The margin for the object, in pixels. Often set to zero.
- background-image—Instead of a background color, an image (of any type that Firefox supports) may be specified.

There are other attributes that may be set; these are examples of common attributes that many users might use.

For example, you might want to change the appearance of Firefox's menus. The code to do this in the userChrome.css is shown in Listing 6.2.

LISTING 6.2   A SAMPLE userChrome.css FILE

```
/* Actual menu bar */
menubar > menu {
    /* Set border to 1 pixel */
    border: 1px solid transparent !important;
    /* set padding top bottom left right */
    padding: 2px 5px 2px 7px !important;
    /* set margins */
    margin: 0 !important;
    /* don't use a solid color, use image as background */
    background-image: url("FeatherTexture.bmp") !important;
}

/* Selected menu item main menu */
menubar > menu[_moz-menuactive="true"] {
    /* default background color to the predefined color named
'Highlight' */
    background-color : Highlight !important;
    /* default color to the predefined color named 'HighlightText' */
    color: HighlightText !important;
    /* Don't use a solid color, use image as background */
    background-image: url("Santa Fe Stucco.bmp") !important;
}

/* Selected menu item popup menu */
menupopup [_moz-menuactive="true"] {
    /* default background color to the predefined color named
'Highlight' */
    background-color : Highlight !important;
    /* default color to the predefined color named 'HighlightText' */
    color: HighlightText !important;
    /* Don't use a solid color, use image as background */
    background-image: url("Zapotec.bmp") !important;
}
```

Now, some more information is in order:

- Images without a path are in the same folder as userChrome.css. If another folder is used for images, a path must be included. You might find it easier to move all images to the same folder as userChrome.css.

- Predefined colors are listed in the cascading style sheet documentation. Try a color; if it does not work well, create what you want as an RGB value.

- Dimensions are usually expressed in pixels (px).

- The keyword `!important` is required to override any other definitions of a given attribute. If you code an object attribute and that definition doesn't seem to do anything, you have probably forgotten the `!important` keyword. This keyword simply sets whether this overrides other definitions or might be overridden itself.

- Groups of attributes for a single object are enclosed in braces {}.

- There is no error reporting for `userChrome.css` (or any other cascading style sheet). Make a mistake and the line (or lines) in error is ignored. Firefox probably won't crash, but it will not perform as expected.

> **NOTE**
> The `userChrome.css` file can be simple or complex. For more extensive modifications, I strongly recommend that you back up your `userChrome.css` files and the entire user's profile folder set.

Creating and Editing `userContent.css`

The `userContent.css` file allows you to modify the way Firefox displays web content. With `userContent.css` you can define defaults for web pages and content.

You might think that a web page doesn't have any defaults at the browser level, but in fact with Firefox there are many defaults you can apply.

From the box, Firefox doesn't have a `userContent.css` file. There is a `userContent-example.css` that you may copy to create your `userContent.css` file.

Some examples of `userContent.css` tweaks are taken from several listed websites. I recommend that rather than attempting to type this code, you go to the original URL and copy and paste.

The website http://db.rambleschmack.net/pc_tips/firefox_tweaks gives examples on how to make error pages look better. This example is fairly lengthy, but shows how each rule contains a number of selectors.

> **NOTE**
> In `userContent.css`, the flag `!important` is used to control how the settings specified are applied to the web page. If there is no `!important` flag, the web page might change the defaults established in `userContent.css`. However, if `!important` is included, your settings in `userContent.css` override the web page's settings.

The following code is from http://cssing.blogspot.com/2004/08/my-own-firefox-usercontentcss-tweaks.html.

```
/* Generally, most users do not get excited with either
 * a marquee (text that scrolls in a box), or with
 * blinking text. With userContent.css you can turn both
 * off
 */

/* Turn off the scrolling Marquee effects */
marquee { display: none !important; }
```

```
/* Do not allow text to blink */
blink { text-decoration: none !important; }
```

A third example is code to block advertisements. This example may be found at www.mozilla.org/support/firefox/adblock.html. Cut and paste the code into your userContent.css file. (If you are using the AdBlock extension, this code is not necessary.)

Using Themes

Themes in Firefox allow the user to quickly change the overall way that Firefox looks. Rather than sit and design a look and feel, themes can be downloaded from the Internet. In addition, all users can create a theme to match their likes and dislikes and maybe even publish their theme for others to use.

Using themes can be as simple as clicking on a link in a website. It is also possible to download and install one of the theme helper tools, or to manually install a theme.

> **NOTE**
>
> The file type Jar (stands for Java ARchive) is a file that holds both files and their relative folder locations. It is like a ZIP file, but without compression. The specifications for Jar files can be found at http://java.sun.com/developer/Books/javaprogramming/JAR/.

Themes are stored in the installation folder's chrome subfolder. A theme is held in a .jar file (the Jar format is used to hold files and folder information to make downloads easier).

Figure 6.2 shows the themes installed on my Firefox installation.

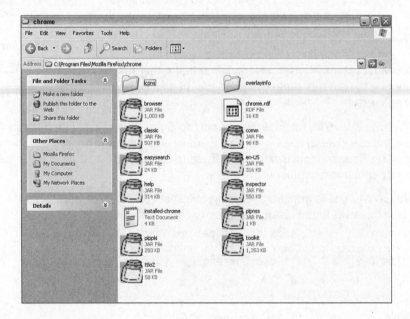

FIGURE 6.2

Jar files are used to hold themes and other collections of files. Use TUGZip *to open them under Windows.*

Themes are discussed in more depth in Chapter 7, "Themes and Plug-ins."

Changing Browser Behavior and Appearance

You can change the way Firefox looks and works in many ways. Both the `userChrome.css` and the `userContent.css` files do just this. However, the interface for these cascading style sheet files is limited at best. Some tools and utilities have been created to improve the process of modifying the way Firefox looks and feels.

Flexbeta FireTweaker

An interesting program that enhances Firefox is Emilsoft's Flexbeta FireTweaker. This program is freeware for personal and noncommercial use.

FireTweaker enables the user to change a number of aspects of Firefox using an interface that is both friendly and well organized. FireTweaker has five categories of tweaks: Appearance, Behavior, Performance, Web Page Appearance, and Rollback.

To download FireTweaker, go to http://www.softpedia.com/get/Tweak/Browser-Tweak/Flexbeta-FireTweaker-XP.shtml.

> **NOTE**
>
> FireTweaker is, like many of the other Firefox additional tools and extensions, updated often. The features described below might be extended or modified by the time you read this. In fact, I'd bet on it!

Appearance

There are seven tweaks to change the appearance of your browser, as Figure 6.3 shows. These tweaks are

- **Use Windows XP Styled Menus**—This tweak makes Firefox's menu appearance match the default Windows XP style (Luna).

- **Use Windows Classic Styled Menus**—Some users have a preference for the user interface from Windows 9x, Me, and 2000. This tweak makes Firefox's menus match the older user interface style.

- **Easy Tabs!**—Using this tweak, you can make Firefox's tabs more easily identifiable. It also allows color modifications. (Users who have extensions, such as Tabbrowser Extensions, installed might find that this tweak interferes with the extension.)

- **Disable Bold Text on Active Tabs!**—By default, the active tab's title text is bold. This allows turning off the bold attribute for the title text.

- **Remove the Close Button from the Tab Bar**—This allows removing the close button and top menu items that you don't use or want.

- **Remove Extra Padding from the Navigation Toolbar**—This allows squeezing together the toolbar buttons to allow more space on the toolbar.

- **Display Sidebar on the Right**—The sidebar (either Bookmarks or History) is moved to the right side of Firefox, rather than being on the left.

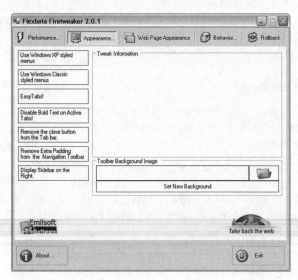

FIGURE 6.3

FireTweaker Appearance options control how Firefox looks. Be careful to not set options that conflict with installed options.

Behavior

Figure 6.4 shows the Behavior section. This section contains tweaks that affect how Firefox feels. There are eight tweaks in Behavior:

- **Open External Links in New Windows or Tabs**—Tells Firefox not to reuse the existing window when another program requests that Firefox open a document or page.

- **Disable `target='_blank'`**—Firefox's built-in pop-up blocker does not stop `target='_blank'` or `target='_new'` pages from opening in a new window. What this option does is make Firefox open all links in the same browser window/tab, ignoring above targets (if so specified in a web page).

- **Always Display the Stylesheet Switcher**—This tweak displays a Stylesheet Switcher button in the toolbar.

- **Use Error Pages Instead of Dialog Boxes**—When an error (page not found or the like) is detected, Firefox uses a dialog box to display the error. Internet Explorer displays this information in the browser window, and this tweak forces Firefox to do the same.

- **Tweak Find As You Type**—The Find As You Type feature is a nice addition to Firefox. This tweak allows setting some hidden preferences for this feature, such as sounds, time out, and sounds.

- **Change the Search Mode in the Address Field**—A search term in the Location Bar causes a Google search using the I'm Feeling Lucky feature. This tweak allows the search results page to display instead.

- **Disable Other JavaScript Window Features**—Access to some additional JavaScript options is added to Firefox with this tweak.

- **Disable Bookmark Icons**—As the name says, it sets Firefox to not display Bookmark icons.

FIGURE 6.4

FireTweaker Behavior options control how Firefox works.

Performance

In Performance (see Figure 6.5) there are tweaks that improve the performance of Firefox:

FIGURE 6.5

FireTweaker Performance options control settings that change Firefox performance.

- **Speed up page rendering**—Firefox does not start to render a page until either all of the page's data has arrived or when 250 milliseconds (1/4 second) have passed, whichever happens first. If this delay (1/4 second doesn't sound like much, does it?) is reduced or set to zero, Firefox more quickly attempts to render the page. The downside of this tweak is that it can slow Firefox's performance on some pages.

- **Enabling pipelining**—By default, Firefox queues a single request to the server at a time. Pipelining allows Firefox to queue multiple requests to speed up requests. Some web servers choke on this option, causing a page error.

- **Memory cache usage**—The amount of memory that Firefox uses for the cache. Usually Firefox allocates the cache memory dynamically based on the free memory available. It is possible to specify zero to have no cache, a positive number to specify memory in kilobytes, or -1 to allocate dynamically.

- **Specify where to store the cache**—No, not memory cache, but page cache, which is stored on the hard drive. It is possible to set the cache location to a different (non-default) location. Why? Some systems are set up where the default cache location is on a network device, which might limit Firefox's performance. This functionality is built into Firefox version 1.1.

Web Page Appearance

The web page look and feel is settable in userContent.css. FireTweaker allows a few easy changes without going through building a userContent.css file (see Figure 6.6). These tweaks include

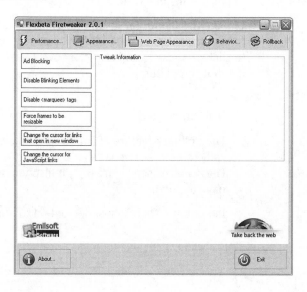

FIGURE 6.6

FireTweaker Web Page Appearance options control a web page's look and feel. These tweaks work using userContent.css.

- **Ad Blocking**—This is a tweak that allows Firefox to block many of the advertisements that are contained on web pages.

- **Disable Blinking Elements**—Although Internet Explorer doesn't support the <blink> HTML tag, Firefox does! If you are like most of us, blinking is disliked at best. This tweak turns off the <blink> tag.

- **Disable <marquee> Tags**—While blinking is just disliked, the <marquee> tag is a downright scrolling annoyance.

- **Force Frames To Be Resizable**—Allows you to make all frame borders resizable. That way when a web page has a frame too small for the contents, you can resize it.

NOTE

FireTweaker uses Microsoft .NET Framework 1.1. If you do not have Microsoft .NET Framework 1.1 installed, you must download and install it first before FireTweaker will install and run. The install file for Microsoft .NET Framework 1.1 is 24MB in size; a fast Internet connection or a large pot of coffee is needed for this download. FireTweaker should be checked before installing to be sure that it will work with your version of Firefox. If it is listed as not compatible, you might need to obtain either an upgrade to Firefox or to FireTweaker.

- **Change the Cursor for Links that Open in New Window**—Some links are hardwired to open in a new window. Some people find this annoying, and this tweak allows the user to spot these links prior to clicking. An earlier tweak in Behavior showed how to modify this behavior.

- **Change the Cursor for JavaScript Links**—Links can also perform a JavaScript command. Again, sometimes you don't want to click on these, so this tweak shows these links with a different mouse pointer.

Rollback

The Rollback feature of FireTweaker allows you to automatically remove all tweaks that have been installed by FireTweaker (see Figure 6.7). It also removes all tweaks you have applied.

In Rollback, there is a single option to remove tweaks.

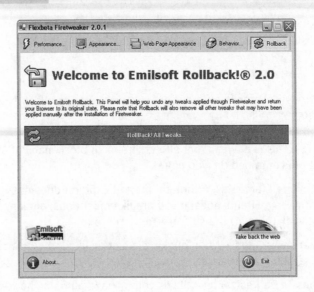

FIGURE 6.7

Rollback allows you to remove tweaks that have been applied manually and with FireTweaker.

ChromEdit: User Profile File Editor

Somewhat less sophisticated than FireTweaker is a small extension for Firefox called ChromEdit. This extension loads Firefox's current user configuration files (`userChrome.css`, `userContent.css`, `user.js`, and `prefs.js`) and allows editing of these files. One main benefit of this little utility is that it ensures the user is editing the correct profile.

ChromEdit's main window is shown in Figure 6.8.

FIGURE 6.8

ChromEdit is a useful editor to modify the Firefox configuration files. It has the ability to edit and save, and not much else.

ChromEdit is a very useful utility, and there are more improvements you can make to Firefox, as seen next.

Other Browser Performance Improvements

Other improvements enhance Firefox's performance. These improvements include more than just improving rendering or communication. Rather they might make a combination of changes to Firefox's configuration

RENDERING AND RASTERIZATION

What is rendering and rasterization?

Rendering is the process of creating an image from graphical objects such as polygons, textures, lines, and so on. Generally, rendering is performed by the application program and not the operating system.

Rasterization is the process of taking the rendered image and placing it into a display device. This process is done by the operating system (and sometimes hardware as well) and not by the application program.

You can do little to improve rasterization—perhaps installing higher perform-ance graphics hardware, improved and faster CPUs, or even an operating sys-tem that has a faster rasterization engine.

With rendering, you have much more control over performance. Rendering is a complex process that is far more complicated than many of us realize. For example, an optimization is made to avoid rendering objects that are not visi-ble. This might be an object that is obscured or covered by another object that is higher in the Z order. (The Z order is the ordering of layers on an image; what is topmost is always visible and layers below the topmost layer are usually at least partially obscured by higher layers.)

No rendering engine is perfect. Some software is better than others, however. With Firefox, the goal is to improve the rendering as much as possible without trying to rewrite the program's rendering engine. (The author has written ren-dering engines for GIS applications, and can assure you that it is not a trivial process!)

Rendering and rasterization together are often referred to as painting.

Firefox waits for about a quarter of a second (250 milliseconds) before it attempts to render a document if the document has not been fully received. (A document is always rendered as soon as it is fully received, even if this time is less than a quarter second.)

It is possible to tell Firefox to start painting the page as soon as enough information has been received to allow painting to start. By default this is on, with that delay of a quarter second. Setting the time value to a lower value (or zero) shortens the wait before painting:

```
// Last value in milliseconds (default is 250)
user_pref("nglayout.initialpaint.delay", 0);
```

When pages are painted, there are cases where the page must be reflowed, or adjust-ed, to allow content received after painting has begun to fit properly on the document. This reflowing is controlled by a preference:

```
// ontimer is boolean, either true (1) or false (0)
user pref("content.notify.ontimer", 1);
```

The default value for this preference is true (1), and this value will probably provide the best performance. However, for some documents adjusting this to false (0) might help speed the painting process.

The time steps for reflows are defined by the `content.notify.interval` preference. There will only be a limited number of reflows before Firefox simply waits for the content to be received without doing a reflow.

```
// Interval is in microseconds (millionth's of a second)
user pref("content.notify.interval", 120000);
```

Recommended values are between 100,000 and 500,000 (one-tenth to one-half second). Some examples set this to a very low value; however, values below 100,000 typically hinder performance, not enhance it!

Firefox tries to reflow the document a certain number of times, and then simply stops and waits until the document's content has been received. If this preference is set to -1, a reflow never happens. Typical values are between 5 and 20, and vary with both the speed of your Internet connection and your computer's speed.

```
// Number of reflows before waiting for complete document:
user pref("content.notify.backoffcount", 10);
```

The `backoffcount` preference can be set by trial and error. If you change computers or connections, you will need to retune this value, however.

Pipelining More Speed

One of the topics I studied when I got my graduate degree was queuing theory. It was a difficult task—optimize the serving of customers in a number of scenarios. It is actually more complex than that because these theories can be applied to manufacturing processes as well.

It gets even better—now I can apply my training in queues in computer software. You can do this, too!

Traditionally browsers have followed a simple process in retrieving a web page from the server. The server asks for a certain element. After it gets that element, the browser asks for the next element. The process is simple, and in theory should work just fine.

Let's look at a set of log entries for a web page. In Table 6.1 is a typical session to get a page. This session spans a total time of about one second. During this time, a total of six requests were made by the client. This is not an example of a dial-up Internet user with a slow connection; some of those requested objects were large. In fact, the web server received requests to send to this user more than 600KB of information in the span of one second. The time to send this information would be between five and ten seconds.

TABLE 6.1 WEB PAGE REQUESTS

Time	Command	Size (KB)
23:09:56	GET /photo.htm	12
23:09:56	GET /photogallery/photo26003/MISC4.jpg	142
23:09:57	GET /photogallery/photo26003/mycat.jpg	18
23:09:57	GET /photogallery/photo26003/HMR4.gif	92
23:09:57	GET /photogallery/photo26003/MISC5.jpg	159
23:09:57	GET /photogallery/photo26003/MISC6.jpg	163

But notice what the client did—it issued six GET commands prior to receiving the information from the previous GET. This is an example of pipelining by a browser. Multiple requests have been queued and are being responded to by the server.

IS PIPELINING THE SAME AS MULTIPLE CONNECTIONS?

There is a misconception that pipelining opens multiple connections to the web server (though this was true with HTTP 1.0, it changed with HTTP 1.1.) This is not true—there is only one connection between the server and the client. What pipelining does is issue multiple requests without waiting for previous requests to complete.

The advantage of pipelining is that the server is better used (the idle time is reduced) because it does not have to wait for a new request when a previous request has been fulfilled. Good? Often times, yes.

However, there is a rub. Some servers have connections or other hardware that cannot handle the number of simultaneous requests pipelining can generate. This results with issues of connectivity and performance that must be addressed.

By default, Firefox has pipelining turned off. Pipelining is configured with the following three preferences, accessible through about:config (see Chapter 9, "Changing Preferences and Settings," for more information about about:config):

- network.http.pipelining—This preference is set to false by default. To enable pipelining, set it to true.

- network.http.pipelining.maxrequests—By default, maxrequests is set to four. A good number to use is between four and eight. The (undocumented) maximum is eight requests; setting a value greater than eight has no additional effect. This value has no effect if pipelining is not enabled.

- `network.http.proxy.pipelining`—This preference is set to false by default. To enable proxy pipelining, set it to true.

A good document to learn more about pipelining is www.w3.org/Protocols/HTTP/Performance/Pipeline.html. This page gives you background information on the implementation of HTTP pipelining.

A good reference on pipelining in Firefox can be found at the Firefox pipelining FAQ at www.mozilla.org/projects/netlib/http/pipelining-faq.html. Again, if you are interested in pipelining, visit the page.

The Firefox pipelining support is contained in the source folder `\mozilla\netwerk\protocol\http\src`. Do a search for pipelining in these folders to determine what files are involved in pipelining.

To get the most out of pipelining, a number of other preferences should be tweaked. These tweaks are very effective for users who have a high-speed connection (such as DLS or cable modems):

```
network.http.max-connections 32
network.http.max-connections-per-server 8
network.http.max-persistent-connections-per-proxy 8
network.http.max-persistent-connections-per-server 4
network.http.pipelining true
network.http.pipelining.maxrequests 8
```

The first four preferences increase the number of connections for a server. The final two are preferences that tune pipelining. However, on a few websites, this preference setting might provide only a nominal increase in performance, but for most, the differences are very noticeable.

Miscellaneous Performance Preferences

Some preferences that can be set to improve Firefox performance include the ones in the following list. Some deal with rendering (those whose name begins with `content`), and some are used in other locations. In most items where a time is listed, the time is in microseconds. A microsecond is one millionth of a second. Many times computers deal in milliseconds (thousandths of a second). In cases where milliseconds are needed, Firefox divides microseconds by 1,000 to convert to milliseconds.

> **NOTE**
>
> Most of the following preferences are used in `nsHTMLContentSink.cpp`. This file has some comments that describe the process of drawing content. `nsHTMLContentSink.cpp` is part of the Firefox source code. See Chapter 18, "Browsing the Code," for information on how to retrieve the Firefox source. Consider this: Three objects need to be drawn. None of these objects has been fully received, but if the browser waits until each one is fully received, the rendering is much slower. Rather, while waiting, the browser draws what it has, even if it's not complete.

The following preferences may be added to user.js or be set using about:config (see Chapter 9 for more information about about:config):

- browser.cache.disk_cache_ssl—This preference is set to -1 if memory is determined dynamically, to 0 if there is no cache for SSL, and a positive value to specify memory in kilobytes. This preference is frequently set to indicate that there is to be no caching, although you can experiment with other values.

- browser.cache.memory.capacity—This preference is set to -1 to dynamically determine the capacity, to 0 if none, or a positive value to indicate the value in kilobytes.

- browser.xul.error_pages.enabled—This preference tells Firefox to use XUL error pages instead of pop-up windows when a page load error is detected. Pop-up windows require that the user explicitly close them, while XUL error pages do not. Also, when this preference is set, the Show Failed URL extension makes a valuable addition to Firefox.

- content.interrupt.parsing—If set to true, the parser might be interrupted. This can improve performance if turned on. The *parser* is the part of the program that interprets the HTML code.

- content.max.tokenizing.time—This preference specifies how long you stay away from the event loop when processing a token. A lower value makes the application more responsive but might increase page load time. Usually this value should be three times the content.notify.interval preference, which is what Firefox does if it is not specified.

- content.notify.interval—Dynamically effects how long Firefox initially waits before displaying a page when Firefox is being used on a slow connection (dialup, for example). Values below 100,000 might adversely affect page loading performance. Values above this will improve page load performance. The default value is 750,000 (3/4 second); a typical value might be 200,000 (1/5 second).

- content.notify.ontimer—A true or false setting to determine whether Firefox does notifications based on time. This preference is usually set to true.

- content.notify.backoffcount—This preference specifies the number of times the counter might be decremented before it reaches 0. If this preference is set to -1, the counter is never decremented.

- content.switch.threshold—Setting this preference to 750,000 (3/4 of a second) sets the switching interval. See content.notify.interval for additional information.

- network.http.max—Specifies a limit to the number of connections that can be established for all hosts. This effects all connections to hosts or the proxy server, if there is one. By default, this preference is set to 24.

- `network.http.max-connections-per-server`—Limits the absolute number of HTTP connections to a single server and specifies the number of connections that can be established for a given host. There is some controversy on this preference as higher numbers of connections can cause adverse server operation, as the server might think it is busier than it really is. This affects either the host or the proxy server, if there is one. By default, this preference is set to eight.

- `network.http.max-persistent-connections-per-proxy`—When using a proxy server and when `network.http.keep-alive` = `true`, this preference limits the number of persistent connections to the proxy server. The default value for this preference is four.

- `network.http.max-persistent-connections-per-server`—When no proxy server is used and when `network.http.keep-alive` = `true`, this preference limits the number of persistent connections. The default value for this preference is two.

- `network.http.keep-alive`—When false, neither `network.http.max-persistent-connections-per-proxy` nor `network.http.max-persistent-connections-per-serve` are used.

- `nglayout.initialpaint.delay`—This preference sets the delay for the initial paint. The default value is 250 milliseconds (1/4 second; unlike many other time related specifications, this is milliseconds, not microseconds!).

These are some of the commonly known preferences that affect performance. There might be many others. To find them, however, requires a careful search of the Firefox source code, an in-depth understanding on how Firefox works, and programming experience.

An example of using one of these preferences would be to add the line:

```
user_pref("nglayout.initialpaint.delay", 500);
```

to your `user.js` file. This doubles the delay before the document is rendered.

Reporting Broken Websites

Broken websites exist. However, some websites are broken in Firefox but continue to work well when viewed with other browsers. This is usually the result of a rendering or other issue where Firefox received data from the site that either was not properly designed or uses a functionality that is not supported. Of course, this could also result from programming bugs.

To report a broken website, select Help, Report Broken Web Site from Firefox's menu. The first time you use this feature it asks you to accept Mozilla's privacy policy.

After you have accepted the privacy policy, the Report a Broken Web Site dialog box is displayed. The current website's URL is placed in the Web Site URL field (which, if you are not at the broken site, you must change). If the website is password protected, you must mark the check box.

You can choose a problem type from a provided list:

- Browser Not Supported

- Can't Log In

- Plug-in Not Shown

- Other Content Missing

- Behavior Wrong

- Appearance Wrong

- Other Problem

Below this list is a text box where you should provide whatever details might help Mozilla in determining the problem's cause. Provide as much information as you can; something that seems of little importance to you might be the key to solving the problem.

A final field is provided for your email address. This is optional. However, if you don't provide an email address, your report is therefore anonymous and if Mozilla is unable to determine the problem, they cannot do anything more. Providing an email address allows Mozilla to contact you if they have any questions.

Power Firefox Tricks and Techniques Secrets for Power Users

Here are a few ideas from the experts:

- Find your configurations files. There are configuration files for Firefox and for the user. User configuration files are in the user's profile, while Firefox default configuration files are found in Firefox's defaults folder.

- Each operating system family stores configuration files in a different location. You saw how to find your user configuration files, and where the Firefox default configuration folder is.

- Firefox global preferences and properties are used to hold preferences for all users, and to initialize a new profile's preferences.

- Defaults.ini and components.ini are used to tell Firefox to load additional configuration files. Use this option to add your own global configuration changes.

- Creating and editing `user.js` allows a user to set the highest priority preferences. Everything in `user.js` overrides settings from all other sources.

- Cascading style sheets are used to control both the look and feel of web pages, as well as Firefox's user interface. Cascading style sheets are standardized and substantial documentation on them is available on the Internet.

- `userChrome.css` and `userContent.css` control the look and feel of Firefox, and the default look and feel for a web page.

- You can use themes to change Firefox's look and feel, much like other programs use skins. Themes modify `userChrome.css`, `userContent.css`, and other configuration files.

- Flexbeta FireTweaker is a powerful tool to improve Firefox's performance, look, and behavior. FireTweaker is a standalone program, not an extension.

- ChromEdit is a user profile editor. Although you may edit `userChrome.css`, `userContent.css`, `user.js`, and `prefs.js` yourself, ChromEdit makes the task a bit easier.

- Many additional browser performance improvements were covered in this chapter, including pipelining and rendering tweaking.

- Along with everything else, the preferences that affect performance are described fully, with default and recommended values for most.

Themes and Plug-ins

Both themes and plug-ins are ways to enhance Firefox's capabilities and usability. Themes change the look of Firefox, the way that skins change how some applications look. Plug-ins enhance Firefox's ability to deliver enhanced content to the user. Many of the most popular plug-ins add the capability to use video, audio, or graphics.

We will work with these two ways to extend Firefox in this chapter:

- **Themes**—Control the look and feel of Firefox and web page defaults

- **Plug-ins**—Add functionality to web pages

A third way of extending Firefox is using extensions. *Extensions* extend Firefox's capabilities, adding functionality to do specific tasks, such as blocking advertisements. We cover extensions in depth in Chapter 8, "Making Extensions Work for You."

While working with themes and plug-ins, we'll cover the Mozilla update site and plugindoc (http://plugindoc. mozdev.org). These websites are where we can get Firefox updates, themes, plug-ins, and extensions.

7

IN THIS CHAPTER

- Browsing Mozilla Update

- Installing a Theme

- Plugging In Content with a Plug-in

- Installing Plug-ins

- Themes and Plug-ins Secrets for Power Users

Browsing Mozilla Update

The first thing we'll do is go to Mozilla's update website. The URL http://update.mozilla.org takes you to the correct page, using a redirect to http://addons.update.mozilla.org.

The update page allows you to obtain updates for all Mozilla projects, including Firefox, Thunderbird, and Mozilla (see Figure 7.1). However, we are only interested in Firefox right now.

| Chapter 7 | Themes and Plug-ins |

Firefox themes and plug-ins are here.

FIGURE 7.1

Mozilla's update web page covers all its products. We will go to the Firefox pages.

Once at the Mozilla update page, there are links to extensions, themes, and plug-ins for Firefox.

Installing a Theme

Themes change the look and feel of Firefox. With a theme, you can customize how Firefox looks, its button sizes, color, and anything else having to do with the look of it. Hundreds of themes are available to Firefox users, and in Chapter 15, "Creating Your Own Theme," you will actually create your own theme!

On Mozilla's Firefox themes page is a list of all the themes available from Mozilla. All these themes are user-supplied because that's the Mozilla way. You can also find themes on other sites on the Internet; a simple search will find many to choose from.

> **NOTE**
> A theme can change the look of Firefox. However, a theme can't change the actual organization of menus or toolbars.

On the left side of Firefox's themes page are categories, while on the right are some of the more popular themes (see Figure 7.2). Popularity is determined by the download count for the previous week.

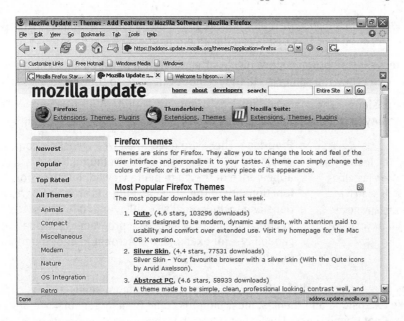

FIGURE 7.2

Install these popular themes and see what the excitement's all about.

How many themes are there? Mozilla's website has almost 100 themes. Some are similar to each other (providing color changes and so on), whereas others are more radical and different. New themes are added almost every day, so check back often to find the latest theme!

Plugging In Content with a Plug-in

With plug-ins, a browser can display more than just native HTML documents. Plug-ins allow showing full-motion video, audio, 2D and 3D graphics, and a host of other functionalities the browser isn't capable of on its own. For example, with plug-ins, you can watch TV, listen to radio, or hold a videoconference.

TIP

Themes can be installed directly from the Mozilla site, or they can be downloaded and installed from a local location, such as your downloads folder. Sometimes the themes don't install automatically. This can be due to Firefox's security settings. You could reset Firefox to allow a theme to install, or just follow these instructions: Open Windows Explorer and navigate to your download folder. Open Firefox's themes manager (Tools, Themes in the menu), drag the theme JAR file, and drop it on the left side of the Firefox Themes Manager window. This installs the theme.

A Firefox user can see which plug-ins are installed by entering `about:plug-ins` in the Firefox location bar. This displays a document listing all the plug-ins currently installed.

Before we install plug-ins, let's discuss the difference between a plug-in and an extension. Aren't they the same? Well, they're not even close to the same:

- **Extensions**—These are additions to Firefox (or Thunderbird) that add a new functionality to the base program. They extend the base program's capabilities.

> **CAUTION**
>
> A plug-in can affect the browser's security. Use care when installing plug-ins and do a web search to see whether there are any negative side-effects with the plug-in.

- **Plug-ins**—These are used to allow a website's content to be displayed in the browser window. Plug-ins deal with the appearance of the page being viewed, but they don't add new functionality to the browser. Plug-ins are third-party applications and include Real's RealPlayer and Adobe's Acrobat Reader. Often a plug-in uses a program to provide the actual capability—for example, the Acrobat Reader plug-in uses the Acrobat Reader program.

Many plug-ins are available for Firefox. Some are common; some are less common. Unlike extensions and themes, most plug-ins come from larger software developers and are not open source. This is not to say that they cannot be open source or user developed, but most are not.

Common plug-ins are supplied by Adobe Systems, Microsoft, Macromedia, Apple, Real Networks, and other larger companies.

Firefox also uses plug-ins to extend the built-in searching capabilities of the browser. Literally hundreds of search plug-ins are available to Firefox users. At last count, I found between 500 and 1,000 search plug-ins (and you thought you were limited to Google, MSN, and Yahoo!).

Other plug-ins are less common, although the actual count varies between platforms (Windows has more than 50, Linux has about 15, and Apple OS/X have about 10).

Most users need only a few plug-ins on their systems. The most popular plug-ins include

- Adobe Acrobat Reader

- Adobe SVG Viewer

- Java Plug-in

- Macromedia Flash Player

- Macromedia Shockwave Player

- QuickTime

- RealPlayer 10

- Windows Media Player

Plug-ins are an important part of Firefox because many of today's web pages use content that requires a plug-in.

Installing Plug-ins

To install general plug-ins, go to http://plugindoc.mozdev.org/. At the top of the page, click your operating system (Microsoft Windows, Linux, Mac OS X, and so on); you will go to the page listing the plug-ins that are compatible with your operating system.

Some of the plug-ins described here will want to find Firefox. More exactly, they need some Registry entries that might not be created when you install Firefox. There is an easy fix to this problem.

If you find that your plug-ins are not working correctly, try the following: Enter the following listing into Notepad and save it as `Firefox.reg`. Then double-click `Firefox.reg` in Windows Explorer and confirm that you want these items added to your Registry. And with that, you are all set! Here's the code to use:

```
REGEDIT4
[HKEY_LOCAL_MACHINE\Software\Mozilla\Mozilla Firebird]
"GeckoVer"="1.0.1"
[HKEY_LOCAL_MACHINE\Software\Mozilla\Mozilla Firebird\bin]
"PathToExe "="C:\\program files\\MozillaFirebird\\MozillaFirebird.exe "
[HKEY_LOCAL_MACHINE\Software\Mozilla\Mozilla Firebird\Extensions]
"Plugins"="C:\\Program Files\\MozillaFirebird\\Plugins"
"Components"="C:\\Program Files\\MozillaFirebird\\Components"
[HKEY_LOCAL_MACHINE\SOFTWARE\mozilla.org\Mozilla]
"CurrentVersion"="1.5"
```

If you want to learn more about the Registry, my most recent Registry book, *Windows XP Registry* (Sybex, 2002), is a good starting point.

Acrobat Reader

Adobe's Acrobat Reader is a program that displays the formatted contents of Portable Document Format (PDF) documents. PDF files are created using Acrobat and a source application such as Word, PowerPoint, or some other document formatting application.

Many documents are distributed using PDF files. This allows platform independence, enabling the content provider to create a single PDF rather than a multitude of different objects, one for each possible hardware/browser/operating system combination.

Generally, PDF files are WYSIWYG, based on printed page layout. When a PDF file is viewed, it is shown in a print layout type of view. A printed PDF document will look almost exactly like the same document on the screen.

How is this possible? The program that creates PDF files—Acrobat—acts as a virtual printer. Instead of printing the document, it creates the PDF file; this file can then be displayed on any computer using either the Acrobat Reader Plug-in or Adobe's Acrobat Reader standalone program. Either works well, although some users prefer the stand-alone version because it offers more functionality.

Currently, four supported versions of the Acrobat Reader plug-in are available. There are also a number of legacy versions of Adobe Acrobat Reader you might encounter from time to time. These older legacy versions should be run in standalone mode only, and not as a plug-in with Firefox. They include

- **Adobe Acrobat Reader 7.0 Full**—This version of Acrobat Reader supports only Windows 2000 and Windows XP.

- **Adobe Acrobat Reader 6.0.2 Full.**

- **Adobe Acrobat Reader 6.0.3 Update**—This version updates Acrobat Reader 6.0.2. If you are using an earlier version of Windows (98 SE, Me, NT 4.0, and so on), use Acrobat Reader 6.0.3.

- **Adobe Acrobat Reader 5.1**—This version is suitable for early versions of Windows 95 and 98.

Generally, you should install the latest version (Acrobat Reader 7.0) if it is compatible with your system.

Navigate to http://plugindoc.mozdev.org/windows.html#acrobat. Find Adobe Acrobat Reader—it should be in the list of the most popular plug-ins. Click Download and the product/version you are installing. Firefox will prompt you to save to disk; confirm and wait for the download to complete. When the download has completed, either click the Downloads Manager's Open for the file or use Windows Explorer to open it. The file will self-extract the Adobe Acrobat Reader installation and run the install process.

Generally, you should accept the defaults for an installation of a program. With Adobe Acrobat Reader, the defaults are reasonable and should work with all systems.

Test your installation! The easiest test is to navigate to any website with a PDF file. (If you are drawing a blank, Google for the keywords "random pdf.") The first time a PDF file is received, a dialog box will prompt you to either open or save the file (see Figure 7.3). There is a check box to make this choice persistent.

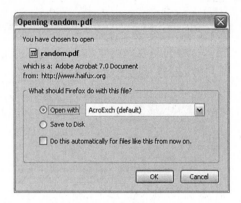

FIGURE 7.3

You will be asked whether you want to open or save a PDF object from a web link. If you choose to open it, you can save it from the plug-in.

As you are testing your plug-in, choose to open with AcroExch (the name for Adobe Acrobat Reader). I do not normally make this the default, but sometimes I want to download a PDF file so I have a local copy.

This test of Adobe Acrobat Reader shows that now you can open a PDF file in Firefox (see Figure 7.4).

> **TIP**
> Whenever you're installing plug-ins, always close and restart Firefox prior to testing them. This enables Firefox to properly configure itself for the new plug-in.

Adobe SVG Viewer

Scalable Vector Graphics (SVG) is a standard that is published by the World Wide Web Consortium (see http://www.w3.org/Graphics/SVG/About.html for more information).

With SVG, you are able to display vector graphics in a browser object. The SVG files (written in XML format) can be compact and create high-quality images.

You use (or will use) SVG to enable device-independent graphics, which are graphics that are smaller than raster graphics and graphics that are editable if needed. Firefox 1.5 provides some support for SVG.

Adobe has created a SVG viewer plug-in. Even though SVG is not yet commonly used, this plug-in is popular with users who want to experiment with this new technology. There are a few notes and cautions on the Adobe SVG viewer.

> **NOTE**
> In the previous paragraph, I said *will use*. SVG is one of the newer things on the Internet, and only a few Internet sites are currently using SVG graphic objects. A few sites have demonstration SVG graphics, but it takes a thorough search to find much SVG content.

The current version is 6.0. However, this version is still being developed and might not be reliable.

SVG Viewer 3.0 does not work and should not be installed with Firefox. I recommend paying heed to this warning and other similar warnings!

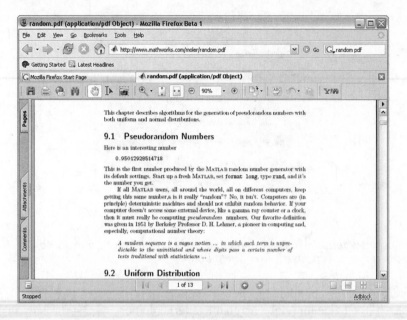

FIGURE 7.4

Now your PDF links will open a Firefox tab, using the plug-in.

Navigate to http://plugindoc.mozdev.org/windows.html#AdobeSVG and click the Download SVG Viewer link.

Currently, the Adobe SVG Viewer requires a manual installation. However, manual installation consists of downloading and then running an executable file that does most of the installation for you.

To get the plug-in to work with Firefox, you must manually install the plug-in itself. The installation program creates, in your `Program Files\Common Files\Adobe` folder, a subfolder for SVG, named (for version 6.0, in this case) `SVG Viewer 6.0`. In this folder is a subfolder named `Plugins`. Copy all the files in the `Plugins` folder (usually there are four of them) into your Firefox Installation Folder's `plugins` folder. (Firefox's plug-ins are usually in your `Program Files\Mozilla Firefox\plugins` folder.)

Do not let the manual installation bit worry you—it installs almost as easily as Adobe Acrobat Reader.

Installation is easy; testing is more difficult. This is because there are few SVG files on the Internet! Even though the first Google hit I did had a site that had SVG files, the site itself was not working. Eventually, however, I found a test SVG file link. The results of this link are shown in Figure 7.5, where the Adobe SVG Viewer plug-in is used to display the SVG file.

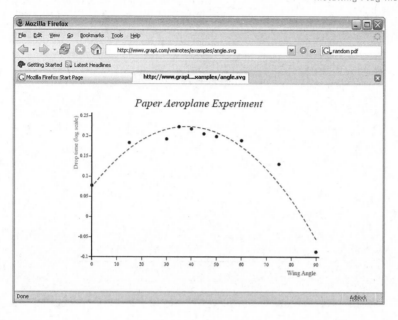

FIGURE 7.5

This graph was created with a simple, 4KB SVG file. SVG files are XML format, and their source can be viewed with Notepad.

For a comparison, Figure 7.6 shows the same SVG file opened with Firefox 1.5's built-in SVG viewer. There are some differences in what is displayed, even though in both cases, it is exactly the same file!

> **NOTE** Sun offers a free product called the Sun Java System Application Server Platform Edition 8. This product can be downloaded from Sun's website.

Java Plug-in

Java is the de facto standard for web browser content programming. It is important to note that Java is a Sun standard and, as such, Sun controls it. This situation might change as time progresses, but the definitive source is still Sun.

When it comes to writing scripts (which is what content programming is made up of), the choices are limited. You can write VBScript (and find that no one likes your website), or you can use Java or JavaScript.

For more information about Java and Java development tools, visit http://www.sun.com/java/ and http://www.java.com/en/.

Installation of the Java plug-in can be either online or offline.

> **NOTE** I prefer to do my installations offline because it leaves me with an installation file should I need to reinstall (and don't want to redownload the file). How you do the installation is up to you, though.
> An online installation can be faster. This is because the offline installation downloads all possible configuration options, regardless of whether they are installed.

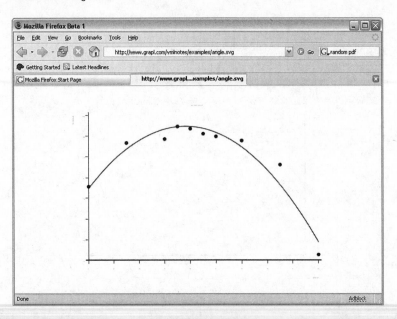

FIGURE 7.6

This graph is displayed using Firefox's built-in SVG capabilities. This functionality is new to Firefox 1.5, and the appearance of the drawing might change as this capability is further developed.

Navigate to http://plugindoc.mozdev.org/windows.html#Java. This page will have links to the Java download page.

The Java installation is more complex than most plug-in installations. There are options for typical installations and custom installations.

One step of the installation tells you to select your browser. Interestingly, Firefox isn't listed. The installation program does inform you that this setting might be changed in the Java Control panel. You can find the Java Control panel in the Windows Control panel.

Open the Windows Control panel, and double-click the Java icon. When the Java Control panel opens, click the Advanced tab and expand the <APPLET> tag support branch. Then select Mozilla and Netscape. When you're done setting any other options desired, click either OK or Apply.

After you have installed your Java plug-in, return to Sun's Java site. Additional content is enabled after the Java plug-in is installed.

Macromedia Flash Player

The Macromedia Flash Player is a system to display full-motion video, text, audio, and graphics. Macromedia claims to have a 98% penetration into the desktop market. This figure is intended to convince content providers that they should embrace Macromedia Flash technology. However, there are other players in the game, including Apple's QuickTime, Microsoft's Media Player, and RealPlayer.

Virtually all Macromedia Flash Player versions are acceptable to Firefox. When this was written, Macromedia Flash Player's current version was 7.0, although Macromedia Flash Player is in continual development.

Navigate to http://plugindoc.mozdev.org/windows.html#flash and find Macromedia Flash Player. Multiple versions might be listed; if so, choose the one you want to install. (Later versions might be less stable but might have better or more features!)

As with many plug-ins, you can choose to either install online or download the installation package for an offline installation. Unlike many plug-ins, though, Macromedia's Flash Player is a relatively small download.

Some plug-ins are browser generic, but Macromedia's are specific to Mozilla (or Internet Explorer, for that matter). You must be sure to install the correct version, and not try to make the Internet Explorer version work with Firefox!

Macromedia Shockwave Player

The Macromedia Shockwave Player is used to create powerful 3D graphics. It's very useful in creating both games and entertainment content, and a provider can create content using Macromedia Director.

After you have downloaded the Shockwave Player, run the executable. This displays the installation program (see Figure 7.7).

NOTE

Some Firefox installations are problematic with the Java installation. When the Java Control panel is opened and the browser support for Firefox is enabled, you get an error message to the effect that the setting cannot be changed. The text of the warning includes the heading `Unable to change Browser Settings`. If you receive this error, try copying the plug-in for Java to Firefox's plug-ins folder (the same process described previously in the SVG installation).

More information about this problem can be found at http://forum.java.sun.com/thread.jspa?threadID=570700. Other users have reported that this is not a problem because the Java plug-in works fine with Firefox even if Mozilla and Netscape are not checked in the Java Control panel. See http://forums.mozillazine.org/viewtopic.php?t=246615&highlight=java+firefox+unable+change+browser+settings for an ongoing thread on this issue.

NOTE

There might be issues installing Macromedia Flash Player 7.0 with Firefox when the Mozilla Firefox installer is used. Instead, use the installer at ftp://ftp.netscape.com/pub/netscape7/english/7.2/windows/win32/bfkprv/flash.xpi.

FIGURE 7.7

Shockwave's installer sees both Internet Explorer and Firefox on my computer.

NOTE

When Firefox is installed using a Zip file (an uncommon installation technique), problems with the Macromedia Shockwave Player plug-in installation can occur. The installation requires a Netscape 4.x or Gecko-based browser plug-ins directory. Firefox is Gecko-based (as are Mozilla and Netscape). Several workarounds for this problem can be found at http://plugindoc.mozdev.org/important.html#shockwave.

Following the installation of the Shockwave Player, the installation program will launch the player. The first start of Shockwave requires some registration information, including your age, name, and email address. If you provide a valid email address, you should uncheck the I'd Like to Receive option.

When this final configuration is complete, you will be at the Shockwave downloads page, which has a simple demonstration of Shockwave.

Navigate to http://plugindoc.mozdev.org/windows.html#shockwave for more information about this plug-in.

QuickTime

Apple's QuickTime player is a plug-in that provides high-quality video and audio. QuickTime 7.0 was first released for the Mac OS-X platform. It should now be available for all platforms; check Apple's website at http://www.apple.com/quicktime/ for more information about QuickTime compatibility and versions.

Firefox is compatible with versions of QuickTime 4.0 and later.

To get QuickTime, navigate to http://plugindoc.mozdev.org/windows.html#QuickTime.

QuickTime is one of the few plug-ins that I personally have a problem with. Apple feels compelled to install additional products at the same time, such as iTunes, a music program. I might have no use for iTunes, but it installs automatically. Also, when you download the player, check that you turn off the sign-up options (free this, free that, news, and whatever). The download page also prompts you for an email address. I used a disposable one to limit emails.

The QuickTime installer asks to install a desktop shortcut, make iTunes the default player for audio files, and to make QuickTime the default media player. Set, or clear, these options as desired.

An undesirable side effect of installing QuickTime is that it can make itself the default player or plug-in for Flash content. This usually breaks sites that are using Flash. Read about this problem athttp://mozilla.gunnars.net/mozfaq_use.html#quicktime_plugin_hijacked_flash.

> **NOTE** The Shockwave Player installation program will ask to install the Yahoo! Toolbar for Internet Explorer. Because of the way Firefox manages search plug-ins, this functionality is not available to Firefox users.
> Google toolbar users will find that the Yahoo! toolbar is similar. Whether you install is your choice, but consider whether you're really going to be using that other browser anymore.

RealPlayer 10

RealPlayer is a media player that performs well. Like QuickTime and other similar products, it allows content providers to offer content to users.

RealPlayer comes in two versions: Basic RealPlayer offers basic media reproduction and is free. A more advanced version of RealPlayer costs about $15 (a one-time fee), but it is important to be sure you are getting the correct product. Real offers several packages that are by subscription, so be careful to not inadvertently get the wrong one!

Navigate to http://plugindoc.mozdev.org/windows.html#realone to install RealPlayer. Installing RealPlayer involves downloading the file and running it. Much like QuickTime, RealPlayer asks whether you want some additional settings: a desktop shortcut for RealPlayer, a desktop shortcut for Free Games and Music from Real, and an icon in the Windows Quick Launch Toolbar. I deselected all to keep things less cluttered. RealPlayer's installation program also prompts to make RealPlayer the default media player (all the media players do this!) or to allow you to select which media types are associated with RealPlayer.

RealPlayer's user interface is complex and can confuse first-time users. On the flip side, it is also very powerful, offering a lot content—both free and paid.

Windows Media Player

The Windows Media Player plug-in is another video- and audio-centric plug-in. It is a reasonably featured product, which I have no complaints about.

We seem to associate Windows Media Player with Internet Explorer and not Firefox. But in reality, Windows Media Player works well with Firefox.

Two versions of Windows Media Player (9 and 10) are available. For Windows XP users, install Windows Media Player 10; for earlier versions of Windows, install Windows Media Player 9.

To view information about Windows Media Player, visit http://plugindoc.mozdev.org/windows.html#WMP. This page shows the current status of Windows Media Player and Firefox. It seems that more compatibility issues exist with Windows Media Player than with some other plug-ins. You can read an excellent discussion of Windows Media Player issues at http://forums.mozillazine.org/viewtopic.php?t=206213.

Other Plug-ins and Toys

Some other interesting plug-ins are listed here. Some of these plug-ins are not fully compatible with Firefox, although they can be installed if you want:

- ActiveX Plug-in
- Adobe Atmosphere
- AXEL Player
- Beatnik Player
- Corel SVG Viewer
- Crescendo Player
- DjVu Plug-in
- FastBid
- Hyperstudio
- Macromedia Authorware Player
- MDL Chime
- Pulse Player
- WildTangent
- XVL Player
- Yamaha MIDPLUG for XG

Themes and Plug-ins Secrets for Power Users

Here are a few ideas from the experts:

- Visit Mozilla Update to get the latest information about updates, themes, plug-ins, and extensions.
- Themes can be installed easily using either a drag-and-drop method or a small extension that puts an Install button on the Themes manager dialog box.

- Any user can create a theme. If the theme is popular, interesting, or attractive, it can easily be distributed over the Internet.

- This chapter showed the basics of creating a theme. The best way to get started is to simply start with an existing theme and modify it. This will teach you what makes up the theme.

- Even though many plug-ins are available, do not try to install every one of them. Doing so can result in some unexpected interactions.

- Plug-ins are used to enhance Firefox's capability to display content. Many plug-ins are available for Firefox.

Making Extensions Work for You

Extensions are a way to allow the user to easily extend Firefox's capabilities. Just like plug-ins add to the types of content Firefox can use, an extension enables you to add features and extend the interface of Firefox.

We know that not everyone wants the same things. Any program that tries to make everyone happy will be so large and awkward that it will be unusable. Instead, Mozilla has followed the path that the main product should have the common functionality most users will want. Then, when users want special things, these can be added as needed using extensions.

NOTE

A *plug-in* is a separate program Firefox is able to host in a browser window, and it enables you to view content Firefox was not specifically designed to show. An *extension*, on the other hand, becomes an integral part of Firefox and usually extends the features of Firefox.

Chapter 5, "Taking Control of Your Browser," talked about a few useful extensions. In this chapter we expand extensions to show exactly which types of extensions are available, how you install them, and how you manage conflicts.

In Chapter 16, "Writing an Extension," you will actually create a simple extension.

NOTE

The Mozilla website contains more than 500 extensions you can download and install. That's just at Mozilla alone. Who knows how many are scattered throughout the Internet!

Chapter 8	Making Extensions Work for You

Firefox Extensions: Never a Dull Moment!

Extensions, by nature, are chancy at best. For example, here's the good:

- Many, many extensions are available to Firefox users.

- Extensions are easy to add and easy to remove.

- Extensions are, by design, specific to a user profile. If multiple users are sharing the same computer, each can have his own personal set of extensions.

- Extensions are easy to write, and the ability to write an extension is not limited to a specific group or company.

- Extensions can save you an incredible amount of work.

However, here's the bad:

- So many extensions are available that users frequently have a difficult time choosing which ones to use.

- Because extensions can be written by almost anyone, there is no quality control. You might not realize that a certain extension is problematic until you have installed it.

- Because extensions are specific to a user profile, if more than one user on a computer wants a give extension, every user must install that extension.

- There is little documentation for most extensions! Why is it that programmers believe users know all?

> **CAUTION**
>
> Firefox extension names have no controls with regard to ownership. It has happened that two similar extensions have been released with either the same name or a very similar name. This problem can create confusion in the user community! Installing the wrong extension can lead to unexpected, and often unintended, results!

And here's the ugly:

- There are few, if any, standards for extensions. Extension development is driven by what the developer wants. Take what is offered, or do it yourself.

- A badly written extension could cause serious malfunctions within Firefox, and maybe even cause problems with Windows.

- Extensions can break when there is a new release of Firefox, especially when the release is a major change.

- Sometimes extensions interfere with other extensions. Extension writers might not know about all the other extensions and what these other extensions modify in Firefox.

Mozilla organizes Firefox extensions into about 20 categories (see Table 8.1).

TABLE 8.1 FIREFOX EXTENSION CATEGORIES

Category	Extension Description
Blogging	Tools that maintain and update weblogs
Bookmarks	Enhance managing bookmarks
Developer Tools	Assist in XUL and website design
Download Tools	Ease the downloading of files
Editing and Forms	Editing and forms
Entertainment	Fun and games
Humor	Extensions on the lighter side
Image Browsing	Aids in browsing sites that are mostly images
Kiosk Browsing	Useful in web kiosk environments
Languages	Language packs and translators
Miscellaneous	Other extensions
Navigation	Additional navigation between related pages
News Reading	News and RSS readers
Privacy and Security	Useful for protecting your privacy
Search Tools	Help you find information
Tabbed Browsing	Enhance the tabbed browsing features
Web Annoyances	Get rid of annoying content while you surf
Website Integration	Website integration
XUL Applications	Full applications posing as extensions

Before we discuss each of these categories, let's first show what you must do to find, download, and install an extension. And, just to be complete, we'll also examine how to remove an extension you no longer want.

Installing an Extension

It seems that half the time installing extensions works and half the time it doesn't! Installing extensions need not be difficult, but sometimes things do not go as expected. Perhaps the extension's installation site is not in your approved to install extensions list. In this section you will learn two ways to install an extension. In *automatic* installation, the installation is initiated by clicking an extension's install link. A *manual* installation, on the other hand, can be done when the extension is already available on the computer. When you click to install an extension's install link and it doesn't install, you can use the same manual installation technique. Basically, you use a drag-and drop-installation just like you can use with themes.

> **NOTE**
>
> Extensions, as with many other features, are installed on a user (or profile) basis. If you switch profiles (either because you are a different user or you simply have multiple profiles), you must install the extension again in the other profile.

> **CAUTION**
>
> Many extensions are available from places other than Mozilla. These extensions have not been checked for safety, though; nor are they signed. Installing them could result in a virus; a trap door; spyware; or some other really nasty, horrible, undesirable program or service being installed on your computer. Be careful! Firefox does limit, by default, automatic extension installation to only those sites you have approved. (Go to the Options dialog box and check out the Allow Web Sites to Install Software option under Web Features.)

All of a given profile's extensions are installed within the profile's extensions folder. If you go to your profile location, you will find a subfolder named extensions. Navigate to this folder and you'll see a number of subfolders, each identified using a GUID, a file named Extensions.RDF, and perhaps another file named installed-extensions.txt.

The Extensions.RDF file lists (in XML format) all the extensions and themes that have been installed.

Automated installation is the best way to get started with extensions. When using automated installation, you don't have to figure out where to put an extension's files or do any of the other installation tasks.

A typical extension scenario would begin with a search of extensions available at http://addons.mozilla.org/?application=firefox.

Let's say we've found an extension that seems interesting. For example, Bandwidth tester is an extension that allows you to test your connection speed. Here's how you could download it.

Manual Installation

To manually install the extension, first download the extension's XPI file. These files are usually small, and even slow connections are able to quickly fetch most extension XPI files. To download it, just right-click the extension's install link and select Save Link As. It'll accept the default download location.

After the file is downloaded, open a Windows Explorer window. Next, navigate to your download location. In Firefox, you have to open the Extensions dialog box.

Finally, drag the XPI file from the Windows Explorer window and drop it on Firefox's Extensions dialog box. From this point, the installation process is identical to an automatic installation, as described in the section "All Extension Installations."

Automatic Installation

An automatic installation is possible when the site where the extension is located has been added to your list of approved sites. By default, the Mozilla sites are on the list. Automatic installations simply eliminate the file download and drag and drop to the Firefox Extensions window. For automatic installations, you simply click the link for the extension's installation.

If you trust an extension site, you can add that site to the white-list of approved sites. Select Options in the Tools menu, and then click Content in the Options toolbar. The selection Allow Web Sites to Install Software must be checked; then you can click the Allowed Sites button to display the list of sites that can install software. Sites can be added or removed, or all existing entries can removed.

You click the extension's Install link on the Firefox extensions web page; Firefox then downloads the extension and launches the installer. Now we can continue with the instructions in the next section, "All Extension Installations."

All Extension Installations

A software Installation confirmation dialog box is displayed, allowing you to either confirm (and proceed with the installation) or cancel (see Figure 8.1).

FIGURE 8.1

The view_format *file is dropped from My Downloads onto the Extensions dialog box; then Firefox displays the Software Installation dialog box, enabling you to confirm.*

After the installer completes its task, there is one final step in the extension installation: restarting Firefox (see Figure 8.2).

> **Tip**
>
> If the geek in you is beginning to show, a plethora of Firefox extensions can be found at ftp://ftp. mozilla.org/pub/mozilla.org/ extensions/. Note that the URL type is FTP and not HTTP. The disadvantage to using this location to get an extension is that there is little documentation as to what each extension is or does. In fact, some extensions might be for a product other than Firefox (such as Thunderbird or Mozilla).

FIGURE 8.2

View formatted source is installed as soon as Firefox is restarted.

The Most Popular Extension Categories

TIP

Do not take anything said here to imply that Mozilla is the only source of quality extensions for Firefox. Heaven forbid! Firefox (and Thunderbird and Mozilla) extensions can come from a variety of sources, some of which might not be even known about by Mozilla.

If you don't see the extension you are looking for at Mozilla, try http://mozilla.gunnars.net/mozfaq_addons.html or http://extensionroom.mozdev.org/ or do a web search.

On Mozilla's website you can find out where to get the most popular extensions for Firefox. These extensions are ranked by the number of downloads during the previous week and are categorized into about 20 classifications.

You can find a large number of extensions at Mozilla, and they are often very popular. Mozilla's extensions list currently numbers about 500, and that number will continue to grow (perhaps without limits) as more and more sophisticated Firefox users develop their own extensions.

The most popular extensions (such as the one shown in Figure 8.3) might have more than 250,000 downloads in a given week. The quickest way to find Firefox's most popular extensions is to go to http://addons.mozilla.org/extensions/?application=firefox and click All Extensions on the left side of the page.

In addition to the most popular extensions (which are ranked from highest to lowest), this page also provides categorized access to many other of the extensions available through Mozilla. Within each category, the extensions are listed alphabetically. At the top of each extension's section is a title line listing the extension's name, its version identifier, and a rating between zero and five stars. Clicking the extension's title takes you to the extension's home page on the Mozilla website. You can download the extension at either the Firefox Extensions page or the extension's home page.

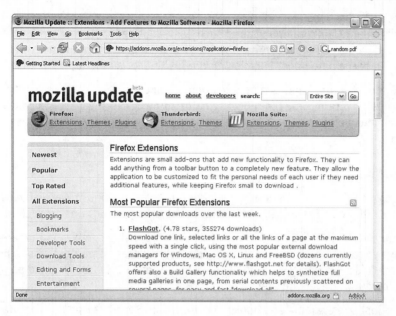

FIGURE 8.3

This week's most popular extension has more than 350,000 downloads, but that's not a record.

The following sections cover the various categories of extensions from Mozilla's web extensions site. I've arranged them alphabetically, not by popularity or number of extensions.

Blogging

Slogging through the world of blogging? On the off chance you have little idea of what a blog, or blogging, is, let's clear that up first. First, *blog* is short for weblog, and many blogs are opinions (editorial) in nature.

In some ways, blogging has been around for many years. We have had Network News Transfer Protocol pages (NNTPs) for many years—these are newsgroups or Usenet groups. Anyone can post their errant mental ramblings should they wish. So, what's the difference between NNTP and blogs?

NOTE

Ratings are from users. If you like (or don't like) an extension, you have the opportunity to rate that extension. Your opinion counts because extension developers look at these reviews, searching for problems, things that don't work well, and usability issues. If you do write a review, be both fair and objective. Don't just say, "This extension sucks." Instead tell the developer which issues you had and what you would like to see improved. Be nice because you might just get what you want! Remember that, with Firefox and Mozilla, you are not dealing with a huge, corporate bureaucracy— extension developers are people just like you and me.

Usenet NNTP groups are topic oriented. Few people have their own Usenet NNTP group just for their random ramblings and such. Instead, Usenet is arranged in a hierarchy of topics, such as `alt.autos.hummer`, a Usenet NNTP group for Hummer owners. A given user can participate in none (called *lurking*), some, or all the topics in a given group.

Blogs, on the other hand, are people oriented, and a single blog can cover a multitude of topics, all intermixed. The blog originator, or owner, is always involved with the blog, though many blogs are multiperson with members dropping out and adding on as time passes.

Bookmarks

Although Firefox offers a good bookmark system, extensions are available to improve what is built in to Firefox. Several of the bookmarking extensions are also interesting.

Do you travel a lot? Are you frequently on the road, using computers that are not always yours? Are you a student, using the college's lab computers? If so, then Chipmark is a great extension that allows you to have your bookmarked pages available to you wherever you are!

This is just one example of a bookmark extension. Several extensions are designed to manage bookmarks, some enable you to synchronize with Internet Explorer, and some are somewhat specialized bookmark-related extensions.

Developer Tools

Developer tools fall into two broad categories: XUL and website design. Many developer tools are available to Firefox users. ShowIP and View Formatted Source are two favorites of mine.

ShowIP

TIP
ShowIP's context menu can be customized by using Firefox's Extensions manager's Options button.

One interesting extension is called ShowIP. This program displays a website's IP address on the right end of the status bar (see Figure 8.4).

One of the things you can do with ShowIP is to look up information about the site in question.

View Formatted Source

I've found an extension that seems interesting: View formatted source is an extension that enables you to view a web page's source code, with formatting (see Figure 8.5). No more kludgey plain text—this extension provides colors, blocks, and more.

Context menu changes for left and right click

FIGURE 8.4

Not only does ShowIP display a site's IP address, but it also adds a context menu to let you get even more information about that site.

FIGURE 8.5

With `view_format` *source, you can see the HTML hierarchy.*

Download Tools

Firefox's download capabilities are acceptable, but they can be made better using some of the downloading tool extensions.

Examples of download extensions include enhancement of the download manager's window, group downloads (where you download multiple files in a single operation), and the ability to save downloads to a variety of locations.

Firefox's default download facility is simple, with the minimum functionality to do the job. For example, the Downloads dialog box has a button called Clean Up. This button deletes all the files from Firefox's download list. The download manager also allows you to remove a single download entry from the list. Neither option deletes the downloaded file, however.

Editing and Forms

Forms are a fact of life, and Firefox has some interesting extensions for forms and form data management.

Extensions can provide something as simple as forms or as complex as a password generator that creates strong passwords, unique to a given site, while allowing you to use a single password. This saves you from having to create unique passwords and then remember or look up those passwords.

Entertainment

Many of us see the entire Internet as entertainment. And, Firefox has extensions that allow for fun and games.

Entertainment extensions are mostly oriented toward games. However, there are some music- and multimedia-oriented extensions, as well.

Humor

A good laugh is important. Not everything, even extensions, need to be serious all the time.

This small collection of extensions adds a bit of light-hearted humor to Firefox. About the only humor extension missing is a joke of the day extension. Hmm, we do need a victim extension for Chapter 16!

Image Browsing

Some sites are almost entirely image based. The image browsing extensions let you more easily manipulate images and even allow you to transfer the image (or its URL) to other applications, such as email.

Additionally, some of the image browsing extensions enhance Firefox to allow functionality such as browsing images on your computer.

Kiosk Browsing

A *kiosk* is a standalone, publicly accessible, object. A telephone kiosk is a telephone (or telephone booth), perhaps in a hotel lobby, for public use. A computer or Internet kiosk is a computer set up for public use. Generally, computer kiosks are limited in functionality to prevent abuse by users.

Some of the limitations that need to be implemented with a kiosk system include making it impossible for a user to break the system or use the system for purposes other than the intended ones.

There is much more to making your kiosk computer secure than just securing the browser, but having a secure browser is an important requirement.

Some extensions to Firefox cause Firefox to return to a known state after a certain period. It is also important to disable task switching, so the user cannot switch to another task.

Languages

Firefox has some language-related extensions. With some of these, you can perform lookups on words. Other extensions in this group modify the language for Firefox without requiring you to build a version for that language.

Miscellaneous

If an extension doesn't fit in any other category, it is placed here. Because most extensions seem to not fit into the other predefined categories, the Miscellaneous category is one of the largest.

Some useful extensions found in this section include

- **Adblock**—An extension that blocks ads from web pages. See Chapter 5 for more information about Adblock.

- **ColorZilla**—A useful tool to determine which colors are being used on a page, along with other functionalities such as a measuring tool and zoom.

- **Copy URL +**—Allows easy copying of the currently viewed document's address, title, and current selection to the clipboard.

- **Show Image**—Allows you to attempt to reload, using a context menu, any images that didn't load from the current page.

Browsing this category can lead to the discovery of some interesting and useful extensions.

Navigation

Oh, my gosh, we're lost—again! There was a time when the Internet was small. Users would often memorize their favorite sites and how to access them. When the user didn't know the exact name for a site, a quick guess often resulted in successfully finding the location she desired.

Today, the Internet is huge. Even though an experienced user can sometimes guess a location, frequently the guesses do not meet our expectations. For example, this book was published by Que Publishing. So, if I were to guess its URL, I'd guess http://www.que.com. And much to my surprise I'd get to a site that has nothing to do with Que Publishing! (Que's web page is at http://www.quepublishing.com.) This is site navigation.

Just as you navigate to a given site or web page, after the page is displayed, you usually need to navigate around that page.

A number of useful navigation extensions exist. Some are trivial, doing simple tasks in an attempt to make things easier. Others are more complex, offering extensive changes to the way the Firefox user interface works.

An example of what a navigation extension can do is Print Hint. This small extension retrieves a web page in a text format (if a text format is available), instead of as a graphical image. You can find this extension at the Mozilla website (see Figure 8.6). It is only 6Kb in size.

Once downloaded, drag the .xpi file to your Firefox Extensions dialog box. Confirm that you want to install this extension; then, after it's installed, shut down and restart Firefox. You will now have a new button on the right end of the status bar, which will be enabled whenever a page has a text printer-friendly version (see Figure 8.7). (If there is no printer-friendly version of the currently viewed page, the Print Hint extension button is disabled.)

FIGURE 8.6

The Print Hint extension allows easy printing of a web page.

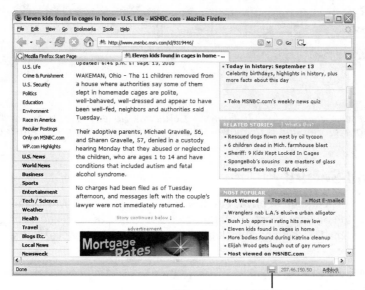

We now have a print button on the status bar.

FIGURE 8.7

After the Print Hint extension is installed, a small printing button appears on the status bar between the current URL and ShowIP's IP display. Click it and you can print the current page in a printable format.

Newsreaders

At one time, news was synonymous with NNTP. However, for Firefox, the term *news* is more traditional—whether it be stock tickers, RSS, newsfeeds, or blogs.

A few Firefox extensions do work with RRS servers. An example is infoRSS, an extension that adds scrolling news to the Firefox status bar (see Figure 8.8).

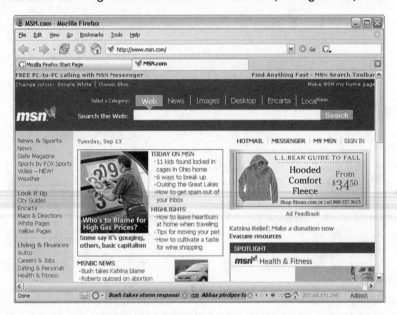

FIGURE 8.8

infoRSS adds a scrolling newsfeed to Firefox's status bar. Hover the mouse over an item and a pop-up with more information is displayed. Clicking it displays the entire item in a new tab.

Privacy and Security

There is no expectation of privacy in this world. Get used to it. When I tell people this, they seem to not want to accept it. But, on the Internet, do not expect complete privacy. There are some interesting extensions for Firefox that will improve your security, however.

A few examples of privacy and security extensions are

- **Add N Edit Cookies**—An extension that allows you to manipulate cookies.

- **ClamWin Antivirus Glue for Firefox**—Integrates the ClamWin antivirus software with Firefox. This enables automatic virus scans of all downloaded files.

- **FraudEliminator**—A useful extension that blocks access to sites that are either fraudulent or phishing sites. The list of sites is frequently updated because these security risks frequently spring up and remain active only a few days before being shut down by authorities.

Search Tools

Searching with Firefox, even without extensions, is easy. Built in to Firefox's navigation toolbar is a search bar. This search bar can be set to search any number of Internet search sites.

Many Internet Explorer converts, however, want functionality such as provided by the Google toolbar. Firefox users need not despair! Although not from Google directly, a similar Google toolbar is available for Firefox.

The Googlebar extension has a number of options to allow customization (see Figure 8.9).

Google toolbar, similar to Internet Explorer.

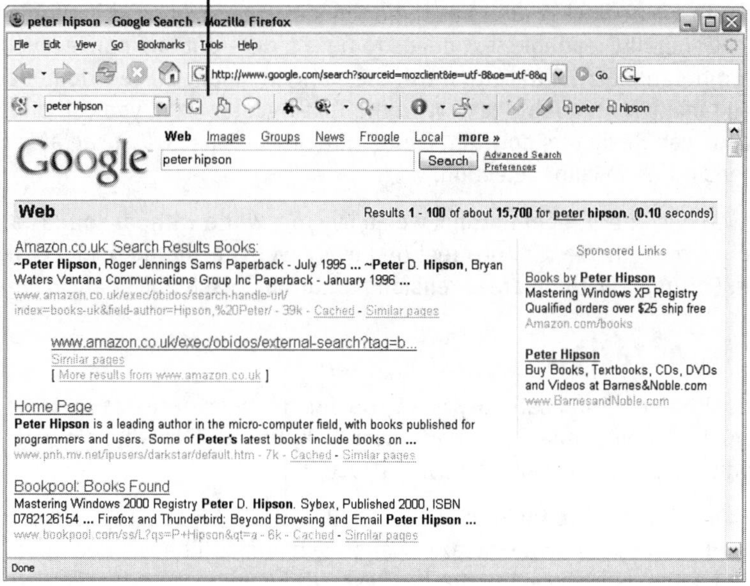

FIGURE 8.9

Like Internet Explorer's Google toolbar, the Firefox version provides a lot of useful functionality.

About the only thing missing from the Googlebar is Google's page rank. Never fear—the Google Pagerank Status extension adds just what you want, a page rank in the Firefox status bar. Of course, you could also try the Googlebar with the Page Rank extension added.

Tabbed Browsing

Firefox has basic tabs built in to it. With the various tabbed browsing extensions, these tabs are made more powerful and useful.

Firefox supports tabs without the need for an extension, but Firefox tabs can be greatly enhanced using a few simple extensions. In addition to the Tabbrowser extension (refer to Chapter 2, "The Power of Tabs and Bookmarks"), there are a number of other similar tab extensions.

Web Annoyances

Pop-up ads, other ads, sounds, and anything you determine to be annoying can be controlled with extensions found in this category.

Red text on a blue background has to be the least-readable combination of colors ever created. Generally, readable text needs to have a different luminance level, not necessarily a different color. Two colors with the same luminance levels do not contrast well and don't make for readable text. With the Text-Bgcolor Fixer, you can undo the damage that some web designers do when creating their web pages. You can also fix some web designer's errors in color selection.

Some web designers seem to think we all live in a world without sounds and that it is their job to make noise. Or, they feel that every website should be peppered with Flash objects. Fortunately, there are extensions to turn off Flash objects.

Website Integration

The website integration category has to be one of my favorites! Is there anyone who has not used eBay at one time or another? Well, Biet-O-Zilla will help you get those last-minute bids in that help you win an auction.

Or, perhaps you want to find out about an eBay user's feedback. Positive feedback (the good kind) is easy—only the sleaziest of eBay users don't have some positive feedback. But some users have hundreds or even thousands of feedback comments, and finding those that are negative can be tedious. Using the Ebay Negs! extension allows you to cull out, automatically, all the negative feedback for an eBay user.

XUL Applications

XUL applications are programs that pretend they are extensions. This enables the XUL application to be called directly from Firefox and (usually) configured using Firefox's Tools menu.

Only a few XUL applications are currently developed for Firefox, although many more are in the works.

It is important to remember that XUL applications work differently from other extensions. They have their own window (and process thread) and work independently from Firefox.

Working with Extensions: Secrets for Power Users

Here are a few ideas from the experts:

- Visit Mozilla's extension room site at http://extensionroom.mozdev.org to learn all about extensions. This location is useful both for creating extensions and using them.

- Firefox extensions can be quirky and temperamental. Often extensions can conflict or interfere with each other.

- You should back up your profile(s) before installing extensions (refer to Chapter 4, "Managing Profiles," for tips on how to back up a profile).

- Extensions are specific to a user profile. If you use more than one profile, you have to install the extension for each profile where it is to be used.

- Extensions normally install automatically. However, some extensions seem to break this functionality, forcing you to install manually using a manual download and a drag and drop into the Extensions manager.

- Mozilla's Firefox extensions pages list about 500 extensions. More are to be found on the Internet!

Changing Preferences and Settings

First introduced with Firebird version 0.6, the `about:` facility enables you to view various settings and change preferences. There are a total of seven options:

- `about:`—Displays an about screen listing Firefox's version information, as well as other useful information.

- `about:buildconfig`—Displays information about the actual build of Firefox. This shows which compiler options were used, as well as the target platform.

- `about:cache`—Lists information about the memory and disk cache. All the cached entries can be listed as well.

- `about:config`—Enables you to modify any of the Firefox preferences and create new preferences if desired.

- `about:credits`—Displays a list of all the people who have worked on Firefox and is retrieved from the Internet so that it is up-to-date.

- `about:Mozilla`—Shows an excerpt from The Book of Mozilla, 7:15.

- `about:plugins`—Shows information about all the plug-ins installed on the computer. Plug-ins are universal, not user specific like extensions are.

All except for `about:config` are read-only and do not allow changes. `about:config` can be used to change preferences for all parts of Firefox.

This chapter is primarily intended to show you how to use `about:config`. The other `about:` components are described here but not discussed in depth unless there is a relationship between them and `about:config`.

about:

The `about:` option, without any argument, displays a web page–like `about` screen. Although much of the information on this page is identical to the Firefox About box (accessed by

selecting Help, About in the menu), the formatting is different. This screen contains a bit more information.

Figure 9.1 shows the results of about: in Firefox version 1.0.4. Other versions of Firefox might have slightly different information.

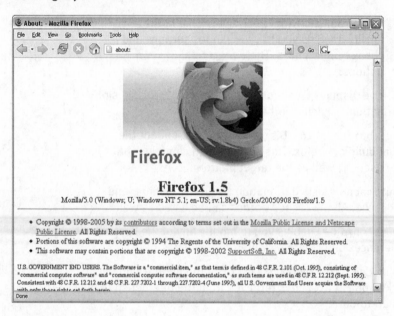

FIGURE 9.1

about: *gives product version information and the browser identification string, which is sent to the web server when a page is requested.*

All browsers will send a string to the server telling the server of the type of browser. Virtually all reference Mozilla (even Internet Explorer) as a browser standard.

about:buildconfig

You can determine which compiler options were used when the current version of Firefox was built. These options include only nondefault options.

Figure 9.2 shows the buildconfig. Compiler options shown in this figure include

- -TC—This option specifies that the source is C (and not C++) code.

- -TP—This option specifies that the source is C++ (and not C) code.

- -nologo—This forces the compiler to not display a logo. This reduces the amount of screen clutter during compiling and building.

- -W3—This tells the compiler to display severe warnings, less severe warnings, and all other warnings recommended for production purposes.

- -Gy—This tells the compiler to use function-level linking.

- -Fd—This is used to rename the program database (PDB) file to the name defined in PDBFILE.

FIGURE 9.2

about:buildconfig *lists compiler and build data, including configuration arguments.*

Configure arguments configure the final product, not the compiler. For example, --enable-extensions=cookies enables the cookie features.

One of the things the compiler information provides is the degree of optimization. This can be interesting if you are a developer and can build Firefox with maximum optimization.

about:cache

Firefox, like many programs, caches information both to memory and to the disk. This is done for performance reasons. With about:cache, you can see exactly what has been cached, and where.

Figure 9.3 shows the root cache statistics page. There are two subpages with additional information.

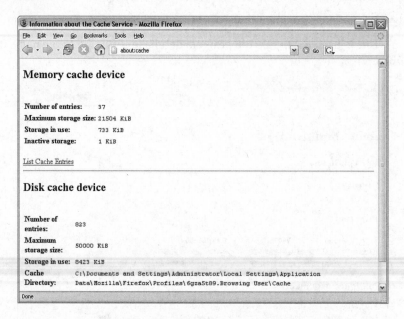

FIGURE 9.3

The root cache statistics page gives overall information. The links on this page are used to retrieve specific entries.

There are two subpages in about:cache. The first displays entries in the memory cache, whereas the second one displays entries in the disk cache. Both cache sizes can be configured using about:config (browser.cache.disk.capacity and browser.cache.memory.capacity).

about:config, Firefox's Configuration Console

about:config is the most powerful way to set options, configuration settings, and preferences (let's just use the term *preferences* from now on). It has a simple interface, has a search capability, and is capable of working with each of the preference data types.

It is an important feature of Firefox because it enables many preferences to be changed that might not easily be set. Certainly it lets you edit prefs.js (refer to Chapter 4,

"Managing Profiles," for more on prefs.js and user.js). However, about:config enables you to change settings while Firefox is running, right in the browser, making things much easier and more manageable.

This section covers about:config.

Chapter 4 briefly described about:config. In this section, we will examine about:config completely and give examples of how it can be used to modify preferences that are not otherwise accessible.

Back Up Before Disaster!

Prior to making any changes with about:config, it is vital that you make a backup of your configuration! If you change something that causes Firefox to act unpredictably or to crash, you need to have a way to recover.

All your alterable files are stored in your profile. This profile can be backed up in its entirety, or you can choose to only back up the critical components. I recommend a full backup of your profile because this enables you to quickly return to the state that Firefox was in when the backup was made.

First—and this is important—close Firefox! Firefox updates the profile when closing and does other housekeeping tasks. You want everything to be stable before backing up.

Take a look at Figure 9.4. In this figure my Firefox profile is named xrjy2cro.default. On May 17, I made two backup copies of this profile. Then on May 18, I made a new backup. To back up, I simply did a right button drag-and-drop and selected Copy Here from the pop-up prompt. (Don't select Create Shortcuts Here because this will not make copies of any files in the profile!)

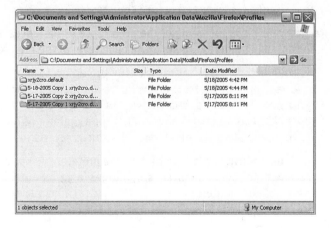

FIGURE 9.4

Drag and drop with the right button in Windows Explorer to make a copy of your profile.

NOTE

The previous example's illustration is for Windows XP. If you are using another version of Windows or another operating system, refer to Chapter 4 for information about finding and backing up the profile.

CAUTION

Extensions and themes are installed as part of a profile. When you restore a profile from a copy made before installing an extension or a theme, that extension or theme is inaccessible until it is reinstalled.

Of course, it is important to not restore any extension or theme that caused Firefox to fail!

Windows won't give me a name that I am happy with, so I renamed my backups using a date and other text to indicate when the backup was made and what the original filename or folder name was. An offline backup, such as to a CD-R or CD-RW disc, keeps this information safe in case of a major hardware failure.

Now, say I destroy my profile by doing something wrong in about:config. I can rename my original profile (in this case xrjy2cro.default) to a different name, saving it just in case the restore fails. Then I can copy—not rename—one of my backups to the original profile name. (I copy so that I don't lose or over-write my profile backup.)

A new or unused profile contains only a few files. As a profile is used, however, it quickly grows in size. Most of the growth is due to the disk cache. You can reduce the size of a profile by clearing the cache by selecting Tools, Options from the menu. Then click Privacy and click the Clear button next to Cache.

Understanding the about:config Display

The about:config user interface is very simple (see Figure 9.5). Don't be fooled, though; it is still powerful and its simplicity makes it easy to use.

In about:config is an edit box where you can enter a keyword, characters, or anything you want to filter by. A Show All button also appears in this box and is active whenever you have used a filter; this turns off the previous filter.

The data in about:config is arranged in four columns:

- **Preference Name**—This is the name of the preference. Preferences are arranged in a hierarchal format using a period to separate each level of the hierarchy.

- **Status**—This column indicates the status of the preference. The three status values are default for any preference that has never been modified by the user; user, which is set for a preference that has been set or changed by the user; and locked for a preference that is read-only. Notice that, after a preference has been changed one time and then reset to the default value, its status reverts to default.

- **Type**—This column indicates the type of data the preference expects. Possible values include Boolean (either true or false), integer (a 32-bit number), or string (a character string without quotes).

- **Value**—The value is dependent on the type of the preference. Firefox makes no attempt to translate between formats; a number entered for a string preference will be a string.

Filter edit area

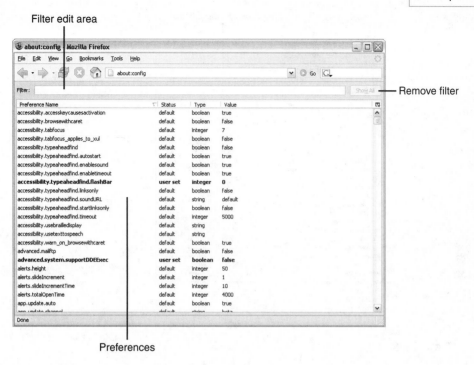

Remove filter

Preferences

FIGURE 9.5

about:config *displays just like a web page in Firefox.*

The final piece of the about:config user interface is a pop-up context menu. This menu, shown in Figure 9.6, is displayed whenever a preference is right-clicked.

The about:config pop-up context menu provides the following functionalities:

- **Copy Name**—This copies the selected preference's name into the Windows Clipboard. It can then be pasted into another application or otherwise used as needed.

- **Copy Value**—The preference's value is copied to the Windows Clipboard. This functionality is useful when the preference is a string.

- **New**—When you create a new preference, you must choose the new preference's type (Boolean, integer, or string). When New is selected, Firefox prompts you for the new preference's name and value.

- **Modify**—This allows changing any preference from its current value to a new value. For Boolean preferences, this toggles the state from true to false or false to true. For Boolean (with no value set), integer, and strings, the new value is prompted for.

Chapter 9	Changing Preferences and Settings

Right click for pop-up menu.

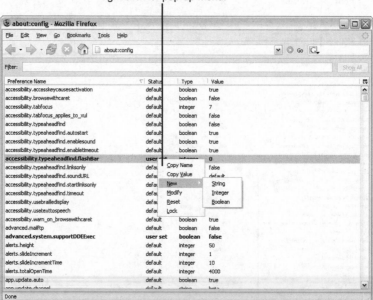

FIGURE 9.6

The about:config *pop-up context menu allows modification of a preference's value and creating a new preference.*

- **Reset**—This option is available only for preferences that have a status of user set. Selecting Reset restores the original value to the preference and changes the status from user set to default.

- **Lock**—This option lets the user lock a specific preference. When it's locked, it cannot be changed by either user.js or prefs.js. This option toggles to Unlock if the preference is locked.

Adding New Preferences

All this makes it seem like every possible preference that can be set in Firefox has been included in about:config. This is not true, however.

In all, thousands of preferences can be set in Firefox; this does not include the thousands of preferences that are part of extensions. With that in mind, you can see that Firefox's about:config lists only a handful of the more popular preferences. One Firefox installation with several extensions installed had about 900 preferences, and another installation with nothing installed still had more than 600 preferences in about:config.

Filtering and Sorting the about:config Display

With hundreds, possibly thousands, of preferences that can be set in Firefox, searching by hand could be somewhat tedious. You have the ability to sort on any of the columns about:config has (Preference Name, Status, Type, and Value), which helps, but manual searching can still be difficult.

Instead of manually searching for a preference, you can use the Filter box. In that box, type characters or words you want to see in a preference name. (You can't filter on preference values—at least not at the time this was written.)

As you type characters, about:config eliminates any preferences that do not have the characters you typed. For example, let's say I wanted to see all preferences that had the word proxy in them. As I typed (first a *p*, then the *r*, an *o*, and the *x*), Firefox would eliminate preferences. So, finally, with prox (I didn't type the *y*), I would see only 20 matching preferences (see Figure 9.7).

> **NOTE**
>
> Why would you add preferences? In fact, many preferences that affect Firefox's operation are not present by default, and a few preferences listed don't do much of anything—they're simply holdovers from earlier versions of Mozilla or Netscape.
>
> There is no exhaustive list of all the Firefox preferences. One of my future projects is to write routines that walk the Firefox source, looking for and flagging all preferences, and create a cross-reference of them. This is not the type of task that could be done manually, though, because preferences come and go.

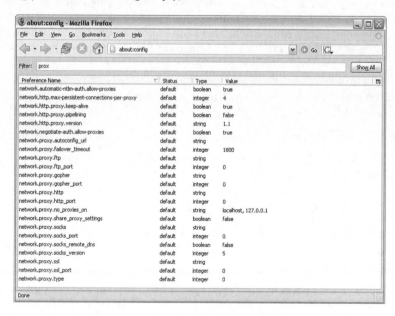

FIGURE 9.7

I've typed prox *in the filter box and now only have to look at about 20 preferences instead of the 600+ I started with.*

When I'm done with the filtered preferences, I can either clear the Filter box or just click the Show All button at the right end of the Filter box. It's that easy.

Using Caution with `about:config`

The `about:config` feature is a great interface, but in reality there is virtually no error-checking for preferences. You can enter virtually any value you might be able to type. In fact, if you create a new preference and choose the wrong data type, the odds are you cannot insert the correct value even if you try!

Because there is no error-checking on the values you enter, pay particular attention to what was originally stored in the preference. Write down the original value (or do a screen print—that's what I do) so you can restore the preference to what it was before you changed it. After you have created a preference in `about:config`, it can be removed only by manually editing `prefs.js`.

And, if all else fails, simply restore the backup you made just before changing anything with `about:config`!

Modifying Preferences with `about:config`

Most of the common configuration settings and preferences can be configured using Firefox's Options dialog box, and I strongly recommend trying that first before using `about:config`. However, with the Options dialog box, you are at the mercy of the Firefox developers as to which preferences are important enough to include in that dialog box. Therefore, you might have to use `about:config` to modify a preference.

To modify a preference using `about:config`, do the following:

1. Find the preference you want to change. If it doesn't exist, you might have to create it.

2. Right-click the preference and select Modify from the pop-up context menu.

3. Write down, or otherwise document, your changes. A week from now, you might not remember what you changed, or why!

4. Enter the new value and click OK when you're done.

Preferences that are Boolean and which are set to a value (a Boolean value can be blank, although that is not recommended) can be toggled with a double-click on the preference name.

Double-clicking an integer or a string preference displays an edit dialog box where you can edit or replace the existing data with your desired changes.

Changing Hidden and Undocumented Options

A few really useful preferences are not in about:config but really should be! Thank goodness you can add these preferences and gain even more functionality with Firefox. We'll look at some of these preferences in this section.

A few interesting preferences you can set in about:config follow.

> **NOTE**
> There is a wealth of information about preferences in the file all.js, part of the source code package. Download the Firefox source code, open the folder modules\libpref\src\init, and edit the all.js file with WordPad.
> Many of the preferences that take an integer value are documented in this file, with comments showing each valid value and its effect.

browser.tabs.showSingleWindowMpdePrefs

This preference is a Boolean value that adds options to the Firefox Options dialog box. Setting this preference to true adds a new section named Force Links That Open New Windows to Open in to the Options dialog box's Advanced Tabbed Browsing section. This new section contains two options: The Same Tab/Window As the Link and A New Tab.

browser.link.open_newwindow.restriction

This preference is in about:config already. However, it is not well documented without digging through the source or the Internet.

Possible values for this preference are

- 0—The default value forces all new windows to be in the current tab or window.

- 1—This tells Firefox to not divert any window that JavaScript spawns.

- 2—Firefox will not divert JavaScript windows that include size, placement, or toolbar information.

browser.xul.error_pages.enabled

When Internet Explorer encounters an error, it displays an error page in the browser window. Firefox, by default, displays an error message box that must be dismissed, requiring extra mouse movement and an extra click. You can tell Firefox to display errors as a page by setting this property to true (the default value is false).

This property should already be in your about:config.

`browser.throbber.url`

The throbber (that funny space at the far right of the menu bar) can be clicked. When clicked, it takes you by default to Mozilla's Firefox home page.

You can change the URL to anything you want by changing this preference's string value. Just make sure it's a fully formed URL!

`browser.blink_allowed`

The blinking text attribute, which does not do anything in Internet Explorer, causes text to blink. Many users find this annoying. If you set this preference to `false`, you turn off a web page's capability to display blinking text.

`layout.frames.force_resizability`

This preference enables you to make all frames resizable, by default. This preference is great when the web designer has failed to include enough room for the frame's content.

Setting this preference to `true` makes frames resizable; however, it can also make some pages look odd because all the frames will have a fixed width border.

`about:credits`—**Who's Guilty?**

There are almost a thousand known contributors to the Firefox project. Each known contributor is listed here, alphabetically. Instructions on the page also include how to add a contributor's name if she is not already listed.

`about:Mozilla`

This `about:` displays the following text:

"And so at last the beast fell and the unbelievers rejoiced. But all was not lost, for from the ash rose a great bird. The bird gazed down upon the unbelievers and cast fire and thunder upon them. For the beast had been reborn with its strength renewed, and the followers of Mammon* cowered in horror."

—*The Book of Mozilla, 7:15*

The number after the reference is actually a date—in this case July 15, 2003, the date that AOL shut down the Netscape browser division. This event is considered by many to mark the beginnings of Mozilla.org. The interesting thing is that `about:Mozilla` is somewhat undocumented. But, regardless, try it.

*Mammon is the demon of money.

about:plugins, **Plugging into Plug-ins**

Each plug-in installed on your computer is available to Firefox. You might feel that you are installing plug-ins into your browser, but in fact they are at the computer level. That is, after a plug-in is installed, it remains available to all users and programs (see Figure 9.8).

> **NOTE**
> Because plug-ins are installed on a machine basis, if for some reason you have to remove and reinstall Firefox, you do not have to reinstall your plug-ins.
> Plug-ins are set as Dynamic Link Library (DLL) files.

FIGURE 9.8

All plug-ins installed on the computer are listed in about:plugins. *Plug-ins are specific to a computer, not a user, profile, or Firefox.*

Working with about: **Secrets for Power Users**

Here are a few ideas from the experts:

- Use about: to display information about your Firefox installation, including version, copyright, license, and other useful information.

- about:buildconfig shows which options were used to create the current version of Firefox.

- `about:cache` displays both the disk and memory cache, and optionally displays individual entries in each cache.

- `about:config`, Firefox's Configuration Console, enables you to configure many features of Firefox without having to edit `prefs.js` or `user.js`. The settings in `user.js` override these settings, however.

- Backing up is the best way to ensure that, if something goes wrong, you can recover. It is better to have too many backups than not enough! Disk space is cheap; your time is not.

- In `about:config` you can add preferences that are not already present. Many preferences that are not in `about:config` can be added to change Firefox.

- Use filtering and sorting to find preferences quickly in `about:config`.

- There are many places to find preferences that are not already in `about:config`. For instance, the Internet has a wealth of sites that list preferences and their options. Also, a file called `all.js` lists many of the possible preferences with explanations of valid settings for them. A good starting point is http://preferential.mozdev.org/preferences.html.

- To find out who has helped work on Firefox, use `about:credits`. This lists the approximately 1,000 people who have programmed, tested, and worked on Firefox.

- The little-documented `about:Mozilla` provides a light moment. Try it.

- Plug-ins are operating system objects, available to all installed browsers. Most plug-ins do not have to be reinstalled when changing or updating the browser.

Using Thunderbird

Part III

Hitting the Ground Running with Thunderbird

Thunderbird is an easy-to-use, complete email and news reader program. Many of the features Firefox offers, such as themes and extensions, are available in Thunderbird as well. Thunderbird and Firefox can be used either together or separately.

A comprehensive set of features is included with Thunderbird that will appeal to all users. Thunderbird has a flexible and powerful spam and junk mail filter. It is a news (NNTP) reader, but to be fair, Outlook Express is also a news reader program. Thunderbird also has a built-in spell checker, so there is no excuse for misspelled words in emails.

Thunderbird Is a Better Alternative

Only a few generally available programs exist for email clients. Included with Windows is Outlook Express, an easy-to-use email program that initially offered such poor security that many users decided to look elsewhere for email. Today, Outlook Express is better, but many users still refuse to even consider using it. Outlook Express offers an NNTP client in addition to email.

Included with Microsoft Office is a more advanced version of Outlook Express named Outlook. Outlook is a somewhat more robust program and offers many good enhancements. Surprisingly, Outlook doesn't offer a news client.

From QualComm comes Eudora, an established name in email clients. It is available in both free and paid-for versions. As with Outlook, there is no NNTP client in Eudora.

Netscape offers Netscape Mail, an email client bundled with Netscape Communicator. This program is probably the least used of the various email clients.

Mozilla Suite also has an email client, from which Thunderbird was developed. This heritage makes the two seem a bit similar, but Thunderbird has many more features.

Finally, Thunderbird is an email client that has the benefits of being free, available for many platforms (such as Windows, Linux, and Macintosh), and easy to use. With Thunderbird, you have both an email and a news client in one compact package.

Thunderbird offers as many features as any competing program. It also adds some interesting capabilities that are either nonexistent in other email programs or severely limited in scope. These are as follows:

- **Themes**—These are supported in Thunderbird in the same way they are in Firefox. This lets you create a look and feel that is your own, or you can use an existing theme to jazz things up.

- **Extensions**—These add new or improved functionality and are available from Mozilla's website. You can also write your own extensions just like Firefox extensions.

- **IMAP/POP/SMPT email protocol support**—This allows Thunderbird to interface with virtually any email system.

- **Built-in RSS reader**—This enables the reading of RSS feeds. (This functionality is similar to the RSS support found in Firefox.)

- **Support for HTML-formatted email**—This is in addition to the plain-text format.

- **Search feature**—This is powerful, fast, and easy to use. The results of searches are saved in search folders.

- **Filters**—The Thunderbird filters enable you to process messages as they arrive from the server. A message may be placed in a specified folder, deleted, or have a number of other actions performed on it.

- **Message functionality**—Messages can be arranged in groups, based on sort criteria.

- **Action labels**—For example, Important, Work, Personal, To Do, and Later can be applied to emails.

- **Return receipts**—If you worry that your message might not be received by the person to whom you sent it, you can use return receipts. If other people send email to you with a return receipt request, Thunderbird can be configured as to whether to send the receipt.

- **Address book**—Thunderbird maintains an address book that holds names of people to whom you frequently send email. The address book can be configured to automatically add the email addresses from your outgoing emails.

- **LDAP**—Thunderbird can use the Lightweight Directory Access Protocol (LDAP) interface to augment its address book features.

- **Import functionality**—A powerful import facility is built in to Thunderbird to enable users of other email clients to import addresses, messages, and settings.

- **Blocking capability**—You can block the loading of remote images that are frequently used by spammers and tracking services, unless the sender is in your address book.

- **Multiple accounts**—Power users with multiple email and newsgroup accounts are in for a treat with Thunderbird because multiple accounts are easy to configure and use.

Thunderbird offers tremendous value for the cost (free) and, as such, is a valuable addition to any user's computer.

In addition to this book, two online documents are useful in learning how to use Thunderbird. The first, "Getting Started with Thunderbird 1.0," is at http://mozillanews.org/?article_date=2004-12-07+16-19-25. The second, "Managing Thunderbird Mail Accounts," is at http://mozilla.gunnars.net/thunderbird_mail_setup.html.

Getting Up and Running with Thunderbird

The first step in setting up Thunderbird is to download the installation package from Mozilla's website. Start at http://www.mozilla.org/products/thunderbird/ and download the installation program. This file is large (almost 6MB), so if you are a dial-up user, you might want to have something to keep you busy while it is transferred to your computer (a 56K modem will take about 20 minutes to fetch this file).

After the downloaded file is safely on your computer, you only need a few clicks of the mouse to get Thunderbird installed. We'll do an installation of Thunderbird on Windows XP and another one on SUSE Linux.

An improvement in Thunderbird 1.5 is the automatic update feature. This feature checks with the Mozilla.org website and, if there is a newer version of Thunderbird, downloads it. After the update is downloaded, you are prompted to restart Thunderbird. (You can defer restarting if it is not convenient at this time.)

Installing on Windows

Thunderbird for Windows is distributed as an executable (Thunderbird Setup 1.5.EXE for Thunderbird version 1.5) file. After it's downloaded, double-click this program; the setup routine will begin.

The first step in installation displays a welcome screen instructing you to close all currently open applications. This is a good precaution, but if you must have a program running, at least save any documents that might be lost if the unthinkable happens and the computer crashes.

The second step is the Thunderbird license. As with all computer software, you need to explicitly accept the license agreement.

As with Firefox, there are two types of installations: standard and custom. The standard installation installs Thunderbird for the typical user. The custom installation lets you set some useful options, so I recommend selecting Custom.

By default, Thunderbird is installed in your Program Files folder, in a subfolder named Mozilla Thunderbird. I strongly recommend accepting this default location if this is your first Thunderbird installation. However, if need be, the installation folder can be any folder accessible to the computer.

You should have selected Custom as your installation type. Figure 10.1 shows the three items this options lets you choose from.

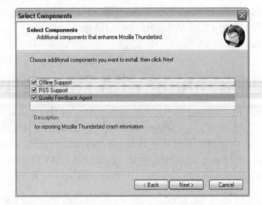

FIGURE 10.1

A Custom installation gives you these three optional components to select if you want them.

Your selectable options are

- **Offline Support**—Most of the time you will be online, connected to your email servers (SMTP and POP3/IMAP). However, for users who are not always connected to the network (perhaps you answer emails while on a coffee break), working offline is useful. To support offline usage and to be able to send outgoing messages the next time the computer is connected to the network, Thunderbird must download your incoming messages and store them locally.

- **RSS Support**—With RDF Site Summary or Rich Site Summary (RSS) technology, Thunderbird is capable of checking RSS Internet sites on a scheduled basis (the default is every 100 minutes) for updates and stories. Thunderbird 1.5 also supports podcasting, RSS feeds that contain audio that plays on devices such as the Apple iPod. If you want to use podcasting, be sure this option is marked.

- **Quality Feedback Agent**—Using this enables Thunderbird to send nonpersonal information to Mozilla whenever Thunderbird crashes. This information is anonymous and helps the developers find and fix flaws in Thunderbird.

You can choose to automatically create icons on your desktop, in the Start menu, and in the Quick Launch bar (the space next to the Start button).

After you have selected your options and configuration, the Thunderbird installation program can begin the installation.

When the installation completes, the final step is to click Finish to close the installation program. The only option on this screen is to select whether to launch Thunderbird at this time. Select the Launch option and give Thunderbird a test drive.

Linux

Installation of Thunderbird on Linux is as easy as with Windows. The size of the download is larger, though (about 10MB, so figure about 35 minutes on a dial-up connection).

After Thunderbird downloads, open the archive (Thunderbird's archive is named `thunderbird-1.5.tar.gz`) in your Linux archive viewer program (File Roller if you're using GNOME). When the archive is open, extract the files (with directory information) to your installation location. Users typically extract the Thunderbird files to a folder in `username/bin`.

> **NOTE**
> Even though the Windows installation of Thunderbird is easy, the Linux installation might be considered to be even easier. With the Linux installation, there are no options to set or folders to install to; all you have to do is extract Thunderbird from the archive and place it into a convenient folder.

After the files are extracted, go to the folder to which you extracted the Thunderbird files and start the Thunderbird shell script—this is the only file named `Thunderbird`.

Importing Account Settings

Most of us already have email. Some people use a web mail interface, such as Outlook Web Access (OWA). Those users should read the section after this, "Setting Up Accounts." But, if you are already a user of Outlook, Outlook Express, or Eudora, read on.

After Thunderbird is installed, the first time it is run it prompts to see whether you want to import your email settings. Importing enables you to import your address books, existing mail from your existing email program, and some configuration settings.

Importing Address Books

Thunderbird can import address books from other email programs, including Outlook, Outlook Express, Eudora, and any email program that is capable of exporting address book information in a text file format (such as LDIF, CSV, TAB, and TXT).

Eudora

Eudora stores address information in separate files in the Eudora program's working folder (typically `c:\program files\qualcomm\eudora\nndbase.txt` and `c:\program files\qualcomm\eudora\nndbase.toc`).

Thunderbird imports these files into your new address book. Because Thunderbird has more detailed information for address book entries than Eudora does, you will likely want to go to the new address book entries and update them to include additional Thunderbird-specific information.

You don't need to own the address book you are importing from Eudora: As long as you have access to this address book, Thunderbird will import it for you. This enables the publishing of a read-only copy of your Eudora address as a network shared resource, and other users can then also import the addresses.

Tip

If you are interested in using Outlook and Outlook Express address books directly without importing them into Thunderbird, visit http://abzilla.mozdev.org/. This document provides information about upgrades to the address book capabilities.

Outlook

Outlook supports address books as a `.pst` file (a personal store), a `.pab` file (a personal address book), or an Exchange Server object. Thunderbird imports the address book the installation of Outlook is configured to use.

To be able to import an Outlook address book, Outlook must be defined as the default email program. After you have installed Thunderbird, when you reach this point, Outlook might not be your default email client. The easiest fix for this problem—which causes the message shown in Figure 10.2—is to start Outlook and click OK when it prompts to be made the default mail program.

FIGURE 10.2

Importing from Outlook is made more difficult because Outlook must be the default mail program.

If you do receive this message, close Outlook if it was open and then restart it. When Outlook prompts whether it is to be the default mail client, click OK. Then the import from Outlook should work. When you're done, make Thunderbird the default email client.

Outlook Express

Outlook Express is the little brother of Outlook. Importing from Outlook Express is easier than from Outlook because you don't have to make Outlook Express your default mail program.

Simply click Outlook Express in the Import Wizard's screen; all Outlook Express addresses will then be imported for you.

Text Files

The various text file formats require the most effort to import. You must tell Thunderbird what the file looks like (which columns are present and the order of the columns).

In Figure 10.3, I am importing a simple comma-delimited text file. The records in this file are

```
Peter, Hipson, Peter5, peter5@hipson.net
Peter, Hipson, Peter6, peter6@hipson.net
```

TIP You might want to import data that has one or more fields that do not match those that Thunderbird expects. Thunderbird has four general-purpose fields named custom 1 through custom 4. And it has a notes field that can be used for this data.
In the exporting program, order the columns in the same order as the Thunderbird fields.

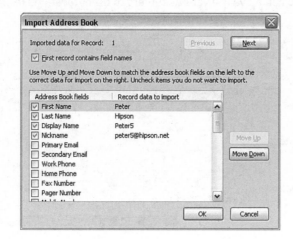

FIGURE 10.3

Any fields that are not in the file being imported are unchecked.

In the Import Address Book dialog box, you can check and uncheck fields and reorder fields to match your file's field order. After you have selected the fields you want to import, simply click OK to perform the importation.

TIP

If you are using a CSV or other file type compatible with Excel, and you have Excel, you can remove columns, sort the data, and reorder columns easily with just a few clicks of the mouse. Change your data to meet your needs and then save it as a CSV file again.

Mail

Transferring the contents of your existing email program into Thunderbird provides a seamless migration in which you lose none of your valuable messages or documents.

A sample import from Outlook Express shows a user with a number of folders and messages. This user then imported the mail, which also imports the entire folder structure, too!

As Figure 10.4 shows, all the messages in Outlook Express were imported into a folder named Outlook Express Mail. The entire Outlook Express folder hierarchy is preserved; if you want, you can move the various folders to other locations in Thunderbird.

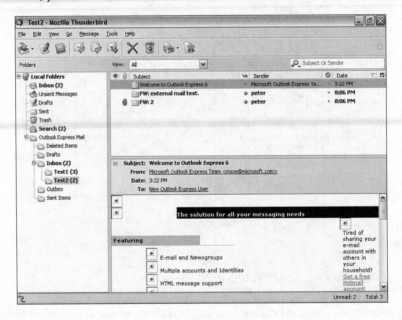

FIGURE 10.4

A simple drag-and-drop lets me move the imported folder Test1 *to my main Thunderbird Inbox folder.*

Settings

The Import Settings selection lets you import various settings and configurations made in Outlook Express into Thunderbird.

Imported settings vary greatly based on the source. Mozilla settings are similar to Thunderbird, so more of them are imported than settings in Outlook Express, for example.

> **NOTE** In Thunderbird 1.0.4, the Import Settings dialog box says that settings and mail and address books are imported. This description is incorrect, however—only the settings are imported. To import mail and address book information, you must select the appropriate option.

Setting Up Accounts

Users seem to see setting up their accounts as one of the more intimidating tasks when setting up a mail program. You have to consider servers, what they do, usernames, mailbox names, passwords, domains, and so on—you get the idea. It's somewhat complicated, to say the least.

To get started, let's figure out as much as we can. First, let's look at how email is done. You start with what is called a Simple Mail Transfer Protocol (SMTP) server. This server is what moves the mail between users, computers, and domains. You send all mail using SMTP because every Internet email system is SMTP based.

When your home domain's mail system receives a message for someone in the domain (using SMTP), it puts that message in a special folder usually called the *drop folder*. Any mail your home domain's email server receives that is not for its domain is then forwarded (or *relayed*) to the correct domain. Years ago, before spam, an email message could be relayed through 5–10 SMTP servers before it reached your domain. Today, to limit spam, relaying is much more limited and is allowed only between domains that trust each other. This keeps you from sending spam through my SMTP server, for example.

Back at your domain, the next link in the chain is the Post Office Protocol (POP3). This server checks the drop folder to see which messages the SMTP server has left for the domain users. Each email is examined to determine who it is intended for. If the user exists, he has a folder (usually called a *mailbox*) and the POP3 server places the email for that user into his mailbox folder. If, on the other hand, the POP3 server cannot find the person who the message is for, it sends a nondelivery receipt (NDR) to the sender's mail system.

Now that POP3 has placed your mail into your mailbox folder, you can begin the process of getting your email. Your email program asks the POP3 server whether there is any email; if there is, it requests the mail. POP3 then transfers the mail to your email program.

> **NOTE**
>
> The Internet Message Access Protocol (IMAP) is another protocol used to interface with your mailbox. This protocol is similar to POP3, although it is more powerful. IMAP enables you to actually create folders on the mail server, perform searches, and other functionality. This is possible because IMAP always stores messages and attachments on the server (local downloading is optional), whereas on POP3 it is usually the other way around.

This is perhaps an oversimplification of the process, but it covers the basic issues. Mail is transferred between domains with SMTP; POP3 collects email from the SMTP server; and users collect their email from POP3.

Security is the issue that sometimes makes setup difficult. You must protect your security, so POP3 wants you to use a user ID and password to ensure your email is delivered to you and not someone else. (SMTP wants you to use a password to ensure that you are allowed to send email, too.) Even this wouldn't be so hard were it not for the fact that with some systems, your username and mailbox names are not the same. Fortunately, many systems are identical, making the setup process simpler.

To set up your mail accounts, first you must gather some information:

- **Your mail domain name**—For example, my mail domain is `hipson.net`.

- **Your mailbox name**—For example, my mailbox name is `thunderbird_user`.

- **Your logon ID**—For example, on my email system mine is `thunderbird_user@hipson.net`.

- **Your logon password**—For example, mine is `apple-pear-grease`.

- **The incoming mail server**—For mine, the server is `ishtar.hipson.net` and the POP3 port is 110. Were this server to be IMAP, the port number would have been 143. A secure POP email account uses port 995. (Virtually all email systems that support IMAP also support POP3.)

- **The outgoing mail SMTP server**—Mine is `ishtar.hipson.net`, and the SMTP port is 25.

After you have collected this information, setting up an email account is relatively painless. Just do the following:

1. Click Account Settings under Tools in the Thunderbird menu. The Account Settings dialog box lists currently defined accounts and has buttons labeled Add Account, Set As Default, and Remove Account. Click Outgoing Server (SMTP) in the list on the left.

2. Thunderbird allows multiple outgoing SMTP servers, but you usually need only one. Fill in the server's name (for this example, it's `ishtar`; the `hipson.net` part is unnecessary because it is a local server). The port, 25, is the default SMTP port. If your SMTP server uses a different port, change this value. Virtually all SMTP servers

require authentication before they will allow sending email to any other SMTP server. In this case, you use your POP3 name and password. You will be prompted for the password when the account is used the first time, and Thunderbird can be told to remember the password for later use. If the SMTP server uses secure connections, set them as well. You might have to ask your network administrator (or ISP help desk) if you do not know the correct setting. You can always try with the default of no secure connection.

3. Next, you must create a POP3 email account. This is the account where you receive your email. Click the Add Account button in the lower-right part of the Account Settings dialog box.

> **NOTE** The Create Accounts Wizard asks for outgoing (SMTP) server information only if no outgoing server is defined.

4. Thunderbird uses a wizard to create accounts. The first wizard page lets you specify the type of account you are creating. In this example, you are creating an email account, which is the default for the wizard.

5. The second page of the Account Wizard lets you enter your name and email address. The email address is what someone will use when they reply to an email from you. The name is simply a people-friendly name.

> **NOTE** You can have an outgoing email server in a different organization from your incoming email server. Your outgoing email server (SMTP) need only be willing to accept your email; it does not have to concern itself with your incoming email at all.

6. On the third wizard page, choose which type of email protocol the incoming mail server will use. The two choices are IMAP and POP. My email server supports only POP3, and not IMAP, so I use the default: POP.

7. The incoming account name is almost always the same as the mailbox name, and frequently the same name is used for both incoming (POP3) and outgoing (SMTP) servers. A few systems do use different names for the account and the mailbox.

> **TIP** Whenever a POP3 mail account is created, you have the option of using the global inbox (also called the Local Folders' inbox), using another account's folders, or creating a new set of folders for this account.
>
> This enables you to keep email from different accounts separated, so you don't mix personal email with business email, for example.

8. Next, you give your account a friendly name. This name is just for your use and does nothing except make the account look pretty. Choose a name that makes sense (such as Work Emails), or just use the default associated with this account.

9. You are done. The Account Wizard displays the account information, which you should review to ensure that no mistakes have been made (see Figure 10.5).

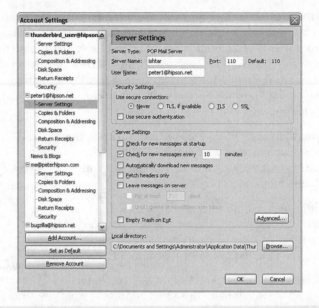

FIGURE 10.5

You can change settings made when you created the account and a few other settings, as well.

Server Settings

After an account has been set up, you can set settings and configurations for it. The first choice, Server Settings, enables further customization and modification of the settings for the incoming (POP or IMAP) server.

Server settings you can modify include those you initially configured, as well as a number of new settings.

Check for New Messages at Startup

When this is checked, each time Thunderbird starts all incoming email accounts are checked for new messages. This option is on by default, and most users leave it turned on.

Check for New Messages Every 10 Minutes

Email comes at anytime; there is no schedule or appointed time for email to arrive. You can check frequently for new email using the interval specified in this option. If the time interval is too short, it could affect your system's performance; if it's too long, you might wait longer than necessary for emails. Again, the default (check every

10 minutes) seems to work well for most users. However, if you frequently receive time-critical email, you might want to set the interval to a smaller value, say 3 minutes. Regardless of the setting, you can tell Thunderbird to check for new emails at any time.

Automatically Download New Messages

If this option is turned off, Thunderbird displays a message that you have new email but does not get the email or headers. If you don't see the new messages in your folders, this option is turned off. Virtually all users turn on this option.

Fetch Headers Only

Instead of fetching the entire message, Thunderbird can be instructed to retrieve only the message headers. The body of the message remains on the email server. You can then examine the header fields, such as Subject and From, to determine whether you want the see the message (download it) or just delete it. This option is usually turned off, but users with slow connections should consider turning it on.

Also see the options under Disk Space, where you can choose to not download messages that exceed a certain size or download only a portion of large email messages.

Leave Messages on Server

If you check email from several computers, you might choose to leave your messages on the server. This option enables you to retrieve the messages later during another email session or on a different computer.

The most important consideration is your server mailbox's maximum size. If your mailbox grows too large, you might lose new emails that are refused with the message `Mailbox full`.

> **TIP** If you routinely leave email messages on your server, you can create a filter that deletes emails that are older than a certain age or that moves the older emails to a local folder.

Empty Trash on Exit

The Trash folder, where everything you delete goes, can be emptied manually or every time Thunderbird closes. I prefer to manually empty the trash, which is the default option.

Creating Your Own Mail Start Page

The mail start page is displayed in the Message pane of Thunderbird. This file, by default, is an HTML file, although an image can be used as well.

To modify the mail start page, click Options in Thunderbird's Tools menu. The Options window's General section displays the Thunderbird Start Page settings (see Figure 10.6). This option can be turned off if you want—however, turning it off doesn't improve anything.

FIGURE 10.6

The Thunderbird Start Page location is set here, but you can restore the original by clicking the Restore Default button.

A location specification exists for the file to be used for the mail start page. The syntax, for Windows users especially, is a bit odd. Because this will be a disk-based file, you specify it as follows:

```
file:///c:/folder/filename.ext
```

Notice in this example that the Windows backslash character (\) is replaced with a forward slash (/). Also notice that you must prefix the file's location and name with `file:///`—and those three slashes are important! In the example shown in Figure 10.7, I've replaced the start page with an image.

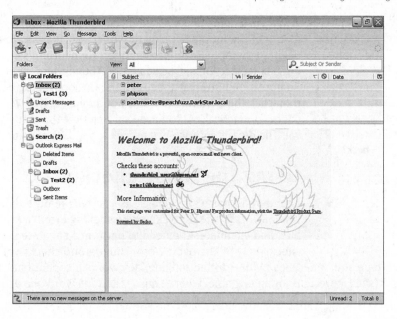

FIGURE 10.7

Originally Thunderbird had an HTML start page, but I've used an image to get the effect I want.

Composing and Sending a Message

To create a new email message, click the New Message toolbar button (the blue pen and paper button). This displays the Compose New Message window, where you can address and compose your message.

In the compose window, you should first address your message. You can enter either a complete email address or a name from your address book. If you want to CC (courtesy copy) or BCC (blind courtesy copy) the message to another recipient, click the down arrow to the left of To in the address field section.

After the addressing is done, begin by typing the message in the message area. After composing the new message, you can send the message by simply clicking the Send button in the message's Compose window toolbar.

One useful trick that allows you to compose a message from the Thunderbird desktop icon is right-clicking the Thunderbird icon and selecting Compose Message from the pop-up menu. This is accomplished using a Registry change. The items you must change in the Registry and a description of this process can be found at http://collingrady.com/2004/12/12/thunderbird-static-desktop-icon/.

TIP

Thunderbird's automatic spelling checker can be turned off. Select Tools, Options and click the Composition button at the top of the Options dialog box. Then click the Spelling tab to get to the spelling options. Once there, check the first option, Check Spelling Before Sending, to tell Thunderbird to always spell-check your message before it is sent.

When you compose a message, Thunderbird automatically saves a draft of the message using the Auto Save feature. To enable (or disable) the Auto Save feature, open Thunderbird's options dialog box (select Tools, Options in the Thunderbird menu). Click the Composition button at the top of the Options dialog box, and then click the General tab if it is not already active. You can then check (or uncheck) Auto Save Every and set the auto save interval. The default interval is 5 minutes, but I set mine at 2 minutes.

Using the Spell-Checker

Thunderbird has a spell-check-as-you-type feature that is new in version 1.5. This feature can make spelling errors a thing of the past and eliminates the need to perform a separate spelling check. As with Microsoft Word, Thunderbird checks your spelling as you type and underlines (with a dotted red line) any words it cannot find in the dictionary (see Figure 10.8 for an example, where I misspelled the word *one* as *wone*).

A simple right-click allows you to select possible correct spellings for the word in question. Thunderbird also lets you easily add words to your custom dictionary (that way, those special terms and names won't always be flagged as spelling errors).

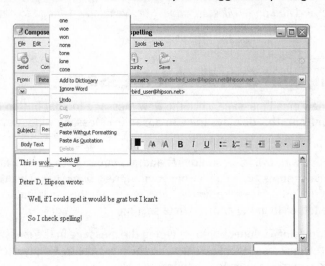

FIGURE 10.8

The word not found is underlined in red, and a right-click gives you some suggested replacement words.

Thunderbird supports languages other than English, so messages written in other languages can be checked.

Replying to Mail

Many times your email consists of replying to messages sent by others. Any message in any folder (even the Trash folder) can be replied to or forwarded. On Thunderbird's toolbar are three buttons: Reply (an envelope with a green arrow), Reply to All (two envelopes and a blue arrow), and Forward (an envelope with a violet arrow).

When you reply to an email, the To address(es) is retrieved from the original message. The subject is the original subject with RE: added to the front of it.

When replying, you can choose to have your reply quote the original message. Then you can configure your reply to start above the quoted message, start below the quoted message (the default), or have the quoted message text selected. These options are set in Account Settings, Composition & Addressing, in the Composition section.

Your reply header (by default, it's <author> wrote:, where <author> is the author of the quoted message) can also be changed by setting a preference as described on this web page: http://mozilla.gunnars.net/mozfaq_use.html#change_reply_header_text.

After you have composed your reply, either click the Send button in the Compose window or press Ctrl+Enter (Return on the Mac).

> **TIP** Other language dictionaries can be downloaded from Mozilla's website. This site has almost 50 dictionaries covering about 35 languages.
> Additional dictionaries can be found at http://www.mozilla.org/products/thunderbird/dictionaries.html.

> **TIP** Be careful of the Reply All button. One of the most serious breaches of email etiquette is to reply to all when you really want the reply to go to only the sender. Reply All sends your reply to the original sender and everyone else the sender sent the message to.
> I have seen disastrous results when Reply All has been used and the reply was not a polite answer. If you call someone a raging idiot in your reply, think about what will happen when others, or that person, see the message. I've seen people lose their jobs due to this type of error.

Creating HTML Mail

Even though many traditional users abhor HTML-formatted email, younger users find that personalizing their emails with HTML content gives them the originality they crave.

To create an email message that contains HTML, simply use the formatting tools (fonts, colors, and so on) and apply them to your message. If the recipient has not been marked as being able to receive HTML-formatted email, Thunderbird displays a prompt to allow you to send only HTML, send both HTML and plain text, or just convert the message to plain text.

The safest choice is to either convert to plain text (and lose the formatting) or send both. Sending HTML to an email client that is incapable of displaying HTML-formatted messages can make your email difficult or impossible to read.

Creating and Using a Template

A template serves as a visual model of how a message should look. You can have a template message with your favorite background, formatting, and other HTML attributes. The template can also contain text, a signature, disclaimers, and anything you want to put in a message

To create a template, do the following:

1. Create a new email message. If this template is being sent to the same address every time, put that address in the To field. In the same manner you can load the other header fields, such as the subject, attachments, and so on.

2. Select File, Save As; then select Template in the Compose window. The message is saved as a template in your Templates folder. The name of the template is the subject line for the message, so include a subject line that is descriptive of what the template is to be used for.

Using a template is easy: Just click the Templates folder and then double-click the specific template you want to use. The Compose message window is loaded with the template's contents.

Creating a Signature

Each email account can have a signature. A *signature file* is typically an HTML document that can easily be created using Thunderbird. First, to create the actual signature HTML code, follow these steps:

1. Create a new email message.

2. Create your signature in the body of the message. Anything valid in HTML can be used, such as images and character formatting.

3. Select the signature text, and images if you have any.

4. In the Compose window, select HTML under Insert.

5. The HTML code that creates your signature will be in the displayed window. Select and copy this text to the Clipboard.

6. Open Notepad, WordPad, or any other plain-text editor, and paste the HTML from the Clipboard into Notepad (or whichever editor you're using).

7. Save this file as your signature file. I named my file `signature.html`. The name choice is yours, though; it is not critical.

8. Close Notepad and the Compose window.

The next step is to tell Thunderbird to use your new signature. In Thunderbird's Tools menu, select Account Settings. Next, click the account with which you want the signature to be associated. (Each account can have only one signature.) In the Account Settings section, check the box labeled Attach This Signature. After selecting this option, click the Choose button to select the file you saved in step 7 of the previous steps.

If you absolutely must have more than one signature for an account, it can be done like so:

1. Click Account Settings in the Tools menu.

2. Select the account to which you want to add another signature. Click the Manage Identities button.

3. Add a new identity, or select an existing one.

4. In the Identity Edit or Identity Add window, provide the information (all of which, excluding the name and signature, can be identical to another identity).

5. Add a signature to the identity being edited or added, and then save the identity.

Now, when you create an email message you can choose which identity is to be used in the From field. You can even switch identities anytime before sending the message.

Subscribing to RSS Feeds and Blogs

Much like Firefox supports RSS feeds using live bookmarks, Thunderbird supports them as folders in which each news item is an item in the RSS folder. To set up a RSS account to read RSS feeds, you must first create an RSS account:

1. Click Account Settings in the Thunderbird Tools menu.

2. Select Add Account, RSS News and Blogs, Next.

3. Give the account an account name. (Make the name as descriptive as possible.) Click Next and then click Finish.

After you have created your RSS account, select it and click the Manage Subscriptions button. In the RSS Subscriptions window, click Add to add a new feed. You must provide the RSS URL—for example, the CBS News top stories RSS feed's URL is http://www.cbsnews.com/feeds/rss/main.rss.

After you're done, you will have a main folder, News and Blogs, containing a folder for each feed you added in the RSS Subscriptions window. Blogs are added in the same manner; an example is http://www.achievo.org/blog/feeds/categories/2-Tips-n-Tricks.rss, which is a blog feed for tips and tricks. Be careful, though, because this stuff can be addictive—and fun.

Podcasting

Thunderbird 1.5 has support for podcasting (a good reason to upgrade if you haven't already). With podcasting, you can retrieve audio RSS content and send it to devices such as the Apple iPod.

OPML

Users of Thunderbird can use OPML to import (and export) RSS feed information with Thunderbird. This feature makes migration from another RSS client program much easier. A search of the Internet will find many OPML files, and even OPML editors to make modifying an OPML file easy.

Reading Newsgroups

Newsgroups, specifically NNTP, are forums in which people discuss given topics. Unlike blogs, which are people centric, NNTP feeds are subject or topic centric.

An example of a news server is msnews.microsoft.com. This publicly accessible NNTP site allows you to ask questions and give advice about various Microsoft products. Here's how:

NOTE Many ISPs maintain NNTP servers for their customers. To use these, you might need a user ID and password. If necessary, your ISP will provide a password and basic instructions on how to configure the NNTP connection. If the NNTP server you want to connect to requires a user ID and password, select Account Settings, click the newsgroup's Server Settings, and check the Always Request Authentication when Connecting to This Server option.

1. Open the Account Settings window. To access newsgroups, go to the Account Wizard and click Add Account. Then select Newsgroup Account and click Next.

2. Provide your name (I recommend a nickname or just your first name because this name will be visible whenever you post to the NNTP group). Also provide an email address if you want. Most NNTP users obfuscate their email accounts, such as: thunderbird_userREMOVETHIS@hipsonREMOVETHISTOO.net; then they let the other party fix it if they want to send an email. Another trick is to use a disposable email account. This is important because posting in an NNTP group will almost certainly generate an enormous amount of spam email.

3. After clicking Next, specify the NNTP server's name. For the Microsoft groups, use msnews.microsoft.com. Click Next and, optionally, make the account name more user friendly; then click Finish.

After following these steps, you will have a new folder. Clicking the folder itself displays the Thunderbird manager window, and selecting Newsgroups, Manage Newsgroup Subscriptions enables you to subscribe to the various newsgroups available on that particular NNTP server.

Thunderbird Secrets for Power Users

Here are a few ideas from the experts:

- Thunderbird is probably the most configurable and customizable email program available today. No other email program allows the extensions, user interface look and feel, and features that Thunderbird offers.

- Thunderbird is easy to install, involving just a simple download (like Firefox) from http://www.mozilla.org. Versions of Thunderbird are available for Windows, Linux, and Mac OS X.

- Thunderbird does an excellent job of moving your email, folders, and settings from Outlook, Outlook Express, and Eudora to Thunderbird.

- Account setup is straightforward and easy. Wizards are provided to help make the setup steps easy and understandable.

- The Thunderbird email editor is easy to use and offers spell-checking and formatting.

- If you like HTML email, Thunderbird is capable of creating your formatted email without relying on complex and difficult-to-use HTML editors.

- Thunderbird is ready to work with RSS feeds and blogs, requiring only a simple setup to get going.

- With Thunderbird, you can access NNTP newsgroups much like Outlook Express does.

Organizing Email with Thunderbird

Most of us save our email so we can refer to it at a later date. How long you save messages varies (I have some messages that are about 5 years old), but it is common enough to find several hundred emails in a folder.

Then one day someone refers to an old email, or you remember something in a message and want the details. Opening and reading hundreds of emails is not practical, but using the power of Thunderbird enables you to do these tasks easily.

In this chapter you cover message management. We'll discuss how you store, filter, sort, and perform other tasks involving your email messages.

Managing Folders

Your email folders in Thunderbird are similar to folders you have on your disk drive. The mail folders are located in your profile, with Local Folders being located in a subfolder called mail. This would look like this: `\profiles\xxxxxxxx.default\mail`, where *xxxxxxxx.default* is your profile.

Under Local Folders, Thunderbird creates some more folders:

- **Inbox**—The default location in which Thunderbird places your newly received email messages. You can set an option to send incoming emails to a folder specifically for the account or another account's folders.

- **Drafts**—Folder where you save messages without sending them. At a later time, these messages can be reopened, edited, and saved or sent.

- **Templates**—Patterns used to create email messages. The template can have formatting, text, and header information included.

- **Sent**—Folder where a copy of each email you send is saved. This way, you can later review any messages you have sent.

- **Trash**—The location where deleted messages are placed. The Trash folder can be emptied explicitly, or Thunderbird can empty the trash when closing.

New folders can be created by right-clicking an existing folder and selecting New Folder in the context menu.

Looking at Figure 11.1, you see Thunderbird, as of the end of the last chapter. You see News & Blogs, Local Folders, a set of folders for one of the two email accounts (peter1@hipson.net), and a set of folders for the other email account (thunderbird_user@hipson.net).

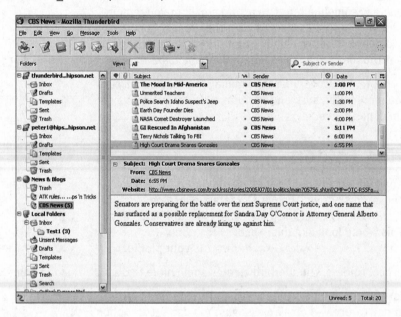

FIGURE 11.1

Folders, in the default Classic Thunderbird view, are listed on the left side. They are displayed in a tree-view format.

Labeling Messages

Messages have one label—the subject (this is almost always true because the sender might occasionally forget to enter one). You can, however, add other labeling to your messages in Thunderbird.

Thunderbird allows you to label messages with an attribute, such as the following:

- 0—None, where there is no special label on the message. This is the default value. Messages with a none label are listed in black text, bold for unread, and normal for read messages.

- 1—Important, for messages you feel are important, or at least more important than others. Important messages are listed in red, so they stand out.

- 2—Work, for messages that are work related. Your work messages are listed in orange.

- 3—Personal, which marks your personal messages to differentiate them from non-personal messages. A personal message is listed in green.

- 4—To Do, indicating that you need to do something, such as research and reply, or some other deferred action. A to-do message is listed in blue text.

- 5—Later, which lets you mark a message as being one you will take action on at a later time. Messages marked for later are listed in magenta.

All the label colors can be reset in the Options dialog box (see Figure 11.2). Select Tools, Options in the menu; then click the Display button on the left side of the Options window. Label colors are located near the bottom of the Options window.

FIGURE 11.2

Label text and colors can be set, and you can click a button to restore the defaults.

Using labels creates visual clues as to the message and what each message's current state is. If you want to change the descriptive text for the file labels, edit the label's text. In the figure, I changed the label Important to read Important to Me.

Change the text to whatever text you want to use. Labels can be used to allow you to quickly see messages in a label group by selecting View, Messages in the menu.

Filtering Messages

To keep things simple, I want to organize my life as much as possible. For example, I teach at the college level and have a folder (named FPC) for messages from the college (students mostly, but occasionally other faculty and staff). That way, I can easily find college-related messages and they don't get lost in my Inbox.

I can drag and drop messages I want to have moved into the FPC folder, but a better solution is to have Thunderbird do this automatically. The tool for automatically processing a message is called a *filter*. Most email programs support filters, and Thunderbird is no exception.

A filter starts by looking at the message's header and body fields. The filter tests the values found with your test value. For example, I would check the Sender field to see whether it contains the text fpc.edu. If the text is found, it is a message from someone at the college and I can move it to the FPC folder. The header fields that Thunderbird checks are

- **Subject**—The message's subject field
- **Sender**—The name and email address of the sender
- **Body**—The actual message body text (this is significant only if you are fetching both headers and body text)
- **Date**—The message's date stamp
- **Priority**—The message priority, which can be set by the sender
- **Status**—The message status (junk or not junk)
- **To**—The specified recipient of the message (which might not be you)
- **CC**—The courtesy copy list
- **To or CC**—The To and CC fields, which are both tested
- **Age in Days**—Messages that are older than the specified number of days

Thunderbird's filters enable you to do more than just move a message to another folder, however. Filters support the following actions:

- Move to folder—Tells Thunderbird to move the message to the specified folder. Messages can be moved between different accounts. When a message is moved, it is removed from the Inbox and placed in the destination folder.

- `Copy to folder`—Enables you to create a copy of the message and move that copy to another folder. The original message is unaltered and remains in the Inbox.

- `Label the message`—Used with the message labels, described previously in the section "Labeling Messages."

- `Change the priority to`—Sets the message's priority to one of the five priority values: `Highest`, `High`, `Normal`, `Low`, and `Lowest`.

- `Set Junk Status to`—Flags the message as either `Junk` or `Not Junk`.

- `Mark the message as read`—Sets the message's status to read (even though you might not have read the message). If the sender has asked for a read receipt, this request is processed as part of this action.

- `Flag the message`—Sets the message flag.

- `Delete the message`—Deletes the message, sending it to the trash folder.

- `Delete from POP server`—If you have left the message on the POP server, delete it there. This does not affect the local copy of the message, if one exists.

- `Fetch body from POP server`—Tells Thunderbird to get the message's body from the email server. This option is significant only if you have set Thunderbird to retrieve headers and not message bodies.

- `Forward Message to`—With this option Thunderbird forwards any messages that match the filter's criteria. You specify the email address to which to forward the messages. The only problem with this feature is that you cannot add any body text to the message.

- `Reply with Template`—Most users utilize this as an out-of-office message. However, sometime you might want a standard response sent to the sender of the message.

- `Ignore thread`—Tells Thunderbird to ignore the entire newsgroup message thread; threads are defined as the thread's initial message and all replies to the message.

- `Watch thread`—Tells Thunderbird that this newsgroup thread is important and that it should track the thread.

> **NOTE**
> There are more header fields than those shown in this list, and Thunderbird allows you to create custom header tests for your filters if you want.

> **TIP**
> To match all incoming messages for an out-of-office response, simply define a rule that specifies that the subject not contain a long string of random characters. Because no emails will have those random characters in the subject, all will be processed by the Reply with Template function.

With filters, the actions are not exclusive. You can choose one or more actions (such as `Move to folder`, `Mark the message as read`, and `Change the priority`).

To create a message filter, do the following:

1. In Thunderbird's Tools menu, select Message Filters.

2. In the Message Filters dialog box, click the New button.

3. In Filter Rules, name and create your filter.

4. Click OK to close Filter Rules, and then click OK again to close Message Filters.

> **TIP**
> When using filters, you should check to see that the filter is doing what you expect—at least for the first few times the filter is used.

Creating a filter is probably easier done than said, and after you create your first filter, the next one will be easier.

For my email, I use about 15 filters. These filters look at subjects, senders, who the message is being sent to, and other information. Then most messages are moved to folders based on the results of these tests. Some messages are deleted, although that is an action that must be used carefully so as not to lose any important messages. (I usually delete messages that contain sexual terms; drug names; or words such as *mortgage*, *loan*, *free*, *opt-out*, and a few other words or phrases I have found to be common in spam.)

Each filter is applied in order, so a message processed with an earlier filter might not necessarily be processed with a later filter—for example, when the earlier filter deletes the message.

After you have filtered your messages, you can organize them, too. Sorting and grouping are valuable tools.

Sorting and Grouping Messages

Message sorting is an often-ignored but very powerful tool. The easiest sort is to click the various message list headers, such as subject, sender, date, and so on. Click one time to sort in ascending order and a second time to toggle the ascending/descending order.

Most Thunderbird users have only a few columns displayed, and using the click-to-sort technique is useful only if the column to be sorted is displayed. Sometimes you sort on fields other than those you can see; to do this, you use a more advanced sort technique.

In Thunderbird's View menu, you can select Sort by (see Figure 11.3). Under Sort by is a list of fields: Ascending, Descending, Threaded, Unthreaded, and Grouped By Sort.

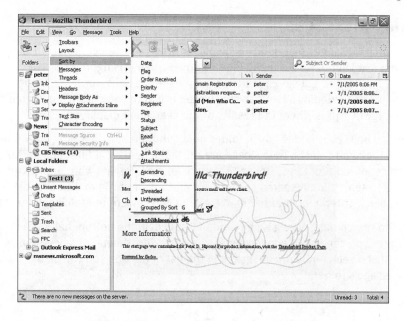

FIGURE 11.3

Sorting on fields that are not displayed is possible from the Thunderbird menu.

The fields are mutually exclusive, as are Ascending/Descending and Threaded/Unthreaded/Grouped By Sort. Thunderbird allows sorting on only one field at a time.

The three mutually exclusive options (Threaded, Unthreaded, and Grouped) let you organize messages either by topic (threaded) or into groups.

For example, you can sort by date and then group based on that sort. This could result in groups for old mail, last week, yesterday, and today. Grouping by sender would create groups for each sender. Any field that can be sorted can also be grouped.

> **TIP**
> You can add fields (columns) in the view by clicking the button at the far right of the view's header bar. This button is to the right of the Date column in Figure 11.3.

Searching

Thunderbird supports two searches. The first enables you to search for specific messages. The second searches addresses in any of your address locations.

Both searches are useful, but I find I search messages much more frequently than I search the addresses.

Searching Messages

The Search Messages dialog box is displayed when you select Edit, Find, Search Messages in Thunderbird's menu (see Figure 11.4). In this figure I searched for either eBay or PayPal and got seven matches (all phishing emails, too). The Search Messages dialog box is divided into two halves: The top is where you enter your search criteria, and the lower half is where the results of the search are displayed.

In the top half, you choose which folder (and subfolders, if desired) you will be searching for. Then you select a field (these are the same fields you filter and sort on), the search condition (Contains, Doesn't Contain, Is, Isn't, Begins with, or Ends with), and the text to search for. A search can look for multiple items in multiple fields; however, these search criteria must either match all (an AND search) or match any (an OR search).

After the search has successfully found messages, in the bottom half of Search Messages you can select a message(s) and open, file, delete, or save them as a search folder. If you select only one message in the list of results, you can also choose to open the message's folder.

FIGURE 11.4

The Search Messages dialog box can also be displayed by pressing Ctrl+Shift+F.

In addition, a quick search is located at the right end of the view bar. If you are doing a simple search, this tool might be faster than the more complex Search Messages dialog box.

Using Search Folders

Search folders are folders that contain the results of a search. The contents of a search folder are not actual messages, but are virtual copies of the messages. If you delete a search folder, the messages listed in it are not deleted. However, if you delete a specific message (or messages), the original message is deleted as well, so be careful. The same is true about other message modifications; these affect the original message, as well.

A search folder is dynamically updated. This means that new messages are searched as they arrive and, if the search is successful, they go into the search folder. You do not have to manually update the search because Thunderbird does this automatically for you.

When you are through with the search folder, you can right-click it and select Delete Folder from the context menu. This is a permanent deletion; the search folder is lost and cannot be recovered from the Trash folder.

Searching Addresses

The Advanced Address Book Search dialog box is displayed when you select Edit, Find, Search Addresses in Thunderbird's menu (see Figure 11.5). This dialog box is divided into two halves just as Search Messages is. The top is where you enter your search criteria, and the lower half is where the results of the search are displayed.

In the top half, you choose which address book (the Personal Address Book, all imported address books, or collected addresses) you will be searching. Then you select a field (these are the same fields you see in your address books, such as Name, Display Name, Email Addresses, and so on), the search condition (Contains, Doesn't Contain, Is, Isn't, Begins with, Ends with, or Sounds Like), and the text to search for. A search can look for multiple items in multiple fields, but these search criteria must either match all (an AND search) or match any (an OR search).

When the search has successfully found address book entries, in the bottom half of Advanced Address Book Search you can select an address (or addresses) and select Write to compose an email (see Figure 11.5). If you select only one message in the list of results, you can also choose to view that entry's properties.

Searching addresses is also possible while composing a message. If you type the first few characters of an address into the Compose window, a drop-down appears listing all the address book names that match those few characters (see Figure 11.6). Then simply click the name to be used (or press Tab) to select the default (first entry).

Of course, to search for addresses there must be something to search—the Thunderbird Address Books.

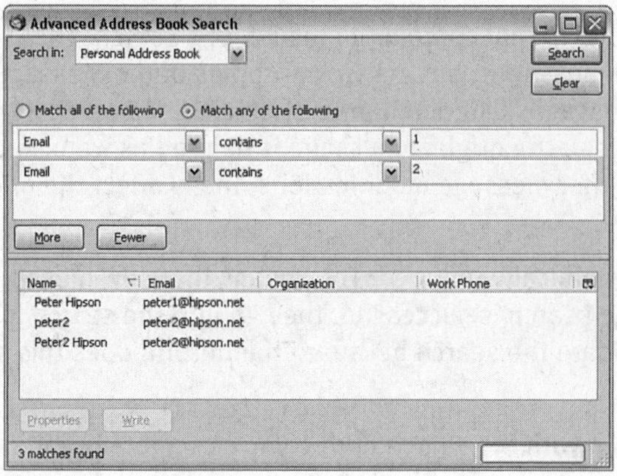

FIGURE 11.5

This search was for all names that have either a 1 or a 2 as part of the email address.

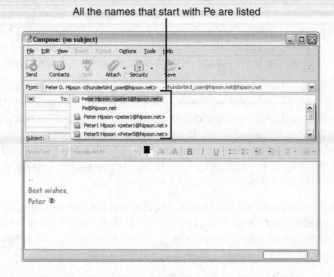

FIGURE 11.6

I typed Pe. *Thunderbird then displayed all the names that begin with these two characters and made the first one the default.*

Using Thunderbird Address Books

Thunderbird has two default address books: your Personal Address Book (abook.mab) and the Collected Addresses address book (history.mab). Additionally, there might be other address books, with various names, created when address books from other applications are imported. All address book database files have an extension of .mab (Mozilla Address Book).

You can move or copy an address book from one Thunderbird profile to another by simply copying the abook.mab and history.mab files to the new profile. (You should do this before using the other profile's address books because the originals would be lost.)

The other, imported, address books can not be copied from one profile to another. This is due to the fact that the linkages to tell Thunderbird about these additional address books are located in prefs.js. Rather than attempt to modify prefs.js, it is usually easier to export the address book (to an LDIF file) from the first profile and then reimport it into the second profile.

Another issue is backups of the address books. Each address book can be backed up by exporting the address book to an LDIF file and then backing up the LDIF file to a disk, CD-R, or other external media.

To export an address book, do the following:

1. Open the Address Book window by selecting Tools, Address Books in the Thunderbird menu.

2. Click the address book to export.

3. Click Tools in the Address Book window (not the Thunderbird window), and select Export.

4. Provide a unique name for the exported address book.

5. Repeat this process for all the address books you have, including the Personal Address Book and the Collected Addresses address book.

Reimporting an exported address book is similar. Just follow these steps:

1. Open the Address Book window by selecting Tools, Address Books in the Thunderbird menu.

2. Click Tools in the Address Book window (not the Thunderbird window), and select Import. The address book information will be imported into a new address book named the same name as the import file.

3. Following the import, you can either rename the newly created address book or copy the entries into one of your other address books.

4. Repeat this process for all the address books you want to import.

If you find that you don't have a good backup of your custom and imported address books but the profile will no longer load, there is a procedure to try to recover these lost address books. One suggested technique is to follow the instructions at http://kb.mozillazine.org/Moving_address_books_between_profiles. Another suggestion is to do this:

1. Create a new, blank profile.

2. Exit Thunderbird.

3. In the profile, rename the abook.mab file to a temporary name—for example, temp-abook.mab (see step 10).

4. Copy your custom or imported address book from the old, nonworking profile to the new profile and rename this file **abook.mab**.

5. Open Thunderbird and open the Address Book window. Check the Personal Address Book and see whether your original addresses are in the file. If they are, follow the next steps (and if not, try the hyperlink noted previously).

6. Create a new address book. In the Address Book window's menu, select File, New, Address Book. Give this new address book the name of your old address book (or any other name you want to use).

7. Copy all the names from the Personal Address Book to your newly created address book.

8. Exit Thunderbird.

9. Rename the abook.mab file to a different name. This file will not be used except as an emergency backup.

10. Finally, rename the address book file you renamed in step 3 (temp-abook.mab) to **abook.mab**.

With just a tiny bit of luck, you should have recovered your custom or imported address book.

Thunderbird's address book features are powerful, flexible, and easy to use.

Organizing Mail Secrets for Power Users

Here are a few ideas from the experts:

- Thunderbird enables you to have multiple sets of folders. Each email account can have its own inbox, and sets of folders or accounts can share folders.

- You can label a message in Thunderbird to indicate which type of message it is, including personal, work-related, important, or a task you want to do at a later time.

- By filtering messages, you can automatically process messages, file them into folders, and perform other actions on your incoming email.

- With message sorting and grouping, you can order your messages and group them into logical groupings.

- Thunderbird has a powerful and flexible search feature. This search lets you quickly find information in emails.

- With Thunderbird's search folders, you have a way to save a search and reuse it at a later time. Search folders are dynamically updated as new email arrives.

- You can delete a message's attachment leaving the message body intact. This keeps your mail box size in check, while allowing you to keep a historical copy of the message.

- Your Thunderbird address books enable you to organize your addresses and other useful information such as telephone numbers and even some custom information.

Fighting Spam

Spam is an unsolicited email attempting to sell a product or service. It seems simple, but the truth is that spam is anything but simple. Spam has become a continuously waged battle between spam senders and everyone who is on the receiving end.

The first recorded commercial message was sent by an employee of DEC, based in Marlboro, Massachusetts, on May 1, 1978. It advertised a DEC computer system and was sent over ARPANET, a network run by the United States Department of Defense that was for official use only. The 1978 message provoked some complaints, but ARPANET was small and the message went unnoticed by virtually everyone else.

We can fast-forward to 1994 and the pivotal message that marked the beginning of spam as we know it today. This event was a mass mailing by a legal firm in Arizona advertising its services. Unlike the DEC example, this message generated an enormous outcry from the computing public. At that time, the Internet was still considered noncommercial, for research and other related work; however, it did not take long for spam to take hold in the following years.

The problems created by spam are enormous. A substantial amount of the Internet's resources are tied up moving spam messages from one computer to another—resources that the users must pay for. Other problems created include wasted time weeding out spam from valid email and other indirect costs.

Today, we rely on two techniques to stop spam:

- **Client-based screening**—The user's email program attempts to block spam using a number of techniques. Thunderbird's spam features are an example of this technology.

- **Spam blocking services**—These scan a user's email, weed out spam, and forward non-spam on to the user. An example of this type of system is http://spamarrest.com/.

For those who want to learn more about spam, an excellent report can be found at http://www.ftc.gov/reports/rewardsys/expertrpt_boneh.pdf. Another good site that has a lot of related content is http://www.theregister.co.uk/2003/11/18/the_economics_of_spam/. This site has links to a number of other articles as well.

For Thunderbird users, several built-in antispam features can be used.

Thunderbird 1.5 contains a feature that attempts to block phishing messages. A *phishing email* is an email that requests you log on to a site with which you might have an account. However, phishing messages have URLs that do not go to the real site—instead, they go to a site run by the bad guys, who then harvest your user ID and passwords. After your user ID and password are saved, these sites either redirect you to the real site or continue to attempt to get more information from you.

The end result of phishing is that you then become a victim of identity theft!

Another problem for users are emails that contain large attachments. Often these attachments are not needed, but the message body text needs to be kept. For these messages, you can choose to delete just the attachment from the message, leaving the message's body text intact so you have a copy of the message. To delete just the attachment, open the message, right-click the attachment, and select Delete (or Delete All, as appropriate).

> **Tip**
>
> Several options can help in your fight against spam. First, in the Thunderbird Options dialog box, click Advanced on the left. Under the Privacy heading, be sure that Block Loading of Remote Images in Messages is checked. (You can optionally check Allow Remote Images If the Sender Is in My Address Book if you want.) Also make sure that Enable JavaScript in Mail Messages is *not* checked.

Security and Privacy Settings

Thunderbird uses a number of techniques to help block spam. The main antispam configuration is found in Thunderbird's Tools, Junk Mail Controls menu selection.

In addition to the Junk Mail Controls, Thunderbird users can configure filters that also scan for spam.

Understanding Bayesian Filtering

Shortly after his death in 1761, Reverend Thomas Bayes's (1702–1761) work in statistical distributions was published by his friend Richard Price. This work is now known as the Bayes Theorem.

Almost 240 years later, Paul Graham published his paper "A Plan for Spam," which proposed using Bayes Theorem (in a slightly modified form, perhaps) to detect spam.

To use Bayesian filtering, you must have a collection of spam emails (several thousand would be best) and a collection of emails that are not spam (again, a few thousand). These messages are then fed to the filter software, which creates lists of words in each category, spam and nonspam. Each word includes a count of how often it occurs (so a word such as *Viagra* might have a relatively high count in the spam messages but not be found in the nonspam messages). After these counts are created, they are plugged into an algorithm to compute the probability that they are an indicator of spam. Here's how it works:

1. Compute the approximate percentage of spam emails. We'll call this percentage Pe.

2. Take the 15 most interesting words. Graham defines *interesting words* as those with the score furthest from average.

3. Compute the combined probability that these words are spam. Each probability is based on the values found in the cache of words and is based on how often these words are found in spam and how often they're found in nonspam.

   Compute the combined probably that these words are in a spam email. Graham provides the following formula for three words:

   $$Ps = xyz \div (x + y + z) + (1 - x)(1 - y)(1 - z)$$

   This formula simply expands based on the number of words.

4. Compute the combined probability that the 15 most interesting words might be found in any email (both spam and nonspam). We can call this probability Pa.

5. Finally, the probability that a message is spam is computed using Ps, like so:

   Probability that an email is spam = $Ps \times Pe \div Pa$

Finally, we take this resulting probability and make a decision. Most systems flag an email as spam when the probability is 90% or greater. Empirical testing shows that few emails fall within the middle probabilities; most fall either at the higher end (and are spam) or at the lower end (and are not spam).

Learning About the Adaptive Filter for Junk Mail Control

Thunderbird's adaptive filter requires that it be trained. You must have both a collection (called a *corpus*) of good email words and one of bad email words:

- If the good corpus is empty, all the messages are classified as spam.
- If the bad corpus is empty, all the messages are classified as nonspam.

These conditions make it clear that the user must train the spam filter before it can be effective.

Part of the filter's configuration are four preferences. (See Chapter 13, "Customizing Thunderbird for Power Users," for information on setting and resetting preferences in Thunderbird.) Here are the four preferences:

TIP

If you are determined to not start from scratch, you can download a starting filter file. However, these files might not reflect spam as it is today. Training your filter is probably the best option because your nonspam emails can vary from other users' emails in their word contents.

TIP

The junk hit list, `training.dat`, is generated automatically as you use Thunderbird. To work correctly, you must not only mark emails as junk, but also mark non-junk emails as non-junk. If you feel that the Thunderbird junk mail filter is miscategorizing non-junk emails as junk, consider resetting the training data. When marking emails as junk, I recommend that you right-click the message and select Mark As Junk from the context menu. A right-click does not display the message or allow malicious content to be activated.

- `mail.adaptivefilters.junk_threshold`—This is the threshold percentage that if a message scores greater than this number, it is considered to be spam. The default is 90%, the same value suggested by Graham.

- `mail.toolbars.showbutton.junk`—This preference determines whether the Junk/Not-junk button is displayed on the Thunderbird toolbar. This button lets you easily toggle a message's status from junk to not-junk, or vice versa.

- `mailnews.display.sanitizeJunkMail`—This setting prevents Thunderbird from displaying images or other content that might contain harmful code (such as viruses).

- `mailnews.ui.junk.firstuse`—The first time the junk mail controls are used, this option displays an information box describing the Thunderbird junk mail (spam) features.

The junk threshold, which is defaulted to 90%, and first use should probably not be modified unless you are sure of the consequences.

Training the Adaptive Filter

Thunderbird's adaptive filter requires training. When you first installed Thunderbird, there was no junk filter list. This list is always created, from scratch, based on your training.

Thunderbird stores the spam filter word list in a file named `training.dat`. This is a binary file, with a file header and a series of variable-length records. Each record consists of a 4-byte hit count, a 4-byte integer specifying how long the *token* (a word or string) is, and then the token's contents. A token is usually a single word, although there are cases where it might be a compound word or other information.

Changing the Junk Mail Settings

Most of the junk mail settings can be changed in the Junk Mail Controls window (see Figure 12.1). This window has the capability to configure the antispam features for each account you have configured.

The Junk Mail Controls window is displayed by selecting Junk Mail Controls from Thunderbird's Tools menu.

FIGURE 12.1

Each account can have individual settings.

White Lists

A *white list* is an accept list; the opposite is a *black list*, where you don't accept the items. With the Junk Mail Settings white list, you can specify an address book in which to check senders' addresses.

If the sender is in your address book, the message is not scanned or tested to see whether it is spam. Instead, the message is left in the inbox.

You can specify one address book as the white list. If you need addresses from two (or more) address books tested, you must create a combined address book containing both sets of addresses.

Handling

The Handling section has three nonexclusive settings:

- **Move Incoming Messages Determined to Be Junk Mail to**—Allows Thunderbird to move messages it feels are spam to another folder, typically the account's junk folder or another account's folders. When this option is selected, you can choose to also delete all junk mail that is older than a specified age (the default is 14 days).

- **When I Manually Mark Messages As Junk**—Tells Thunderbird what to do with the manually marked messages. You can choose to either move them to the junk folder or simply delete them.

- **When Displaying HTML Messages Marked As Junk, Sanitize the HTML**—When checked, this prevents Thunderbird from displaying image and executable content. This feature provides some limited protection from virus programs and can possibly protect your identity. Displaying an image or any other web-based content in a spam email can also send the spam sender a confirmation that your email address is valid and that you have read the message.

Logging

Thunderbird creates a log of mail flagged as junk. This log is accessible by opening the Junk Mail Controls window and clicking Junk Mail Log (see Figure 12.2).

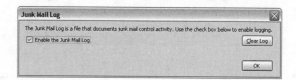

FIGURE 12.2

The Junk Mail Log tells you exactly what Thunderbird did to the suspected junk mail.

To find the actual log file, you can open a command prompt window and enter these commands:

```
cd %appdata%
cd thunderbird
cd profiles
cd xxxxxxxx.default && rem substitute your profile name in place of
➡xxxxxxxx.default
cd mail
dir junklog.html /s
```

These commands list all the junk mail logs Thunderbird has created. These files are in a standard HTML format and can be opened in Firefox.

Handling Spam

I don't mind getting my hands dirty, but I personally feel that handling spam is over the limit for me. I don't like to open it; often just the message's subject line gives me much more information than I want.

My phobia about opening spam comes from the fact that I know how to make an HTML email message notify me that it has been read without the user knowing that this has happened. True, with HTML, it is trivial to write a message that will advise the sending organization that a specific email address has opened a message and displayed its HTML code.

This little trick is done with the image URLs HTML emails always seem to have. They tack on an identifier for your email address to the fetch of the image. This gives them your email address and the IP address of your computer.

Look at this URL, taken from a recent spam message:

```
<"http://0xlb4j03tuiveal.tussurke.net/">
```

It contains an interesting URL, and you can bet that the server at the other end knows exactly what to do with that `0xlb4j03tuiveal` part, now they know they have a good email address. This is the reason for Thunderbird's Sanitize HTML option.

I'll be the first to admit that this is rarely done. Spammers usually do not have the time, or resources, to process this type of information. But it is common enough that I worry about it, and that's why I don't open any spam emails if I can avoid it.

> **NOTE** I have to wonder what kind of person would do business with a Chinese company selling drugs over the Internet? If people would stop responding to spam, we'd have much less of it. No reputable, or honest, company sends spam.

After you have isolated your spam into the junk folders, the only thing left to do is to delete it. You can tell Thunderbird, in Junk Mail Controls, to automatically delete junk emails in 14 days. Or, if you're confident that Thunderbird is not incorrectly marking good mail as spam, you can even shorten that interval.

Catchall Spam

For those of us lucky enough to have our own email domains, one useful way to catch spam is to inspect the catchall account's contents.

A *catchall account* is an account that most email servers use to put all mail addressed to the domain that don't have a valid email address (there is no mailbox matching the name given). Most servers are set up to simply discard such emails after sending a nondelivery receipt (NDR). However, instead it is becoming more common to drop all these messages into an account set up specifically for these undeliverable messages. When spammers send spam, one technique is to try to guess email account names. The result is that many times the catchall account has many copies of a particular spam message.

The difficulty with catchall is that it is server-side technology, so whoever is running your email system needs to implement it. However, after a catchall account is implemented, setting up Thunderbird to handle it is fairly simple:

1. Have the email system administrator create a catchall account. You will need access to this account to use it to train Thunderbird's adaptive spam filter.

2. Create an account for the catchall account. In my system, I've named the catchall account `catchall`. (Use something like `catchall@domain.com`.)

3. Create a filter for this account. This filter must mark everything that comes into the catchall account as spam. I've found that a filter that checks the email date and flags all emails dated after 1/1/1945 as spam work well. (Prior to this time, spam was always sent as food in cans and not as messages.)

4. In the filter, also specify that the emails are to be moved to your junk mail folder for this account.

5. It can be worthwhile to occasionally check the catchall junk mail folder for messages that are nonspam but were misaddressed. However, in my experience this is very rare.

Using the catchall account to train Thunderbird's junk mail filters can lead to much improved performance. I have noted on my system that virtually all junk mail to existing user accounts appears in the catchall account as well. Often the catchall account ends up with many copies of the spam, a sure indicator that the message is spam and not desired email.

Living Without Spam

After you have configured your junk mail filters, the Bayesian word lists have been created, and things are moving along smoothly, you might begin to notice something.

You probably won't be getting as much spam as before.

Well, first, don't panic. This is the way things were back in 1994 before spam became the king of the Internet. Back then, when you got an email, it was significant—it was meant for you and was something you wanted. Today, with our modern antispam tools, we can get almost back to the good old days. You will never eliminate all the spam, but you can certainly minimize the quantity you have to see.

After it's fully set up and running, current estimates are that Thunderbird's junk mail filter can catch as much as 99% of the spam that is sent to you. For many of us, that means we might see one, perhaps two, spam emails a day.

I can live with those numbers.

Organizing Mail Secrets for Power Users

Here are a few ideas from the experts:

- Security and privacy settings enable Thunderbird to control spam.

- Bayesian filtering analyzes the content of an email message and computes a probability of whether it is spam or a legitimate message.

- Training the adaptive filter in Thunderbird is easy. You simply turn on junk mail controls and classify your incoming email as either junk or not junk.

- Thunderbird maintains the capability to have a white list of acceptable email senders. Those senders are never subjected to the Thunderbird junk mail scanning.

- A special server-side account, usually named `catchall`, can be used to enhance the junk mail filter list.

Customizing Thunderbird for Power Users

This chapter discusses how you can customize and enhance Thunderbird using settings, themes, and extensions. With these customizations, you are able to make Thunderbird look and work exactly the way you want it to.

You can add functionality with extensions and modify the look and feel of Thunderbird with themes.

In addition to themes and extensions, you can set many configuration settings directly from the Thunderbird Options window. However, some preferences are accessible only through direct manipulation of the prefs.js file or the user.js file, or by using the about:config extension.

In fact, in Thunderbird both extensions and themes work much like they do with Firefox. However, neither Firefox themes nor extensions are compatible with Thunderbird. Fortunately, the theme and extension managers are able to check compatibility.

You'll learn that, just like Firefox, Thunderbird is very customizable and when you are done, you'll know just how to reclaim your inbox.

Finding and Installing Themes

Themes are the easiest way you can make major changes to the way Thunderbird looks. A theme can alter virtually any part of the user interface, just as a Firefox theme does.

Most themes change background colors or images, button styles, and other interface features such as border styles and fonts.

In this section, we discuss themes, installing a theme switch, and removing themes. We'll also cover some common problems users have with themes.

13

Finding a Theme

There are fewer Thunderbird themes at Mozilla's website than for Firefox, but that should not stop you from checking there first for themes.

Going to https://addons.mozilla.org/themes/?application=thunderbird gives you access to the themes Mozilla knows about. (Yes, there probably are also themes on the Internet that are not listed here.) When this was written, about 20 Thunderbird themes were available, in four categories: compact, miscellaneous, modern, and nature.

Another site with themes is http://nightlybuild.at.infoseek.co.jp/help/themes.html. This site's content is more limited than Mozilla's site is, but it contains some interesting and different themes.

Installing a Theme

Theme installation is only a bit more difficult with Thunderbird than with Firefox. The reason for the additional complexity is that Thunderbird is incapable of actually downloading the theme—to do that, you need Firefox.

You can start your installation by finding your theme. Let's use the theme Outlook 2003 BlueTB, available from the Mozilla website. With Firefox, you first go to the download location (https://addons.mozilla.org/themes/moreinfo.php?application=thunderbird&numpg=10&id=891) and right-click the Install Now hyperlink.

In the Firefox context menu, select Save Link As. In the File Save As dialog box, select a destination folder. You also can optionally change the downloaded theme's filename. I download my themes to a folder named Thunderbird Themes in my Downloads folder.

After the download completes, close the Downloads window and minimize Firefox.

Next, in Thunderbird, select Tools, Themes. In the displayed window, click the Install button (see Figure 13.1). In the Select a Theme to Install window, navigate to the folder you saved the theme in and click the theme's JAR file. Then click the Open button.

Thunderbird prompts you with a confirmation of whether you want to install the theme; click OK. At this point, the theme is installed. Just like Firefox, you must click the theme to use it. Then click the Use Theme button. To see the newly selected theme, you must restart Thunderbird—so close and restart it.

Switching Between Themes

Switching themes in Thunderbird is easy. Simply open Thunderbird's Themes window, click the theme you want to use, and then click the Use Theme button. An even faster way is to simply double-click the theme you want to use.

You must restart Thunderbird to make the newly selected theme active (see Figure 13.2).

FIGURE 13.1

Thunderbird's Themes dialog box is a carbon copy of the Firefox Themes dialog box.

FIGURE 13.2

This theme makes Thunderbird look a lot like Microsoft Outlook.

Of course, if you don't like the way Microsoft Outlook looks, there are many other themes you can use. Maybe you will want to delete that Microsoft Outlook theme.

Uninstalling a Theme

Getting rid of unwanted themes is also done using the Thunderbird Themes window. You can select any theme except for Thunderbird (default) and click the Uninstall button to remove it. Should the theme you are uninstalling be the current theme, Thunderbird switches back to the default theme (ah, so that's why you can't delete it...).

When a theme is deleted, the original source JAR file is not deleted, so you either have to manually delete the theme's JAR file or choose to just ignore it. Ignoring can work best—that way you can reinstall the theme at a later time without having to download it again.

Common Theme Problems

Thunderbird cannot install themes directly from the Internet. Instead, you need to download them (using Firefox) and then install them. One problem some users report is that, when they download some themes, the theme's extension, which should be `.jar`, is incorrect. Mozilla recommends renaming the file, changing the incorrect extension to `.jar`, and attempting to reinstall the theme.

Customizing Toolbars

Thunderbird enables you to do some limited customization of the toolbars. Toolbar buttons can be added, moved, and removed from the toolbar; however, you can do this to only a limited set of buttons.

Additionally, an extension is available to improve Thunderbird's toolbar button support. It's called Buttons!.

Add Buttons

To add buttons to the Thunderbird toolbar, right-click the toolbar and select Customize in the pop-up context menu. The Customize Toolbar window is displayed, with all the unused toolbar buttons.

Each button you add to the toolbar is moved from the Customize Toolbar window to the toolbar, so a button can't be added in two places. This is in contrast to some other applications, in which a toolbar button can be added in several places.

Three special items on the Customize Toolbar window are the Separator object; Flexible Space object; and Space object, which is used to separate buttons on the toolbar. These special items can be added multiple times, but they merely change the look of the toolbar and don't add functionality.

The Space object adds a space that is one half the width of a large icon (this space does not shrink or grow when toggling between small and large icons).

The Flexible Space object adds space that enables you to have some buttons forced to the right side of the toolbar. For example, the throbber is on the right because there is a Flexible Space between the last toolbar button and the throbber.

The Separator object places a single vertical line between two buttons, allowing you to create groups of buttons.

Rearrange or Remove Buttons

Any of the buttons on the toolbar can be removed or rearranged by dragging and dropping them in their new location. To rearrange a button, click and drag the button while the Customize Toolbar window is open.

To remove a button, drag it off the toolbar to the Customize Toolbar window. This puts the button back on the Customize Toolbar window.

Button Extensions

These are a few of the extensions that add buttons or extended functionality to Thunderbird:

- **Buttons!**—An extension that adds a number of useful buttons to Thunderbird (see Figure 13.3). Toolbar buttons included with Buttons! are Archive, Delete Thread, Search, Label, Images, HTML On/Off, Select SMTP, and Delete Junk.

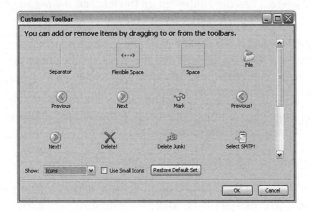

FIGURE 13.3

The Customize Toolbar dialog box shows the buttons added by the Buttons! extension.

- **compactfolder**—Makes available a toolbar button to purge and compact folders.
- **Move Search Items**—Does not add more buttons but allows moving the search bar to the toolbar.
- **Signature Switch**—Adds a Signature Management button to the toolbar. This extension does more than just add to the toolbar.
- **Translation Panel**—Adds a button that facilitates translation of content to different languages.
- **View Headers Toggle Button**—Adds a button that turns on or off message headers. Being able to view the headers is great for trying to track down the source of spam.

Many more toolbar-related extensions can be used but are not listed at the Mozilla Update website.

Changing the Window Layout

The Thunderbird window consists of a title bar, menu, toolbar, folders bar, and display area. At the bottom is a status bar showing connection status, the unread message count, and total message counts.

Three Layouts

There are three layouts for Thunderbird. Each layout displays at least two panes: Folder and the Message list. Each layout can optionally have a third pane with the contents of the currently selected message (if there is one).

The layouts Thunderbird supports are

- **Classic view**—This has the Folder list on the left and the Message list on the right. If the Message pane is on, it is displayed below the Message list.

- **Wide view**—This has the Message pane the full width of Thunderbird's display area, the Folder pane above on the left, and the Message list above on the right. If the Message pane is not turned on, this view is the same as the Classic view.

- **Vertical view**—This has the Folder pane on the left, the Message list in the middle, and the Message pane on the right. Again, if the Message pane is not displayed, this view is the same as the Classic view.

Each layout is selected from the Thunderbird View, Layout menu.

If you have the Message pane turned off, the space that would normally have been occupied by it is allocated to the Message list window.

Folder Pane

The Folder pane shows all the defined accounts and the folders for each account. The Tree List view lets you expand each account and see folders that belong to the account. Each email account has at least an inbox, a Drafts folder, Templates folder, Sent folder, and Trash folder. If Junk Mail Controls are enabled, you'll also have a Junk folder.

News and blog accounts have a folder for each RSS feed and a Trash folder.

Newsgroup (NNTP) accounts have a folder for each newsgroup you have subscribed to. There is no Trash folder in newsgroup accounts because messages can't be deleted. You can, however, attempt to cancel a post you've made. Most servers, though, do not handle this properly.

Message List Pane

The Message list contains all the messages for an account. Messages are in bold if they are unread and are not bold if they've been read. You can mark messages as read or unread at any time. When you mark a message as read and the sender has requested a read receipt (and you have enabled read receipts), the receipt is sent.

Message Pane

The optional Message pane shows the contents of the currently selected message. For email, if the format is HTML, the HTML formatting is applied in this pane. If you have a substantial amount of email, the Message pane is a valuable time-saver because it allows you to quickly peruse your messages without having to explicitly open each one.

Attachments Pane

The Attachments pane is used to show message attachments. Messages with attachments are indicated in the Message list pane with a paperclip icon. Attachments in the Attachments pane can be right-clicked and then either saved or opened. The standard cautions apply when opening attachments: Unless you know that the attachment is safe, you should run a virus scan or not open it!

The Attachments pane is displayed only if the message has an attachment and if the Message pane is also displayed.

Changing the Appearance of Email Messages

How messages look in the Message pane is, to a limited extent, configurable. To changes the settings, go to Thunderbird's menu and select Tools, Options.

In the Options window, click the Display button on the left. In the Message Display section (on the right) are settings for both plain-text messages and HTML messages. You'll also see settings to control the colors for labeled messages; these were described in Chapter 11, "Organizing Email with Thunderbird."

Plain-text Messages

Plain-text messages have a few more formatting options than HTML messages. For a plain-text message, you can choose to wrap long lines so the message fits the window width without scrolling. You can also choose to display emoticons as graphics.

Another setting is whether to use a fixed width font, such as Courier New, or a variable width font, such as Times New Roman.

Message replies often contain quoted text from the original message. The convention is to annotate a quoted line by setting the first character to a greater than sign (>). This quoting can be nested many levels deep, and email etiquette says you should limit quoting to only necessary material.

Quoted portions can be made bold, italic, bold and italic, or regular text. As well, you can set the size to be regular, bigger, or smaller. A final option lets you set the quoted text's color—the default is a medium gray.

HTML Messages

Generally, HTML messages contain all the formatting as part of the message. However, both the default text color and the default background color can be customized.

Whenever no text color is specified, you can choose to have that text displayed in the color of your choice. The color chosen should contrast well with as many backgrounds as possible; otherwise, the message can be difficult or impossible to read.

When a message has no specified background color, you can specify a background color. Recommendations here are that the color should be light, such as a light gray or light yellow, rather than dark to give good contrast with text that is usually in a darker color or black.

NOTE

Windows XP/2000 uses an environment variable to hold the location of many of the user-specific files. This variable is %appdata%, and the value is set when the user logs on. This variable can be viewed in a command prompt, although it should never be changed by the user. In virtually any place that a filename and folder are requested, you can insert %appdata%. If you do so, the folder to which %appdata% points is opened. This functionality is available in most applications' Open and Save dialog boxes, as well. The default for %appdata% in most installations is C:\ Documents and Settings\ [User Name]\Application Data.
You can also use %appdata% in a shortcut's Properties dialog box for Target and Start In.

Locating and Using Your Thunderbird Profile

The Thunderbird profile contains everything that makes Thunderbird unique for a certain user, including the user's email, settings, themes, and extensions. The Thunderbird profile's basic structure is similar to Firefox's.

Finding Your Profile

Your profile's location varies depending on which operating system you are using. The location can also vary if the operating system's defaults for certain file locations have been changed as well. Most users find these locations to be representative of their systems:

- Windows 95/98/Me profiles are usually in C:\ WINDOWS\Application Data\Thunderbird\ Profiles*xxxxxxxx*.default\.

- Windows XP/2000 profiles are usually in %appdata%\ Thunderbird\Profiles*xxxxxxxx*.default\.

- Linux profiles are usually in ~/.mozilla/thunderbird/*xxxxxxxx*.default/

- Mac OS X profiles are usually in ~/Library/Application Support/Thunderbird/ Profiles/*xxxxxxxx*.default/.

In all these examples, *xxxxxxxx* is a series of random letters and numbers. This feature is used to improve security for the user's profile.

What Is in the Profile?

Some of the files and folders located in a typical Thunderbird profile include those in Table 13.1.

TABLE 13.1   THUNDERBIRD PROFILE FOLDER FILES AND FOLDERS

Filename/Folder Name	Optional	Description
20587344.s		Mail account information
abook.mab		Default address book
cert8.db		Certificate database
chrome		Look and feel folder
compatibility.ini		Version compatibility information
components.ini		Component information
compreg.dat		Component registrations
defaults.ini		Defaults
extensions		Installed extensions folder
history.mab		Collected addresses
Imapmail	Yes	Mail folder for IMAP mail accounts, if any are defined
key3.db		Key database
localstore.rdf		Configuration information
Mail		User mail store folder
mailViews.dat		View rules
mimeTypes.rdf		MIME helper file
panacea.dat		Thunderbird files list
prefs.js		Basic (initial) preferences; it overrides user.js and updates these settings

TABLE 13.1   CONTINUED

Filename/Folder Name	Optional	Description
secmod.db		Security module database
training.dat		Bayesian filter word list file
virtualFolders.dat		Virtual folder's version number
xpti.dat		Thunderbird configuration file
XUL.mfl		User interface cache file
user.js	Yes	Additional user preferences; it overrides `prefs.js` and updates `prefs.js`
userChrome.css	Yes	Thunderbird look and feel Cascading Style Sheet file
userContent.css	Yes	Thunderbird content Cascading Style Sheet file

Each subfolder in the profile's mail folder contains files for each account folder in Thunderbird. In Figure 13.4, you see nine accounts defined, with a folder in Mail for each account.

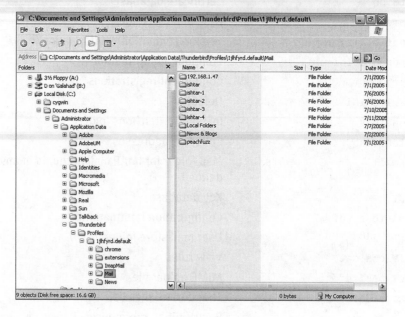

FIGURE 13.4

This profile's Mail folder has nine accounts configured, although most users usually have only one or two.

For example the Inbox for an account's folder would have

- `Inbox`—A text file that contains all the email stored in this account's inbox.

- `Inbox.msf`—Message header information and an index for each message stored in the account's inbox.

- `Inbox.sbd`—A holder for any subfolders for this folder. If no subfolders exist, this folder is empty.

There is no reason to modify many of these files, but a few are editable, either with the `about:config` extension or a text editor.

Other Modifications and Tasks

A few additional tasks should be performed. Backups are vital—your email is stored in your profile and should be backed up on a regular basis.

Backups

Backups are vital to keeping your email data safe from destruction. A minimum backup is to copy a profile into a new location. If this location is on the same computer, and same drive, a drive failure can cause the loss of both the backup and the original data. Only back up locally if you have no other choices, and if you do so, make an offline backup as soon as possible afterward.

If you are running Windows XP and have a CD-R or CD-RW drive, you can easily back up your email to a CD-R or CD-RW disc. It takes just a second to do, while recovery can take much longer.

Making a backup is easy. You need to find your profile; it is usually in `c:\documents and settings\`*userid*`\application data\thunderbird` (where *userid* is your logon username). Then do the following:

1. Close all Mozilla applications, especially Thunderbird.

2. Copy (do not move) the entire Thunderbird folder to a CD-R, CD-RW, or other writable persistent media. Alternatively, copy your profile to a network share on another computer.

> **TIP**
> Before doing a restore, I recommend you back up the bad copy of a folder before overwriting it with the backup copy. This can save you if you find the backup is worse than the damaged profile.

Restoring the backup is as easy:

1. Close all Mozilla applications, especially Thunderbird.

2. Make a second backup of the current Thunderbird folder as described previously.

3. Copy the original backup files you saved in the backup procedure to the same location they were originally located. Make sure you get all the files and folders.

There are third-party backup options as well. MozBackup is a small backup utility for Windows users that backs up the profile folders into a compressed file. The file's extension is `.pcv`, but it is a standard Zip file; if it's renamed, Windows XP's Explorer will open it. You can download MozBackup from http://mozbackup.jasnapaka.com/.

Compact Folders

Thunderbird folders are simply large databases that contain all the messages the folder contains. Like databases, when you delete an item such as an email message, the empty space is not automatically recovered. Instead, the message is marked as deleted and the space continues to hold the message.

To recover the deleted messages space, you have to compact the folder. The compacting process rewrites the folder database file without the deleted messages, making it much smaller and more efficient.

Folders are compacted by selecting Files, Compact Folders in Thunderbird's menu. The amount of time it takes to compact is related to how large the folder is and the performance of your computers. Larger folders with many deleted messages can take longer to compact than smaller folders.

All folders are compacted using this method: To compact an individual folder, right-click the folder and select Compact This Folder from the pop-up context menu.

Profile Management

Unlike Firefox, where one user can have many profiles, Thunderbird users typically have only one. The reason for this difference is that Thunderbird stores more than configurations in the profile. This is where the user's email messages are stored. (For more information, see the section "Backups," earlier in this chapter.)

However, just like Firefox, Thunderbird offers profile management tools. And, Thunderbird does allow multiple profiles. For instance, if a computer is used by more than one person, each person will want her email to be relatively confidential.

NOTE

Speaking of confidentiality, do not assume that your emails are secured in Thunderbird. The mail is stored in the Mbox format (used by many email clients) and is editable with Notepad or WordPad, as shown in Figure 13.5.

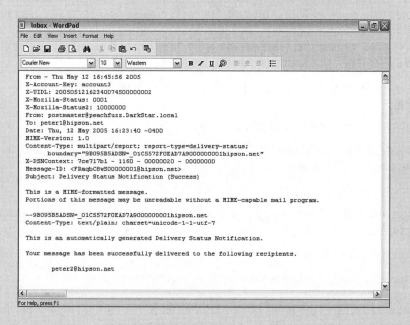

FIGURE 13.5

This shows how easily you can browse the inbox from outside Thunderbird using WordPad.

They are stored in your profile, but you must apply file permissions to really begin to protect your email folders from prying eyes.

The Profile Manager is a part of Thunderbird and works in much the same way. The Profile Manager is started by starting Thunderbird with the -p or -profilemanager switch.

You can tell Thunderbird to start with a specific profile by using this syntax, either in Windows's Start, Run; a command prompt; or a shortcut:

```
"C:\program files\Mozilla Thunderbird\thunderbird.exe " -p
➥"profilename"
```

This assumes you have installed Thunderbird in the default location. Additionally, you need to change `profilename` to the name of your profile.

Antivirus Software Issues

Viruses? We don't need no stinking viruses. Unfortunately, Thunderbird does not get along well with some antivirus software. The main problem is that email messages are stored in a single, large database file, rather than as separate files. If some antivirus programs see a virus in that large database file, they delete it because they are configured to do so. When this happens, you lose your email.

The antivirus software programs most compatible with Thunderbird include the following:

- Alwil Avast! with Thunderbird 0.9, 1.0
- Computer Associates eTrust EZ Antivirus version 6.2.0.28 eTrust v6.4 (this can have some problems, however)
- eset NOD32 version 2.12.3
- Grisoft AVG7 with Thunderbird 1.0, 0.9 (read http://forums.mozillazine.org/viewtopic.php?p=1202435)
- Kaspersky Lab Anti-Virus
- Trend Micro PC-cillin Internet Security 2005 version 12

The following antivirus programs don't work well with Thunderbird. Again, this list is not exhaustive, and these products change on a regular basis:

- McAfee VirusScan
- Panda Antivirus Internet Security
- Symantec Norton AntiVirus version 9.0.1.1000 with Thunderbird 1.0

For any antivirus program, you can configure it to not scan your Thunderbird profile folders. However, because most virus infections come as email attachments, this technique can seriously compromise your computer's antivirus protection.

Account Pane Order

If you are not happy with the ordering of the account names in Thunderbird's folder pane (shown in Figure 13.6), they can be reordered. There are some limitations, however.

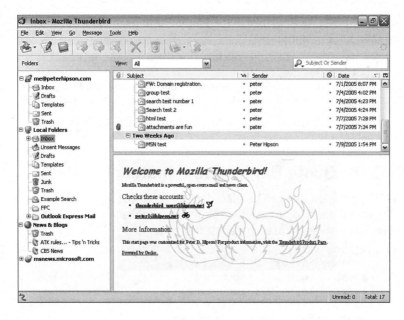

FIGURE 13.6

The Folders pane order can be reset with an edit to prefs.js *or by using an extension.*

The Folderpane extension can accomplish this. Another technique is to manually edit prefs.js. You must follow some rules on account ordering, however:

- Newsgroups are always last, unless they are the default account.

- Local folders are above newsgroups, unless either the newsgroups or local folders are the default folders.

- Email and RSS accounts are always above local folders, unless one is the default account.

- The default account (RSS, email, news, or local folders) is always listed first (at the top). This behavior can't be changed.

If you are willing to live with these restrictions, you can reorder your folder view.

Signature Display in Color Versus Gray

By default, the Thunderbird Compose window displays your signature in gray so that it is set apart from the remainder of the message body text. This color can be changed with a preference. The signature color affects only the display in the Compose window and not the color(s) of the signature as it is sent.

The following lines, when placed in the Thunderbird `userContent.css` file, change the display color of your signature:

```
// Change display color of text and links in signature

.moz-txt-sig, .moz-signature {color: yellow !important;}
.moz-txt-sig > a, .moz-signature > a {color: red !important;}
```

This displays the signature text in yellow and any links in the signature red. Change the colors as you want.

Turn Off Color Quote Bars—Use > Instead

Another modification that can be placed in `userContent.css` and in `user.js` is one that tells Thunderbird to not use the colored bars to mark quoted sections, but to leave the > symbols instead. In `user.js` enter this code:

```
blockquote[type=cite] {
        padding-bottom: 0 ! important;
        padding-top: 0 ! important;
        padding-left: 0 ! important;
        border-left: none ! important;
        border-right: none ! important;
}
```

In `user.js`, enter this code:

```
user_pref("mail.quoted_graphical", false);
user_pref("mail.quoteasblock", false);
user_pref("mailnews.display.disable_format_flowed_support", true);
```

If you do not have a `user.js` file, create one and place it in your profile folder.

Throbber URL

The throbber is the small, animated icon that shows the program is working. There is a throbber in Firefox and one in Thunderbird. To change Thunderbird's throbber, you can change, or add, the following lines in your `user.js` file:

```
// Change throbber URL in main window
user_pref("messenger.throbber.url", "http://kb.mozillazine.org/");

// Change throbber URL in Compose window
user_pref("compose.throbber.url", "http://kb.mozillazine.org/");

// Change throbber URL in Address Book window
user_pref("addressbook.throbber.url", "http://kb.mozillazine.org/");
```

These settings could be placed in `prefs.js`; however, manual modification of `prefs.js` is not recommended.

Finding and Installing Extensions

Just as in the case of themes, the process to get and install an extension is slightly different in Thunderbird. This is because Thunderbird doesn't have the download capability. (Maybe some bright reader would care to take that on as his project?)

The first place to look for extensions is the Mozilla Thunderbird extensions pages. Try https://addons.mozilla.org/extensions/?application=thunderbird for your first attempt to find a specific extension. The Mozilla extensions site categorizes extensions into five groups: contacts, message reading, miscellaneous, news reading, and privacy and security.

Although there are not as many extensions for Thunderbird as for Firefox, you still have a choice of more than 100 extensions in these five categories. Another location to search is http://extensionroom.mozdev.org/main.php/Thunderbird, where more than 75 additional extensions are listed.

Many more extensions can be found using a Google search for the term "Thunderbird extensions download" (without quotes!).

Installing an Extension

Extension installation is similar to that of Firefox or to installing a Thunderbird theme.

When you find the extension you want, you must first download it to the location where you want to save your extensions. I use a folder named Thunderbird Extensions under my Downloads folder.

In the Firefox context menu, select Save Link As. In the File Save As dialog box, select the destination folder; you can optionally change the downloaded extension's filename.

After the download completes, close the Downloads window and minimize or close Firefox.

Next, in Thunderbird, select Tools, Extensions in the menu. In the displayed window, click the Install button. Then, in the Select an Extension to Install window, navigate to the folder in which you saved the extension and click the extension's .xpi file; then click the Open button.

Thunderbird prompts you with a confirmation asking whether you want to install the extension; click OK. At this point, the extension is installed. To use the newly selected extension, you must restart Thunderbird—so close and restart it.

Uninstalling an Extension

Getting rid of the unwanted extensions is also done using the Thunderbird Extensions window. You can select any extension and click the Uninstall button to remove it.

When an extension is deleted, the original source .xpi file is not deleted, so you have to manually delete the extension's .xpi file or choose to just ignore it. Ignoring can work best because, that way, you can reinstall the extension at a later time without having to download it again.

Safe Mode

Like Firefox, Thunderbird offers a safe mode where extensions are not loaded. The default theme is also used. This helps eliminate extensions and themes that can be keeping Thunderbird from starting properly.

You can tell Thunderbird to start in safe mode by using this syntax, either in Windows's Start, Run; a command prompt; or a shortcut:

```
"C:\program files\Mozilla Thunderbird\thunderbird.exe " -safe-mode
```

This assumes you have installed Thunderbird in the default location. Note that there is an embedded hyphen in the option.

Changing Hidden Options with about:config

Firefox has a preferences editor built in, and it's accessed by typing **about:config** in the Location bar. Thunderbird does not have a Location bar and does not have about:config either.

Not to confuse you, but an extension named about:config does exist for Thunderbird. This extension enables you to easily modify or create new preferences.

Installing the about:config Extension

The about:config extension can be downloaded from https://addons.mozilla.org/extensions/moreinfo.php?application=thunderbird& numpg=10&id=423. It is very small, so connection speed is not important.

After the extension is downloaded, open Thunderbird's Tools, Extensions menu item and click Install. In the prompt for the extension to install, click the downloaded about:config extension's XPI file.

Modifying Preferences

On the surface, the only change about:config makes in Thunderbird is to add a menu item under Tools named about:config. Clicking this menu item displays the about:config window (see Figure 13.7). The about:config window has the capability to search for preferences and to let you edit or change any preference listed.

To add a new preference, right-click anywhere in the about:config preferences list and select New, (type) from the pop-up menu. You can also copy a preference's name or value to the Clipboard, modify the preference, and optionally reset it if the preference is not the default value.

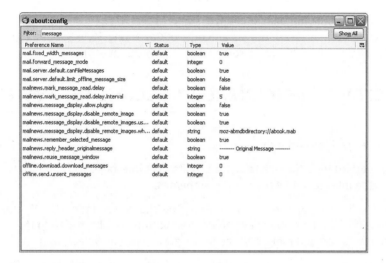

FIGURE 13.7

The filter in the about:config *extension lets me see only those preferences that meet my search filter.*

Editing Thunderbird Configuration Files

Three configuration files are designed to be modifiable by the user. None of these files are present by default, so you must create them:

- user.js—This is the first file you can create, and it's the file that's used to hold preferences that will be merged into the prefs.js file by Thunderbird. If the preference already exists in prefs.js, it is updated with the value from user.js. After they have been merged into prefs.js, user.js serves no purpose until it's modified again. If you delete user.js, the changes that were last loaded from it remain in prefs.js unless specifically removed (with either about:config, or by editing).

- userChrome.css—The way that Thunderbird looks to the user can be customized in this file. It's similar to a theme, although not nearly as powerful, and you can change fonts, colors, and various other attributes for Thunderbird.

- userContent.css—This file controls the way content looks in Thunderbird.

Changing Configuration Settings Manually

Manually changing configuration files can be done with a compatible plain-text editor. Rather than attempting to modify `prefs.js`, it is better to enter your changes in `user.js`.

Creating and modifying `userChrome.css` and `userContent.css`, at least initially, can be tedious. After you learn the ins and outs of Cascading Style Sheets, things get easier (refer to Chapter 6, "Power Firefox Tricks and Techniques").

Thunderbird Customization Secrets for Power Users

Here are a few ideas from the experts:

- Thunderbird uses themes to customize its user interface. You can download themes from the Internet and write your own themes.

- There is limited support for customizing the Thunderbird toolbars. Without using extensions, only a small set of predefined buttons can be added to the toolbar. Extensions can add more buttons to the group you can select from.

- As with any program, it is important to back up Thunderbird's profile. The profile contains the configuration for the user and that user's email. Lose the profile and you also lose your email.

- Extensions create new functionality in Thunderbird. They are easy to install, and you can write your own extensions.

- By using the `about:config` extension, many of Thunderbird's preferences can be altered to suit your needs. The extension frees you from the problems of trying to manually edit `prefs.js` and `user.js`.

WEB DEVELOPMENT AND FIREFOX EXTENSIONS

PART IV

Web Development with Firefox

Web development is more than just creating web pages.

Firefox, as a browser, can affect what a web page will look like. (To an extent, so can Internet Explorer; however, the user has no control over the appearance of a web page. In contrast, Firefox provides control.)

So you are going to look at web development with Firefox. You are not going to develop a website—that's not the purpose of this chapter. If you want to develop websites, there are many good references on the topic, including those listed in the following note.

You can use these capabilities to help you design Firefox themes, extensions, and web pages. An example is a typical Firefox or Thunderbird theme that can consist of Cascading Style Sheets (CSS), images, and supporting files.

An extension might have all the same files that a theme has, plus you will also find JavaScript in it. If you are planning to develop themes or extensions, everything in this chapter will prove useful.

Web page and HTML developers will find that they need to use HTML, CSS, and a scripting language—usually JavaScript.

Hopefully, after you finish this chapter, you'll understand how to use Firefox's tools and the techniques necessary to be a successful web developer. You will also understand the ideas behind CSS.

This chapter covers

- Issues such as Firefox's compliance with web standards
- Some of the tools available to developers
- JavaScript and the JavaScript console
- CSS, the standards, how they are supposed to work, and how you can use them
- Firefox's use of CSS

NOTE

If you want some good references on website building, two interesting titles are

- *Sams Teach Yourself Web Services in 24 Hours* by Stephen Potts and Mike Kopack, Sams Publishing (ISBN: 0-672-32515-2).
- *Special Edition Using Microsoft FrontPage 2003* by Paul Colligan and Jim Cheshire, Que Publishing (ISBN: 0-7897-2954-7).

Both Que and Sams offer other similar books as well.

- The document object model (DOM) inspector, a tool that helps you learn how a page is laid out

Let's start with web page compliance.

Firefox and Compliance with Web Standards

Does Firefox comply with all the web standards? No. But then, neither does Internet Explorer, Mozilla, Opera, or any other web browser! No browser is 100% compliant with the standards.

It is my hope that Firefox is better than other browsers with regard to the standards. And, maybe it is. However, there is a lot of subjectivity in that it is often a case of comparing apples to oranges with compliance and standards. One browser complies with standard A, and the other with B. Which is better? Standard A is different from standard B, so they cannot be meaningfully compared.

First, what are these mythical standards? There is no government-appointed web standards organization—the Internet is strictly hands off with regard to the government (and that includes any government!). Instead, these standards come from many places. General Internet standards are set by the following:

- Internet Architecture Board (IAB)

- Internet Assigned Numbers Authority (IANA)

- Internet Engineering Task Force (IETF)

- The Internet Research Task Force (IRTF)

- RFC Editor (requests for comments describe how Internet standards are created)

That's a lot of alphabetic soup—and this list is not exhaustive. However, for web standards, a few organizations are critical to our usage of the Web. The main web standards authority is the World Wide Web Consortium (W3C).

W3C defines standards, including

- **Cascading Style Sheets**—CSS is used to add styles for web HTML documents. With CSS, you can set styles and override existing styles as desired.

- **DOM**—Document object model.

- **Extensible Hypertext Markup Language**—XHTML is the next step beyond HTML. Looked at as simply as possible, XHTML is HTML wrapped in XML.

- **Extensible Markup Language**—XML is a data format that enables the intelligent transfer of information from one point to another.

- **Hypertext Markup Language**—HTML is the primary language standard for the Web. There are three main versions of HTML: 2.0, 3.0, and 4.0. There are subreleases of these versions as well.

- **Internationalization**—Deals with differences in locations, such as language.

- **Uniform resource identifier**—URIs are sometimes called *uniform resource locators (URLs)*, but the correct term is *URI*.

- **Web Services Description Language**—WSDL uses XML to transfer data or procedures between two points.

As stated at the beginning of this chapter, we are most interested in CSS and the DOM inspector.

The Mozilla Developer Interface

There are some developer tools that you, as a Firefox developer, will find useful. Refer to Chapter 8, "Making Extensions Work for You," and review the developer tools available as extensions.

On the Mozilla add-ons web page, http://addons.mozilla.org/developers, is a hyperlink labeled Developers (see Figure 14.1). The developer section at Mozilla requires that you be a registered developer. If you have not registered, you can do so easily. All you need is your name, an email address, and a password. Register, and Mozilla will send a confirmation email to your email address, which will contain a link to the confirmation page for your developer account. The entire registration process takes but a few seconds.

When you click the Developers link, you go to your own private developer web page (see Figure 14.2). At this page you can publish your extensions and themes. You can also modify your profile, which you created when you registered.

Click this link to get to the developer pages.

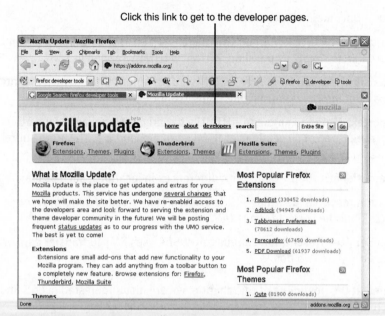

FIGURE 14.1

At the top of the Mozilla add-ons page is a link named Developers.

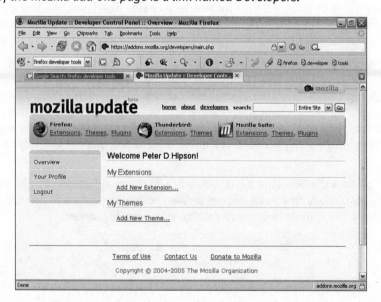

FIGURE 14.2

Sending your themes and extensions to the Firefox community is easy; just add them and they will appear in the proper places on the Mozilla site.

Web Developer Tools

You might find the following developer tools useful when developing extensions or themes. For more information on these tools, visit Mozilla's website.

DebugLogger

The DebugLogger tool is designed for extension developers. This extension provides a way to get information about your extension as you develop it, without resorting to dump() calls. The nice thing about DebugLogger is that it enables you to debug multiple projects at the same time. This is useful when you have an interaction bug, where an extension fails due to another extension's presence.

View Cookies

This extension adds a new tab called Cookies to the Page Info dialog box. This tab displays every cookie belonging to the page and shows the page's cookies, but globally and in detail.

Figure 14.3 shows the cookies for Google. It can be seen that the name of the cookie is PREF and the value consists of identifiers, an equals sign, and a value. For example, NR=100 says that I wish to see 100 results per search page (the default is 10).

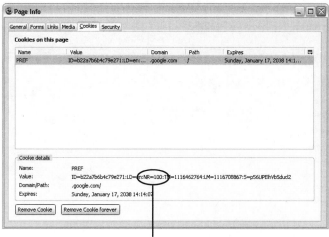

I want 100 results returned on each Google page.

Figure 14.3

Page Info's Cookies tab shows cookies and details about the selected cookie.

View Rendered Source

The View Rendered Source tool is used to help debug a number of object types. This handy extension displays HTML that is color-coded, styled, and formatted. It also displays the source exactly as Firefox would display it. Those who are developing the following code should check out View Rendered Source:

- CSS
- HTML
- JavaScript
- XML

Web Developer

The Web Developer extension adds both a menu and a toolbar with web development tools. Figure 14.4 shows the installed Web Developer toolbar.

FIGURE 14.4

Much of what the toolbar does is always available, but the Web Developer toolbar makes accessing it easier.

The Web Developer extension makes HTML development much easier, although more advanced websites will also want to use scripting—the topic for our next section.

JavaScript for Developers

Some tools and preferences are very helpful to developers. One such tool is the JavaScript console, which is installed with JavaScript. A number of JavaScript-related preferences (some of which exist in about:config and some of which must be added) improve the usability of JavaScript debugging tools.

JavaScript Console

The JavaScript Console is a window (separate from Firefox's browser window) that displays error messages generated in JavaScript code. In Figure 14.5, you can see that the JavaScript Console started after opening Firefox and showed several errors in JavaScript code while running and a final error at shutdown.

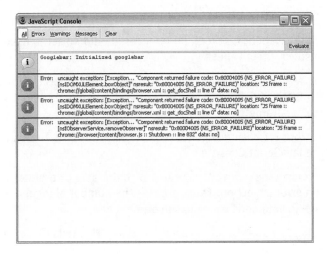

FIGURE 14.5

The JavaScript Console is showing three errors and one information message.

The Venkman Extension

The Venkman extension is a powerful JavaScript debugger. Programmers familiar with systems such as Microsoft Visual Basic 6, Visual C/C++, and other programming development tools will be familiar with Venkman. The Venkman extension does the following:

- Enables you to continue from the current point, perform single-step execution, step over a subfunction call, or step out of a subfunction call.

- Profiles code, showing which parts seem to be consuming the most time. This gives information about which parts of the script should be optimized if possible.

- Saves and restores settings such as breakpoints and variable watches. Venkman enables you to automatically save settings upon exit.

- Opens both a web page and files. Most are displayed in tabs in the source code window, allowing you to easily navigate between each.

> **CAUTION**
>
> Venkman is version specific. A certain version must be used with Firefox (and others must be used with Mozilla Suite). Be sure to use the correct version; otherwise, Venkman will not perform properly, if at all.

Venkman is the most powerful JavaScript development tool. It works well with other JavaScript tools and preferences (our next section).

Debugging Preferences

When developing JavaScript, several preferences should be set to maximize the JavaScript Console's effectiveness:

- `browser.dom.window.dump.enabled = true`—This causes Firefox to enable the `dump()` statement, which prints to the standard console. You must start Firefox with the `--console` parameter.

- `javascript.options.showInConsole = true`—This tells Firefox to log chrome file errors to the JavaScript Console.

- `javascript.options.strict = true`—With the `strict` preference, this tightens the limits on error collection. This increases the number of logged warnings; you will see warnings in your code as well as in other code.

- `nglayout.debug.disable_xul_cache = true`—This tells Firefox to disable the XUL cache. If the XUL is cached, Firefox must be restarted for any changes to be effective.

Firefox Command-line Options

Firefox supports a number of command-line options. These are sometimes referred to as command-line *parameters*— either terminology is acceptable. These options are documented at http://www.mozilla.org/docs/command-line-args.html. This page references Mozilla Suite, not Firefox, but most options listed there work with Firefox.

Understanding CSS

Chapter 6, "Power Firefox Tricks and Techniques," introduced CSS. CSS are an important part of both the Web and Firefox. Without CSS web pages, the Internet pages would not be as consistent as they are today.

There are two levels of CSS: CSS-1 and CSS-2.1. The next level, CSS-3, is under development. With style sheets, you can define the look and feel of web documents. A style sheet can define fonts, colors, character size and spacing, and style definitions that contain a complex number of effects. In fact, CSS are similar to Microsoft Word's style sheets.

In Microsoft Word, a style sheet defines a paragraph's formatting, including

- Paragraph formatting such as line spacing, space above and below, indents, text alignment, and so on

- Font specifications, such as type face, size, color, and so on

- Tabs, both the type and location

- Borders, such as width, style, color, and so on

- Frames, such as location, size, and so on

- Numbering and bullet style

CSS Level 1

The first CSS standard is called Level 1. This standard was created in late 1996 and later revised in 1999. When it was revised, no revision indicator was used. CSS-1 is rather simple and easy to use. It requires that you know basic HTML and understand the concepts and components of style. Some of the major parts of CSS-1 are discussed next. The following items are part of the standards created by W3C.

> **NOTE**
> Throughout this chapter, the term *selector* is used. A selector is the mechanism to select or group elements together to allow them to be styled as a single object.

Pseudoclasses and Pseudoelements

Pseudo means false or not real. CSS uses pseudoclasses and pseudoelements to allow the definition of items that are not part of HTML's classes or elements:

- **Anchor pseudoclasses**—A link on a document is technically referred to as an *anchor*. An anchor that has been visited (this information is usually contained in the history list) can be colored or formatted differently than a link that has not been visited.

> **NOTE**
> When used with a selector, pseudoelements can be used only at the end of the selector. In a selector, only one pseudoelement can be specified. Multiple pseudoelements are permitted otherwise, and can be combined as desired.

- **Typographical pseudoelements**—The first-line and first-letter pseudo elements are defined as typographical pseudo elements:

  - **First-line pseudoelements**—The first line of a block (paragraph) might be formatted differently from following lines. This effect is flexible, in that as the line length varies, the rendering engine compensates for this variation.

  - **First-letter pseudoelements**—Frequently you see the first letter in a paragraph printed as a drop capital. This is where the letter is actually two lines high, spanning the start of both the first and second lines. This is an example of first-letter formatting. The first-letter pseudoelement allows this type of formatting. First-letter formatting is not restricted to drop capitals but can be any valid character-level formatting.

Cascading

> **NOTE**
>
> A style sheet definition can be declared with the !important keyword, making that style override definitions that are not defined with !important.
> An author's !important overrides any preceding normal or important definitions and any following normal definitions.
> A viewer's !important overrides an author's normal definition but not an author's !important definition.

It is expected that more than one CSS will be used to format a given object in the rendered document. Several simple rules define cascading inheritance.

A style sheet need not be complete. Several partial style sheets can be combined to create a complete style sheet. Both authors and viewers can define style sheets (the *author* is the person who has written the web page, for example, whereas the *viewer* is the person using Firefox).

Cascading order says that style definitions follow these rules, in this order:

1. Rank definitions by important or normal. Any important definition always overrides normal definitions.

2. Then rank definitions by source, either author or viewer. Any author important definition overrides a viewer important.

3. Next, rank the definitions by scope. More specific scope overrides less specific scope.

4. If two definitions carry the same weight at this point, pick the last one (later definitions override earlier definitions).

Formatting Model

The CSS formatting model includes the following classes of formatting:

- Block-level elements
- Vertical formatting

- Horizontal formatting

- List-item elements

- Floating elements

- Inline elements

- Replaced elements

- The height of lines

- The canvas

- BR elements

CSS-1 Properties

Various properties that can be set with CSS-1 include notation for property values and how these properties are specified. Additional specifications are

- **Font properties**—These describe the font's look and formatting and include `font`, `font matching`, `font-family`, `font-style`, `font-variant` (such as italic), `font-weight` (light, bold, or normal, for example), and `font-size`.

- **Color and background properties**—These include `background`, `color`, `background-color`, `background-image`, `background-repeat`, `background-attachment`, and `background-position`.

- **Text properties**—These are properties such as `word-spacing`, `letter-spacing`, `text-decoration`, `vertical-align`, `text-transform`, `text-align`, `text-indent`, and `line-height`.

- **Box properties**—These include `margins`, `padding`, `border`, `width`, `height`, `float`, and `clear`.

- **Classification properties**—These include `display`, `white-space`, `list-style-type`, `list-style-image`, `list-style-position`, and `list-style`.

Units

CSS-1 units of measure are defined. These include length units, percentage units, and color units.

CSS-1 Conformance

One final part of CSS-1 is conformance. Conformance specifies how a user agent (such as a browser rendering engine) would conform to the standard.

Conformance also specifies that parsing be forward compatible; that is, any user agent that is compatible with later versions of CSS must also support earlier versions. Thus, a user agent that supports CSS Level 2.1 will also support CSS Level 1.

CSS Levels 2 and 2.1

With CSS-2 (and 2.1, which soon followed it), some important functionalities were added. CSS Level 2.1 is the current standard; CSS-3 won't be a standard for some time, most likely.

In addition to the functionality found in CSS-1, there is some new functionality:

- **Media types**—Describe the media that will display the content. Some examples are `print` (where the content will be sent to a printer), `screen` (content is displayed on the screen), and `Braille`. This example shows both print and handheld media is used:

  ```
  media="print, handheld"
  ```

- **Inheritance**—This is where a child element inherits its parent element's attributes when no matching attribute is specified. For example, in `<H1>The headline <EM>is</EM> important!</H1>`, the subelement `is` would inherit the parent (containing) element's styles such as color, font, and so on.

- **Page**—This specifies that the media will be paged and is often used with printed output (refer to the previous bullet about media types). `@page { size 8.5in 11in; margin: 4cm }` specifies that the page is letter size, with a 4cm margin. The mixing of units of measure (English and metric) is acceptable but perhaps not recommended.

- **Aural or sound**—Indicates a style sheet that will be aural (sound-based). Within aural are items such as `volume`, `voice`, `pause`, and other attributes and styles. For example, `H1{volume: x-loud}` indicates that the sound will be very loud.

- **Internationalization**—Virtually all operating systems and computers take into consideration that styles vary from country to country, so it is important that your style sheets be able to do so as well. CSS-2 includes support for various national and language requirements.

- **Font support**—CSS includes better matching of fonts when a specified font is unavailable, as well as other support. As an example, `BODY { font-family: Baskerville, "Phaisarn" }` specifies that Baskerville will be used for Latin characters and that Phaisarn will be used for Thai fonts.

- **Tables**—These are often used to categorize or group data, adding a powerful layout tool. Tables have rows, columns, headers, and borders.

- **Positioning**—Enables content to be positioned to absolute, relative, floating, or fixed. Using relative positioning, related elements can be positioned based on their relationships. As an example, a child element can be positioned relative to its parent or sibling elements.

- **Boxes**—Can be created with backgrounds, content, padding borders, and margins. Boxes serve to set content elements apart or to draw attention to important elements.

- **Overflow**—Used with boxes, this defines how any child element of a box will be treated should it overflow the box's borders. Overflow can occur under a number of conditions, such as lines that can not be broken because there is no white space in the line. Or, the box might be ill-defined. Overflow values include `visible`, `hidden`, `scroll`, `auto`, and `inherit`.

- **Visual aspects**—For example, minimum and maximum height and widths might be set with visual aspects.

- **Selectors**—These include `descendant`, `child`, `adjacent`, and `attribute` selectors. For example, `H1 { color: green } EM { color: red }` are selectors and the element `<H1>This headline is <EM>very</EM> important</H1>` displays the text in green, with the exception of the word `very`, which will be red.

- **Automatically generated content**—Lets you create content that is automatically numbered (such as page, chapter, or section numbers).

- **Shadows**—Used to make text stand out. An interesting effect is to set the text color to the same color as the background and the shadow color to a contrasting color. This displays only the shadow outlining the text (while the text, being the same color as the background, becomes invisible).

- **Pseudoclasses**—These are elements such as `:first-child`, `:hover`, `:focus`, and `:lang`. They allow content to dynamically respond to user input. As an example, `:hover` might specify a different color for an element when the mouse pointer is held over the element.

- **Color and font**—These add new system colors and fonts and make defining colors that match those that the system uses easier. Color definitions are similar to those in the Windows Display Properties, Appearance tab. However, the names used are not identical to those in Windows.

- **Cursor**—Enables the specifying of a cursor(s) for the document being displayed. Cursors are defined in a cursor resource URL (such as `cursor : url("first.cur")`, `url("second.csr")`. If it's a system-defined cursor, such as `crosshair`, `pointer`, or `move`, it can be defined in lieu of a cursor file.

- **Outlines**—Can be drawn around an object, with the color, style, and width specified. Outlines take no space and need not be rectangular in shape.

- **`!important`**— In CSS-1, an author's `!important` takes precedence over the viewer's `!important`. In CSS-2, though, the viewer's `!important` reigns supreme, taking precedence over the author's.

In CSS-1, `display` has an initial value of `block`. In CSS-2, `display`'s initial value is `inline`.

There are other changes too technical to document in this book. It can be useful to visit W3C's web page and read the standards.

CSS Level 3

First, CSS-3 has been under development since April 2001. Now, more than four years later, it is still not codified as a standard. Not only that, but there is no projected date for its acceptance.

Using CSS with Firefox

Firefox uses CSS in its basic installation set (see Firefox's `res` folder) and with user profiles (`userChrome.css` and `userContent.css`).

All user profiles contain `userChrome-example.css` and `userContent-example.css`. Firefox keeps a standard version of both of these files in the Firefox installation folder (`\defaults\profile\chrome`). Firefox itself ignores both of these files, so they must be copied (or renamed) to be recognized by Firefox. (`userChrome-example.css` should become `userChrome.css`, and `userContent-example.css` should become `userContent.css`.)

Also found in the Firefox installation folder is a subfolder named `res`. In `res` are eight `.css` files:

- `EditorOverride.css` and `EditorContent.css`—These control the editor's WYSIWYG appearance when in Browser Preview mode.

- `forms.css`—This contains styles for old GFX forms widgets.

- `html.css`—This is the overall style sheet for HTML.

- `mathml.css`—This specifies the formatting of math.

- `platform-forms.css`—This loads `forms.css`.

- `quirk.css`—This describes quirks mode, in which Firefox emulates many of Netscape Navigator's and Internet Explorer 4's nonstandard behaviors.

- `ua.css`—This is the style sheet that controls the mapping of HTML elements as block or inline.

- `viewsource.css`—This defines how source looks when edited in Firefox.

These are style sheets used by default in Firefox. However, the important style sheets are those that define themes. Because themes are packaged as JAR files, you don't usually see the `.css` files that make up a theme. A typical complete theme that is well-designed might contain as many as 100 CSS files, along with image files for each visual object (such as buttons, backgrounds, and so on) and other files. In fact, a well-done theme will have 300 or more files. Most of the files for themes are image files (either .gif or .png files).

In Chapter 15, "Creating Your Own Theme," you will create a simple theme. The theme you create won't have this many files and CSS, however.

The two CSS files users might find they want to make changes in are userChrome.css and userContent.css.

userChrome.css

The userChrome.css file is the easiest tool for you to modify the way Firefox looks. Almost anything you might want to set to quickly modify the look of Firefox can be set in this file.

Mozilla provides a sample userChrome.css file (see Listing 14.1). This sample file has a few modifications already written for you. You can take a look at this file and see exactly how the CSS affects the way Firefox looks. (I have reformatted comment lines in the listing to make it more readable.)

LISTING 14.1 userChrome.css

```
/* Edit this file and copy it as userChrome.css into your
➥profile-directory/chrome/ */

/* This file can be used to customize the look of Mozilla's user
➥interface
 * You should consider using !important on rules which you want to
➥override default settings. */

/* Do not remove the @namespace line — it's required for correct
➥functioning */
@namespace
url("http://www.mozilla.org/keymaster/gatekeeper/there.is.only.xul");
/* set default namespace to XUL */

/* Some possible accessibility enhancements: */
/* Make all the default font sizes 20 pt:*/
 * * {
 *    font-size: 20pt !important
 * }
 */
/*
 * Make menu items in particular 15 pt instead of the default size:
 *
 * menupopup > * {
 *    font-size: 15pt !important
 * }
 */
```

263

LISTING 14.1 CONTINUED

```
/*
 * Give the Location (URL) Bar a fixed-width font
 *
 * #urlbar {
 *     font-family: monospace !important;
 * }
 */


/*
 * Eliminate the throbber and its annoying movement:
 *
 * #throbber-box {
 *     display: none !important;
 * }
 */

/* For more examples see http://www.mozilla.org/unix/
➥customizing.html */
```

Taking a close look at the listing, you see that you can set the font size for everything:

```
{
   font-size: 20pt !important
}
```

In this small piece are two important parts of a CSS. The first is a definition of the font size (`font-size: 20pt`), and the other is the `!important` that specifies that this particular setting must be used unless you (the user) say otherwise in another setting.

The same is true for this part of the CSS file:

```
menupopup > * {
   font-size: 15pt !important
}
```

The first line specifies that you are modifying the pop-up menu font size, setting it to 15 points, from whatever the default was (see Figure 14.6). This only affects the pop-up menus, and not the top-level menu, as Figure 14.6 shows.

This change makes things quite large, so a bit of fine-tuning is in order. You could also specify a color:

```
menupopup > * {
   font-size: 15pt !important;
   color: red !important
}
```

Although it's difficult to see in the figure, the pop-up menu items are in red. Notice how we separated each of the attributes we set with a semicolon. Also, each attribute name has a colon following it, and each attribute has its own `!important` specification.

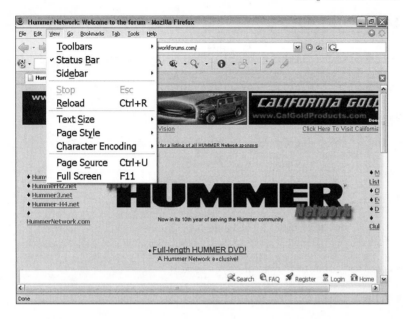

FIGURE 14.6

Notice the size difference between the word View *in the top-level menu and the items in the pop-up menu.*

Following the same concept one step further, consider this code:

```
menupopup > * {
  font-size: 15pt !important;
  background: green !important;
  color: red !important
}
```

Now the pop-up menus will be red text on a green background. Perhaps that's a bit hard to read (both colors have about the same luminosity, or brightness). Therefore, you might be more inclined to make the background a lighter gray and the text a darker color.

userContent.css

The supplied userContent.css example (userContent-example.css) lets you change the way default items in a web page appear. Again, in Listing 14.2, I've reformatted the comments so the listing won't be too large.

LISTING 14.2   userContent-example.css

```
/* Edit this file and copy it as userContent.css into your
➥profile-directory/chrome/ */
/* Each example is commented out in this example */
```

265

LISTING 14.2 CONTINUED

```
/* This file can be used to apply a style to all web pages you view
 * Rules without !important are overruled by author rules if the author
sets any.
 * Rules with !important overrule author rules. */

/* example: turn off "blink" element blinking
 *
 * blink { text-decoration: none ! important; }
 *
 */

/* example: give all tables a 2px border
 *
 * table { border: 2px solid; }
 */

/* example: turn off "marquee" element
 *
 * marquee { -moz-binding: none; }
 *
 */

/* For more examples see http://www.mozilla.org/unix/customizing.html
 */
```

Looking at this example, the first change it makes is to the `blink` tag. Perhaps you don't like blinking text on web pages. If you're an Internet Explorer user, you probably don't (yet) know what blink is because Internet Explorer does not support blinking text. But, you can set blink to off:

```
* blink { text-decoration: none ! important; }
```

First, you have the tag's keyword, `blink`. Then you set `text-decoration` to none. You can set `text-decoration` to any of these values:

- none—Specifies that the text won't have any special attributes.

- underline—The text will have an underline.

- overline—The text will have an overline.

- line-through—The text will have a line through it.

- blink—The text will blink.

Not all these values are exclusive; the text could blink and have an underline, overline, or line-through. Naturally, setting `text-decoration` to none precludes setting any of the other attributes.

Another example from `userContent.css` is shown here:

```
/* example: turn off "marquee" element
 *
 * marquee { -moz-binding: none; }
 *
 */
```

This example deserves special attention because it has a nonstandard setting: "`-moz-binding:`". This property is used to associate a URI and is used to specify that the property is to be inherited, or is set to `none`.

DOM Inspector

The document object model (DOM) is an interface standardized by W3C to allow programmers a methodology to create dynamic content. This is referred to as Dynamic HTML (DHTML) by some. DOM includes such functionalities as CSS, HTML, XML, and other components.

Figure 14.7 shows the DOM Inspector window. In this figure you are looking at eBay's home page.

The DOM Inspector is useful to show the layout and hierarchy of your document's code.

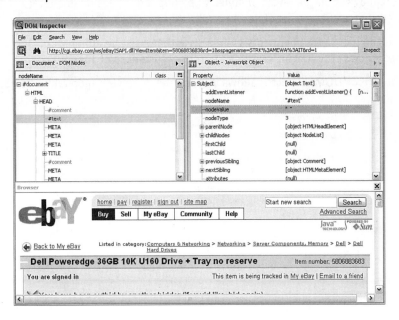

FIGURE 14.7

The web page is shown in the bottom pane, with DOM Inspector information in the upper two panes.

Working with Web Development Secrets for Power Users

Here are a few ideas from the experts:

- Firefox attempts to comply with all web standards. However, just like all other browsers, there are areas that do not comply.

- Firefox has a basic built-in developer interface. Additionally, a number of extensions can be used to improve the developer support.

- CSS are the way that documents appear. Both the document's author and the viewer can apply style sheets to modify the document's appearance.

- Firefox uses CSS for the browser's look and feel and for content. All styles are created using CSS and images.

- Chrome refers to how the program (Firefox) appears to the user. When a custom style is used, the Chrome is modified.

- Content refers to the content displayed by Firefox. You can either accept the author's styles or apply your own styles to content.

- CSS allows multiple levels of styles to be applied. Styles loaded later can take precedence over earlier styles.

- You can use !important to signify a style that must be adhered to. Of course, the last loaded !important overrides earlier occurrences of !important.

- The Firefox DOM Inspector allows viewing the document hierarchy and object properties.

Creating Your Own Theme

Firefox uses themes to change the look and feel of its interface with the user. You can either download themes or create your own themes. *Themes* and *skins* are both terms for changing the look and feel of a program. An example of using skins is the Windows Media Player.

In this chapter you will create a theme. Not a complete, ready-for-the-public version (to do that we'd have to dedicate most of the book to themes), but a theme that performs some formatting changes.

Theme creation is only a bit harder than modifying `userChrome.css`, allowing you to make Firefox's browser window look the way you want.

NOTE

All the files described in this chapter can be downloaded from the book's website at http://www.quepublishing.com/title/0789734583.

THE MAGIC OF CHROME

Some of the more technical readers might wonder what magic allows Firefox to use themes. After all, it is the Windows (or Linux or OS/X) interface, right?

Wrong. It is Firefox's interface. Most applications are made up of hundreds of windows, arranged in a tree structure of parents, children, and siblings.

A window might have a menu, toolbar, or other attached objects (such as scrollbars), but these smaller objects are actually windows, too. The application depends on Windows to manage these objects. So when you click a menu item, for example, Windows sends a message to the application's menu handler.

Firefox, however, has none of the detail windows other applications have. Instead, Firefox creates the menu, toolbar, or other item by drawing them itself rather than having Windows do the management. Instead, Firefox determines which menu item was clicked and calls the handler itself.

So, if Windows isn't providing the menus and toolbars, who is? Firefox is, using the Gecko rendering engine. This engine is the same engine that makes web pages appear in Firefox. It also creates the menus, toolbars, and other similar objects. Because Gecko understands Cascading Style Sheets (CSS), creating a theme is much easier.

Why do this? Well, you'd think that using themes might be the entire answer, but it is not. In fact, Firefox does this so that it can be as platform independent as possible (although there are a few platform-dependent features in the Mozilla products). After all, were Firefox to use Windows support for this, how would you (easily) make it work on Linux or OS/X?

Preparing Your Theme

To create a theme, you have several tricks of the trade that you can employ to help you get started. Some of these are mandatory, and some are just highly recommended. The next few sections give you the basic setup for a new theme.

One thing you will do is to copy an existing theme. You could copy virtually any theme, but one of the best starting points is the Firefox default theme that is installed with Firefox.

Open your favorite text editor. WordPad works for text editing, but there are better choices. A graphics editor is necessary, as well. The graphics editor must support transparent background graphics (which rules out Windows' Paint program). A visit to http://www.sourceforge.net will lead to many examples of both text and graphics editors.

If you did not install the DOM Inspector when you installed Firefox, do so now (installing Firefox again and selecting the DOM Inspector is the easiest way to do this). It is a useful tool for theme developers.

Creating the Working Theme

First, if you are using a theme other than the default theme, start Firefox and select the Firefox (default) theme. Then close Firefox, restart it, and ensure that the default theme is active.

Themes are contained in JAR files when they are distributed. However, that format is awkward to use while developing and testing your theme. Instead, a theme can be created in a directory structure using folders and files.

To create this working folder, you will need a JAR file unpacker. Three programs that will do the job are TUGZip, Ultimate Zip, and WinZip. Windows XP's built-in Zip file functionality does not seem to work with JAR files.

Firefox's themes are stored in the Firefox installation folder (usually `program files\mozilla firefox\chrome`). In this folder you will find at least one JAR file, named `classic.jar`. This is the default theme for Firefox. There might be more JAR files in the chrome folder, especially if you have installed a number of themes already.

After opening the `classic.jar` file, create a new folder in Firefox's `chrome` folder. I suggest naming it `classic`, at least for your first theme.

Now extract all the files in the `classic.jar` file into the `classic` folder. Make sure you keep the JAR file's folder/directory structure. This will create a number of files and subfolders under your `classic` folder.

> **TIP**
>
> If possible, you should start developing themes with a new installation of Firefox and a new profile. Doing this keeps your Firefox installation as simple and uncluttered as possible. After you have more experience developing themes, you can consider using an installation of Firefox that is more customized.

After the theme has been extracted, close your unpacking program (WinZip, TUGZip, or whatever you used). This is important: Copy the `classic` folder (with all of its contents) to a backup location. I chose the name `classic_backup` and placed that backup folder in my Firefox `chrome` folder. This leaves you with a copy of the original files should you irreparably damage any file.

This leaves you with `classic.jar`, a new folder (with files and subfolders) called `classic`, and a backup of the classic folder called `classic_backup`.

Next, make a backup copy of the file named `installed-chrome.txt`. You will be modifying the original file, and after you want to restore the original settings, you will have a copy for that purpose.

Edit your `installed-chrome.txt` file using a good text editor. I use WordPad, but if you have a favorite text based editor, use it.

With the `installed-chrome.txt` file open, search for the string `classic.jar`. You will find about five occurrences of this filename in the `installed-chrome.txt` file. Each occurrence needs to be changed. (A safety check is that each of these lines should start with the word `skin`.)

Originally the line that must be changed was

```
skin,install,url,jar:resource:/chrome/classic.jar!/skin/classic/browser/
```

You should change each line to read:

```
skin,install,url,resource:/chrome/classic/skin/classic/browser/
```

There are two changes to make in each line. First, locate the characters `jar:resource:` and change them to read `resource:`. That means you must delete the `jar:` part. Next, find `classic.jar!` and change that to `classic` (or whatever folder you extracted the files and folders to earlier). In this edit, you are deleting `.jar!` — don't forget to delete that exclamation point, too. This change tells Firefox that the theme won't be packaged in a JAR file.

After you have changed all the lines that contain `classic.jar` as described, save this file and close your editor.

Finally, test your work. Open Firefox, and it should look exactly like it did before. If you notice differences, you have made an error; close Firefox and find what went wrong.

Configuring Firefox for Theme Development

Firefox is almost ready to develop themes; only a few more changes are necessary. Start Firefox and open `about:config`. You need to disable the XUL cache so that your changes will become immediately visible without having to restart Firefox. The XUL cache is used to cache the user interface, improving performance because Firefox does not have to deal with the JAR file each time the theme is needed.

The preference you need to set is

```
nglayout.debug.disable_xul_cache
```

> **TIP**
> Check your user.js file and make sure there is not a setting for nglayout.debug.disable_xul_cache that sets the preference to false. This would override any other settings of this preference.

Set this preference to `true`. (Don't forget to reset it to `false` when you're finished creating your theme; otherwise, Firefox performance will suffer.)

One final setup is to ensure that there is no `userChrome.css` file. Anything in `userChrome` will override the theme's settings. You do not want settings in `userChrome.css` to affect the results of your theme development!

Graphics Images

Each theme consists of many Cascading Style Sheet settings that control size, color, shape, font, and so forth. Also set in CSS are the theme's background and button images.

Menu, Toolbar, and Dialog Box Backgrounds

Background images generally are one of the following:

- Browser background
- Toolbar/menu background
- Dialog box header background

This list is not exhaustive, and you will probably use the same background for several purposes.

The theme I am working on will give a wooden appearance to Firefox. To start with, I took several pieces of wood and created digital images of them. Using a graphics editor, I resized each image to fit the needs of my theme. When finished, I had created four images. Eventually, I will probably create another four or five wood-based images.

Button Images

Button images need to be created for both small buttons and large buttons. The background needs to be transparent so the toolbar background will show through the button as needed. Buttons that are disabled can be made with a transparent background and a semitransparent face, so that only a ghost of the button image shows.

Initially start with the existing button image files. Each image file usually contains many button images, which are then indexed for display. Figure 15.1 shows a sample button image.

FIGURE 15.1

Space for four rows of 15 images exist in this image, but the bottom row is not fully utilized.

Creating Themes

At first, creating a theme might seem to be a daunting task, but it is really not that difficult. To create themes, you need to know about a few standards such as CSS, be able to create icons and other graphics images, and know some basics of XML.

I will not try to minimize the amount of work it takes to create a theme. It is not a trivial, do-it-in-an-afternoon type of job. In fact, it could take weeks or months before your theme is complete enough for distribution. But it can be done—others do it, and so can you.

I do not recommend creating themes from scratch, especially for your first theme. Instead, you should start with Firefox's existing classic theme. You do the preparation as described previously in "Configuring Firefox for Theme Development," and start by modifying simple aspects of the theme. This will give you some experience in how the parts of the theme relate to each other.

The classic theme has the following folder structure:

- skin—The skin folder is the folder that serves as the theme's container. There is one folder in skin, named classic.

- skin\classic—This folder contains four subfolders: browser, communicator, global, and mozapps. The most important folder for your theme is browser.

- skin\classic\browser—Contained in this folder are the main CSS files, some image files, and two subfolders (bookmarks and pref).

- skin\classic\browser\bookmarks—This contains theme elements dealing specifically with bookmarks. You will probably find two CSS files and the bookmark's toolbar button image file.

- skin\classic\browser\pref—The pref folder holds style objects for the Tools, Options dialog box, buttons for the major categories (General, Privacy, Web Features, Downloads, and Advanced), and the pref.css file.

- skin\classic\communicator—This folder contains a subfolder named cookie and two other files.

- skin\classic\communicator\cookie—In cookie are toolbar images for cookie management and a taskbar button image.

- skin\classic\global—The global folder is the heart and soul of a Firefox theme. Virtually everything that might be set is done in global. It contains 11 subfolders (listed next) and many image and CSS files.

- skin\classic\global\alerts—In this folder is the alert.css file. This CSS file describes the alert box.

- skin\classic\global\arrow—This contains up arrows, down arrows, left arrows, right arrows, and arrows of many styles. These are all image files; there are no CSS files in this folder.

- skin\classic\global\checkbox—Items (typically menu items) that are checked are marked with the check image files contained in this subfolder.

- `skin\classic\global\console`—These items are used by the JavaScript console. This folder typically has a `console.css` file and some image files.

- `skin\classic\global\icons`—Contained in this folder are various icons and images that are used for warnings, and general control buttons (such as the Close button).

- `skin\classic\global\menu`—This folder contains menu item–related images. There can be toolbar-related items here as well.

- `skin\classic\global\radio`—Radio button (sometimes called *option* buttons) images for checked and not checked are located here.

- `skin\classic\global\scrollbar`—This has scrollbar images and usually one image for the slider.

- `skin\classic\global\throbber`—Contains throbber images, a minimum of a small throbber image. (The *throbber* is the image at the right end of the menu bar.)

- `skin\classic\global\toolbar`—This folder might contain several toolbar-related, special-purpose images.

- `skin\classic\global\tree`—Contains images used with tree views, such as in the DOM Inspector's window lists.

- `skin\classic\mozapps`—The `mozapps` folder holds about eight subfolders, described next. There might also be a `contents.rdf` file.

- `skin\classic\mozapps\downloads`—Contains images, CSS files, and other files related to downloading and the Download dialog box.

- `skin\classic\mozapps\extensions`—Contains images, CSS files, and other files related to extensions and the Extensions dialog box.

- `skin\classic\mozapps\help`—The Firefox help system styles are contained in this folder, as are a number of CSS files and images.

- `skin\classic\mozapps\pref`—Contains miscellaneous files, check images, dot images, and the `pref.css` file.

- `skin\classic\mozapps\profile`—The Profile Manager CSS files and images are found in this folder.

- `skin\classic\mozapps\shared`—Contains `richview.css` and some related images.

- `skin\classic\mozapps\update`—In this folder are images and the `update.css` file, which is used as part of the Firefox update system.

- skin\classic\mozapps\xpinstall—Contains images and the xpinstallconfirm. css file. The XPInstall system is Firefox's cross-platform installation system.

Classic

The Classic folder is the home folder for your theme. It contains files and subfolders. Eventually, you will package this folder into a distributable JAR file.

Usually four files can be found in the root of the theme's JAR folder.

AN EASIER WAY TO USE JAR FILES?

A new JAR file is needed for the new theme. There are programs that can create JAR files, but the following process might be easier because it enables you to use just the Windows Explorer program.

First, create your theme. You can extract an existing theme, modify it, and use that as the basis for your theme. Virtually all themes are clones of other existing themes.

Next, follow these steps to get started:

1. Copy any existing theme JAR file, giving it the name of your new theme. You can copy the JAR file of the theme you used to build your theme from.

2. Rename this JAR file by changing its name to the theme's name and its extension from .jar to .zip. Ignore the warning Explorer gives. Open this Zip-compressed folder in Windows Explorer, and delete all its contents. All you want is an empty Zip-compressed folder at this point.

3. Create your theme as described in this chapter. Do not forget the RDF files, preview.png, or the icon.png files.

4. Copy all the theme's folders and files into your new Zip-compressed folder that you created in step 2. You can drag and drop your theme's files (but not the folder itself) into the new Zip-compressed folder.

5. Rename the newly created compressed folder to have the extension .jar. For example, rename my_theme.zip to my_theme.jar. As before, Windows might display an error message; if so, click OK and ignore it.

Does this work? No, not fully. It is necessary to start with an original JAR file. If you create a new Zip file and change the extension to .jar, it will not work. Instead be sure to copy an existing JAR file to a new name as your starting point.

Each of the four files in the JAR root needs some modification. You can start by modifying the RDF files first. That creates a new theme in name only—the actual look and feel will mimic the original theme. After the RDF files are modified the way you want, change the `icon.png` and `preview.png` files.

After the root folder files have been updated, it is only necessary to move through the remaining files and subfolders and update the CSS and image files as appropriate. Now, if you work carefully, you should have a theme that reflects what you wanted. Your first try might not be as good as you want, but now you have experience and a much better understanding of what makes up a theme.

The root folder files you need to update are discussed in the next sections.

contents.rdf

`contents.rdf` describes what the theme consists of, such as a list of folders for the theme and other information.

The `contents.rdf` file contains a description of the files that make up the theme (see Listing 15.1).

In Listing 15.1, you need to replace all occurrences of THEME-NAME with the name of your theme. Replace YOUR NAME HERE with your name, a nickname, your company name, or whatever name you want to use. It is recommended that you include an email address as well in this space. In the `chrome:description` line, enter any description you want.

If you do not have all the folders described in the `contents.rdf` file, edit or delete as necessary. Each of your theme's subfolders must be listed in the `contents.rdf` file. The `contents.rdf` file describes what makes up your theme. You should replace text that is in bold and italic in this listing. The text THEME-NAME should be changed to your theme's name.

LISTING 15.1 THE contents.rdf FILE

```
<?xml version="1.0"?>

<RDF:RDF xmlns:RDF="http://www.w3.org/1999/02/22-rdf-syntax-ns#"
         xmlns:chrome="http://www.mozilla.org/rdf/chrome#">

  <RDF:Seq about="urn:mozilla:skin:root">
    <RDF:li resource="urn:mozilla:skin:THEME-NAME" />
  </RDF:Seq>

  <RDF:Description about="urn:mozilla:skin:THEME-NAME"
       chrome:displayName="THEME-NAME"
       chrome:author="YOUR NAME HERE"
```

LISTING 15.1 CONTINUED

```
        chrome:description="THEME-NAME is based on an example from a
➡book on Firefox. It is compatible with Firefox Versions 1.x and
➡later. There is for basic items, calendar, downloadstatusbar, tabx,
➡quicknote, offline, rss-reader, sage, and tbx. Tested with (whatever
➡versions of Firefox you have tested your theme with)."
        chrome:name=" THEME-NAME"
        chrome:accessKey="1"
        chrome:image="preview.png">
    <chrome:packages>
      <RDF:Seq about="urn:mozilla:skin:THEME-NAME:packages">
        <RDF:li resource="urn:mozilla:skin:THEME-NAME:communicator"/>
        <RDF:li resource="urn:mozilla:skin:THEME-NAME:global"/>
        <RDF:li resource="urn:mozilla:skin:THEME-NAME:browser"/>
        <RDF:li resource="urn:mozilla:skin:THEME-NAME:inspector"/>
        <RDF:li resource="urn:mozilla:skin:THEME-NAME:mozapps"/>
        <RDF:li resource="urn:mozilla:skin:THEME-NAME:help"/>
      </RDF:Seq>
    </chrome:packages>
  </RDF:Description>


  <!-- Version Information -->
  <RDF:Description about="urn:mozilla:skin:THEME-NAME:communicator"
➡chrome:skinVersion="1.5"/>
  <RDF:Description about="urn:mozilla:skin:THEME-NAME:global"
➡chrome:skinVersion="1.5"/>
  <RDF:Description about="urn:mozilla:skin:THEME-NAME:browser"
➡chrome:skinVersion="1.5"/>
  <RDF:Description about="urn:mozilla:skin:THEME-NAME:inspector"
➡chrome:skinVersion="1.5"/>
  <RDF:Description about="urn:mozilla:skin:THEME-NAME:mozapps"
➡chrome:skinVersion="1.5"/>
  <RDF:Description about="urn:mozilla:skin:THEME-NAME:help"
➡chrome:skinVersion="1.5"/>

</RDF:RDF>
```

install.rdf

The install.rdf file describes the installation of your theme. This file has a relatively simple format (see Listing 15.2). You do, however, have to create a globally unique ID (GUID) for your theme. A GUID can be created using the tool at http://kruithof.xs4all.nl/uuid/uuidgen. This is only one of many sites on the Internet to do this. (You can, if you have Microsoft's development platform, generate a GUID on your own computer.)

In Listing 15.2, do not forget the four lines directly below the line:

```
<doc:InlineComment> The Firefox versions that
your theme will work on</doc:InlineComment>
```

You must enter both the earliest version of Firefox and the latest version of Firefox that your theme will work with. If you want the latest version of Firefox to be greater or equal to the version specified, add a plus sign (+) after the version as shown in Listing 15.2.

As with the `contents.rdf` file, you should edit and change any text shown in bold and italic in this listing.

> **NOTE**
>
> If you feel more comfortable generating your own GUIDs, you can download Microsoft's GUIDGen program at http://www.microsoft.com/downloads/details.aspx?FamilyID=94551f58-484f-4a8c-bb39-adb270833afc&DisplayLang=en. To avoid typing in this complex URI, go to Microsoft's website (http://www.microsoft.com/downloads). When in the Download Center, search for GUIDGen. This will take you to the GUIDGen download page.

LISTING 15.2 install.rdf REQUIRES A UNIQUE GUID AND SOME MINOR CUSTOMIZATION

```
<?xml version="1.0"?>

<RDF xmlns="http://www.w3.org/1999/02/22-rdf-syntax-ns#"
     xmlns:em="http://www.mozilla.org/2004/em-rdf#">

  <Description about="urn:mozilla:install-manifest">
    <em:id>{XXXXXXXX-XXXX-XXXX-XXXX-XXXXXXXXXXXX}</em:id>
    <doc:InlineComment>
          Replace the above xxx's with your theme's GUID.
    </doc:InlineComment>

    <em:version>1.0.9</em:version>

    <em:targetApplication>
      <Description>
        <em:id>{ec8030f7-c20a-464f-9b0e-13a3a9e97384}</em:id>

        <doc:InlineComment> This GUID is for Firefox, so don't change
        ➥it!
        </doc:InlineComment>
<doc:InlineComment> The Firefox versions that your theme will work
➥on</doc:InlineComment>
        <em:minVersion>0.8</em:minVersion>
<doc:InlineComment> The earliest verson of Firefox that your theme will
➥work
on</doc:InlineComment>
        <em:maxVersion>1.0+</em:maxVersion>
<doc:InlineComment> The newest verson of Firefox that your theme will
```

LISTING 15.2   CONTINUED

```
work on</doc:InlineComment>
      </Description>
    </em:targetApplication>

    <em:name>Bingo</em:name>
    <em:description>MY_THEME, my ultra simple theme</em:description>
    <em:creator>Your Name Here</em:creator>
    <em:contributor>Your name or company name</em:contributor>
    <em:homepageURL>Your web site URL</em:homepageURL>
    <em:internalName>MY_THEME</em:internalName>
  </Description>

</RDF>
```

> **NOTE**
>
> A complete sample of our theme can be downloaded from http://www.
> quepublishing.com/title/0789734583. This sample is stored as a JAR file and
> can be installed into Firefox if you want; however, it won't differ from the default
> Firefox theme.

icon.png

This is your theme's icon as a PNG file. Convention says name it `icon.png`. This icon should be 32 × 32 pixels, 72 DPI, and 256 colors.

Your icon can provide a transparent background using alpha channels. Either edit the existing file or create a new one. I recommend editing the original file for your first theme.

preview.png

This small image in Mozilla's themes web page shows the user what your theme looks like. Most developers usually take a screenshot (cropped and resized) of part of Firefox with the theme loaded. Some theme developers use some form of a logo instead.

The `preview.png` image can be any size, but a recommendation is that it be between 150 × 75 pixels and 438 × 89 pixels, true color.

If you want, you can use `preview.jpg` or `preview.gif` for this file, but I recommend `preview.png`, which is easily created using a screen capture and Windows XP's Paint program.

Other Folders and Files

All the other theme files can be edited and modified as necessary. Other than the four previously mentioned files, each file that is part of the theme is located in a subfolder.

Many theme developers create the images next and then rewrite the CSS files to reflect these images. Although your sample theme might have images of one size, you are not limited to that size—your images can be as small or large as practical.

When I start a theme, I begin with my background images. I like to use real things for backgrounds (such as wood and other textured surfaces). However, there is no reason not to use whatever fits your ideas for the theme. After the background images are installed correctly, I then start working on the button images. There are many of these, so a good idea is to print the existing images (blown up in size to show detail). After they're printed, I can sketch my ideas on top of the printouts and then transfer these ideas to the actual image files.

You do not have to create all the buttons at one time; replace those you want. Later, you can replace other buttons with custom images. For my wood theme, I started with the main default browser toolbar buttons. I created back, forward, refresh, stop, and home buttons. After I situated these buttons, I created the remaining images.

Not all themes are complex. Some Firefox themes are simple, consisting of a few files and only changes in backgrounds, icons, and the like. Other themes are extensive, modifying many aspects of the Firefox user interface. Start simple, learn, and then go for more lofty goals.

> **TIP**
>
> An old programmer's rule is to change only one thing at a time. That way, should things break, you are more likely to know what caused the failure.
>
> At least initially, I recommend you do the same—work in small steps, changing one thing at a time and slowly building your theme.

Multibutton Images

Many of the button image files in Firefox have multiple button images. This reduces the number of files that must be opened, improving Firefox's performance.

The image portion to be used is specified as shown in the following code snippet:

```
menuitem.bookmark-item   {
  list-style-image: url("chrome://global/skin/icons/folder-item.png")
!important;
  -moz-image-region: rect(0px, 16px, 16px, 0px)
}
```

In this code, the image comes from the graphic file named `folder-item.png`. This image is 32 × 48 pixels in size. The part you want is defined by the `-moz-image-region`, specifically the `rect()` part. In `rect()` there are four parameters. In order (left to right) they are `top`, `right`, `bottom`, `left`. Think of a box and follow the perimeter in a clockwise manner, and you should remember which parameter is which.

Now, for this example you see that

top = 0

right = 16

bottom = 16

left = 0

So, the top and left are 0,0, or the upper-left corner of the image. (All images have an origin of 0,0 at their upper-left corner.) You also see that the right and bottom are both 16 pixels. You are taking a piece of this image starting at 0, 0 to 16, 16 to use as your button image (see Figure 15.2). The image is 16 pixels square, starting at pixel 0 and ending at pixel 15. The pixel at 16 is not included in this image.

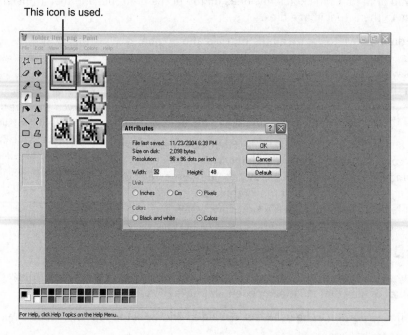

FIGURE 15.2

The icon will be the one in the upper-left corner of the image.

After you have created your button images, you need some background images for the menu and toolbars.

Background Images

You need to have images for backgrounds. In my example, I used wood that I'd digitally scanned into the computer. (Using a scanner creates better-quality images if the source is reasonably flat.)

I started with three scans. I had two samples of wood (one was not real wood, but a laminate product) that I scanned. The scans I liked best were the scans of some teak I had. I adjusted the color balance to bring out the grain some, but otherwise the scans were usable without serious editing.

My theme has seven general wood images:

- `Page_wood.gif`—A background for the browser's display area. It is almost always covered by browser content (for example, web pages).
- `Vertical_wood.gif`—A vertical band of wood, 70 × 1020 in size.
- `Menubar_wood.gif`—Used as background in menu bars and toolbars.
- `Treecol_wood.gif`—Used for tree view backgrounds.
- `Dark_wood.gif`—A darker version of `Treecol_wood.gif`.
- `Dialogheader_wood.gif`—Used as a dialog box header.
- `Button_wood.gif`—A 64 × 65 image used with buttons.

It was necessary to work with about 16 CSS files, adding the background-image attribute lines.

An Example: `global.css`

There is no way to show all the modifications that went into generating my sample theme, wood. Instead I will concentrate on the `global.css` file, which was modified as needed.

In the `global.css` which I started with, was the following section:

```
/* :::::: root elements :::::: */

window,
page,
dialog,
wizard {
  -moz-appearance: window;
  background-color: -moz-Dialog;
  color: -moz-DialogText;
  font: message-box;
}
```

This piece of code defines the look of windows, pages, dialog boxes, and wizards. All four are defined with the same attributes (the attributes are enclosed in braces).

Originally the background color was defined as -moz-Dialog (a predefined color constant that varies with the background color of the user's operating system dialog box).

The text color was defined as -moz-DialogText. Again, this color will be the same as the operating system's dialog box text color.

The font for these four is message-box, a predefined font used as the default in message boxes. This is also based on the user's operating system dialog box font.

Now, let's split the four objects into two groups. The first group will have window, dialog, and wizard. The second group will be page:

```
/* ::::: root elements ::::: */


window,
dialog,
wizard {
  -moz-appearance: window;
  background-color: -moz-Dialog;
  color: -moz-DialogText;
  font: message-box;
  background-image: url(vertical_wood.gif);
}
```

For window, dialog, and wizard, you will use the image named vertical_wood.gif. This image is shown in Figure 15.3.

For page, a different image is used:

```
page {
  -moz-appearance: window;
/*  background-color: -moz-Dialog; */
  color: -moz-DialogText;
  font: message-box;
  background-image: url(Page_wood.gif);
}
```

page is set to the image page_wood.gif. This image is one of the largest images used in the theme (see Figure 15.4). It also has some graphics on it.

In global.css, I also added images to the following:

- Statusbarpanel—Located at the bottom of the Firefox window.

- Sidebarheader—Sidebars are along the left side of Firefox's window (by default, some extensions allow moving them).

FIGURE 15.3

Vertical wood is a tall and not very wide (70 × 1020 image).

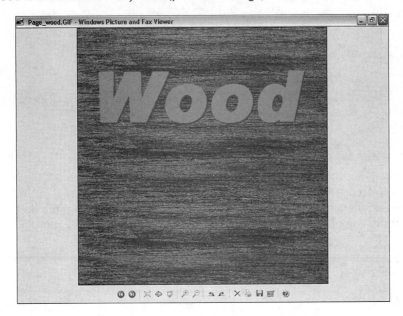

FIGURE 15.4

The page_wood.gif *image has the theme name on it.*

Chapter 15   Creating Your Own Theme

TIP

I strongly recommend checking the effect of your work after a few modifications. That way, if something breaks, you might be able to track down what is causing the problem.

After I made my changes, I saved the `global.css` file and moved to the next CSS file until I had checked, and possibly modified, every CSS in the theme.

Final Results

In creating my wood theme, I did the minimum necessary to show what can be done. Figure 15.5 shows Firefox before I created and installed my theme.

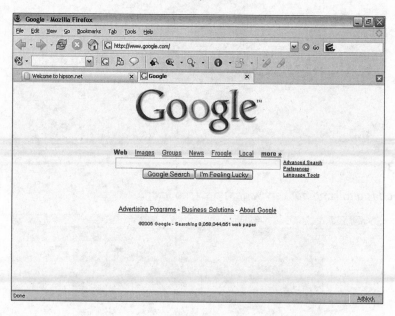

FIGURE 15.5

This is Firefox with the default theme installed.

After I created my wooden theme, I created a JAR file and installed it in Firefox. Once installed, I then made it the active theme by clicking Use Theme at the bottom of the Themes dialog box (see Figure 15.6).

After I made wood the current theme, I needed to restart Firefox. Once restarted, I was using my new wood theme (see Figure 15.7).

This is our new theme.

Click here to make the new theme active.

FIGURE 15.6

Firefox's Themes dialog box shows both my theme (selected, but not yet in use) and the default theme.

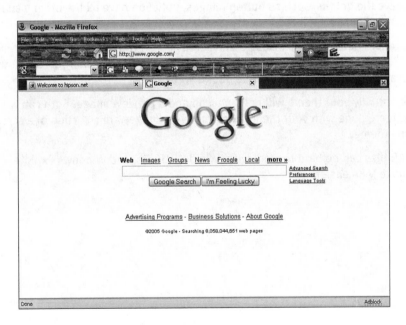

FIGURE 15.7

This is Firefox with the new wood theme installed.

You have now completed your theme. Like any good wood product, it will need sanding, polishing, updating, and additions before it is ready to publish.

Theme Writing Secrets for Power Users

Here are a few ideas from the experts:

- Backing up is very important. You will make mistakes and will need to restore files.

- Some minor changes in Firefox's configuration, such as disabling the XUL cache and telling Firefox to load a theme that is not yet packaged in a jar, will make theme development much easier.

- Determine what the theme should look like. Metal, wood, and animals are all possible theme topics. Check the Mozilla web pages to see whether there is already a theme similar to yours; if there is, find a different topic.

- Create your background images to match your ideas on how the theme should look. Images can come from virtually anywhere, such as nature, people, or surfaces. Surfaces are the most common.

- Leave the details, such as button images, until you have all the other visual aspects of the theme completed.

- Firefox's default theme, classic, can serve as a starting point for your theme, but you will have to provide a `contents.rdf` and an `install.rdf` file. You can download examples of both files from this book's website.

- Eventually your theme will need an icon and a preview image. Both can wait until you are done with your theme. Most preview images are a section of a screenshot of the theme.

- JAR files can be hard to work with. WinZip, TUGZip, and Windows Explorer can help make JARs easier.

Writing an Extension

Firefox uses extensions to enhance its functionality. An *extension* is a package consisting of chrome modifications and executable content (usually in JavaScript). Extensions are installed using the Extensions Manager, found on the Tools menu.

Extensions provide varied functionality enhancements, variety, and versatility. There are navigation extensions, humor extensions, searching extensions, and so on—in all, there are about 20 categories of extensions for Firefox. The actual number of possible extensions is impossible to estimate. The Mozilla website has perhaps 500 extensions for all its products, with many more posted on its developer's website.

In this chapter we will cover tools and extensions for extension development. We'll also discuss the Extensible User Interface Language (XUL), JavaScript, and resources for extension developers.

Setting Up the Development Environment

First, the suggestions in this section are not absolute. You can install and configure Firefox differently and still be a successful extension developer. However, my experience has taught me that these steps are very useful in starting extension development.

I recommend a new, clean installation of Firefox. If Firefox is already installed, I recommend uninstalling it and checking to make sure the Firefox program folder has been deleted.

Next, delete your profiles! Back them up if you want, so you can later reinstall them, but for now, you will want a clean profile.

After you have uninstalled Firefox and cleared all your profiles, reinstall Firefox.

Now, your Firefox installation will have all components from the same installation source, thereby avoiding corrupt installation files. As well, because the profiles will be clean, you will be starting out clean.

After you have installed Firefox, launch it. Firefox will go to the default home page. In the Location bar, type **about:config** to go to the preferences configuration page. You will change several preferences to values that improve your development environment.

Preferences for Extension Developers

In the about:config window, check the following preferences. Set them as indicated, and then restart Firefox. (Restarting ensures that your changes have taken effect.)

If you determine any preferences are missing during the Firefox installation, add them using about:config. Check the following preferences:

- nglayout.debug.disable_xul_cache = true—Setting this preference to true turns off the XUL cache. Any XUL changes made will not require that you restart Firefox.

- browser.dom.window.dump.enabled = true—Setting this preference to true causes the dump() statement to print to the JavaScript Console. You must restart Firefox with the –console option to use this preference. Try creating a shortcut icon on your desktop with the –console option added to the command line (see Figure 16.1).

- javascript.options.showInConsole = true—This preference enables the JavaScript Console to log chrome errors.

- javascript.options.strict = true—With this preference, warnings are also sent to the JavaScript Console. This can generate more messages because warnings for all the extensions are sent to the JavaScript Console, not just those generated by your extension.

The two JavaScript preferences require that you run Firefox with the console for them to be useful. To start Firefox with the console active, modify your desktop shortcut to Firefox as shown in Figure 16.1. Add **-console** after the final quotation mark in the Target string. If you add it before the final quotation mark, it will not work.

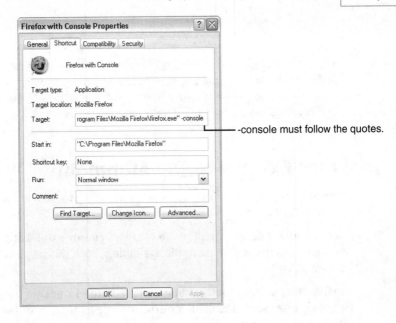

FIGURE 16.1

Set your Firefox -console *option as shown.*

Now, start Firefox one final time. Check about:config to be sure your four development preferences are correctly set. Switch to the console and see what it looks like. Figure 16.2 shows the Firefox console during a run of Firefox.

FIGURE 16.2

The console is a separate window that looks a bit like a command session.

> **NOTE**
>
> When `javascript.options.strict=true` is set, the console displays in addition to errors generated by your code errors that are generated by other code (such as other extensions). This is a good reason to not have any unnecessary extensions loaded while developing your extension.

Tools for Extension Development

There are several useful development tools, most of which are implemented as Firefox extensions.

Prior to starting development, go to Mozilla's Firefox extensions page and see which developer extensions are currently available. Check this page frequently because the list changes often.

The following section contains information on the Extension Developer extension. This particular extension, designed for extension developers, can save you a great deal of time if used properly.

The Extension Developer Extension

One of the most useful tools for extension development is the Extension Developer. This tool was written by Ted Mielczarek and can be downloaded at http:// ted.mielczarek.org/code/mozilla/extensiondev/.

Extension Developer installs a new pop-up menu under Firefox's Tools menu selection. The eight choices in this menu are

- Extension Builder
- Toggle Debugging Prefs
- JavaScript Shell
- JavaScript Environment
- JavaScript Injector
- HTML Editor
- XUL Editor
- Reload All Chrome

You can quickly try each of these options, as described in the following.

Extension Builder

The Extension Builder is the most powerful and useful feature of Extension Developer. Shown in Figure 16.3 is the dialog box that appears when this feature is selected.

Editing the install.rdf file is easy.

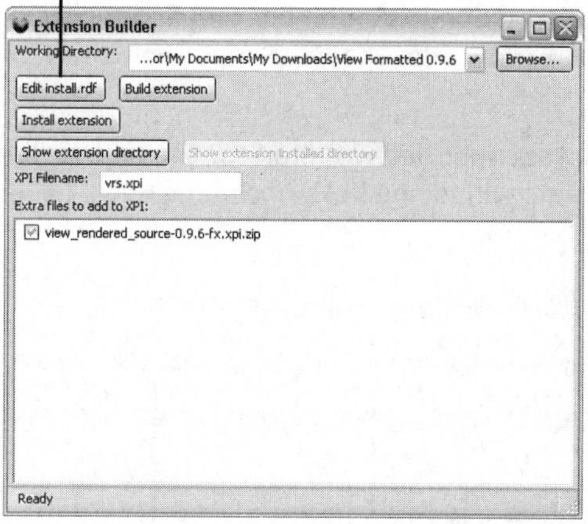

FIGURE 16.3

One useful part of Extension Builder is its capability to edit the install.rdf *file automatically.*

Other features of the Extension Builder include the capability to build the extension, install it, determine its folder location, and show its installed folder.

The install.rdf editor is able to read the extension's install.rdf file. All extensions must have an install.rdf file (this file tells Firefox all about the extension).

Toggle Debugging Prefs

In the previous section, "Preferences for Extension Developers," you set some preferences when developing extensions. The Extension Developer's menu item Toggle Debugging Prefs toggles three of the four recommended extension building preferences:

- `nglayout.debug.disable_xul_cache`
- `browser.dom.window.dump.enabled`
- `javascript.options.showInConsole`

Being able to toggle these preferences is important because, when they are set, Firefox performance can be seriously compromised.

The one preference that is not toggled is `javascript.options.strict`. If your extension uses JavaScript and you are encountering problems, manually enable `javascript.options.strict` preference, as earlier described.

JavaScript Shell

Sometimes the JavaScript Console's one-line JavaScript evaluator is not sufficient for testing pieces of JavaScript code. The JavaScript Shell interface can be very useful in such cases.

In Figure 16.4, the JavaScript Shell was started. The first six lines in the window are welcome text, complete with some links (including `Math`, `help`, and `enumerate Windows()`).

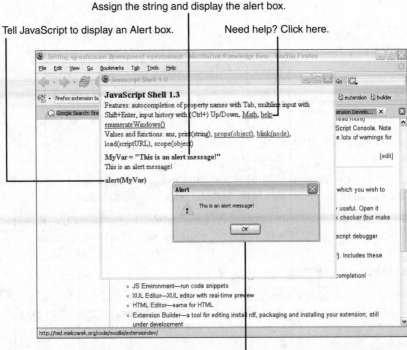

Assign the string and display the alert box.

Tell JavaScript to display an Alert box.

Need help? Click here.

JavaScript displays our Alert box with the text contained in MyVar.

FIGURE 16.4

The variable `MyVar` *is assigned a string; then* `MyVar`'s *contents are displayed in an Alert box.*

The steps to display the Alert box shown in Figure 16.4 are shown here:

1. On the seventh line, MyVar = "This is an alert message!" is the first line typed into JavaScript Shell's window.

2. The JavaScript Shell responds by printing the new value of MyVar, in the eight line.

3. In the final line, alert(MyVar) is typed and Enter is pressed. The Alert box is displayed, using the text you saved in MyVar.

If you click the help link (end of the third line), a short but useful help page is displayed. After using this small window for a while, you might find that it is indispensable when developing simple JavaScript code.

JavaScript Environment

The JavaScript Environment is similar in concept to the JavaScript Shell. The most important difference is that the JavaScript Environment allows you to develop more complex JavaScript code.

The JavaScript Environment window is shown in Figure 16.5. In this example, I've written a simple JavaScript program that prints the squares of numbers between zero and five. (When you start the JavaScript Environment, you will see the inspiration for this program.) To make this example a bit more than trivial, I've created a function to do the square function.

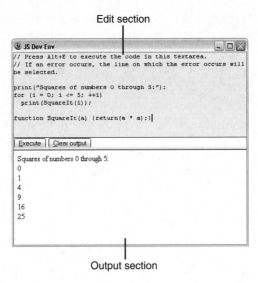

Edit section

Output section

FIGURE 16.5

In the JavaScript Development Environment window, the top half is the window where you enter your code.

Here's my sample code:

```
print("Squares of numbers 0 through 5:");
for (i = 0; i <= 5; ++i)
  print(SquareIt(i));

function SquareIt(a) {return(a * a);}
```

This small JavaScript program created the results shown in Figure 16.6.

The JavaScript code

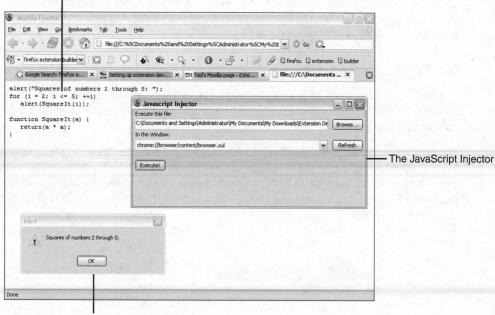

The JavaScript Injector

The results of the execution

FIGURE 16.6

The browser window shows the actual code; the JavaScript Injector window shows the file being executed; and the Alert window shows the results.

JavaScript Injector

The JavaScript Injector enables the user to execute JavaScript that has been saved in a file. This allows easy testing of complete JavaScript files without having to cut and paste.

Shown in Figure 16.6 is Firefox with a small sample JavaScript program. This program is similar to the one in the previous example; however, the previous example's `print()`

statements have been replaced with `alert()` statements. This was done because the JavaScript Injector runs the JavaScript program in a true JavaScript environment, whereas the other two examples have a text output area available.

In the end, all three of these JavaScript tools are very useful.

> **TIP**
>
> Don't forget that the JavaScript Console is available when these JavaScript tools are used. For example, if you use the JavaScript Injector and the code doesn't execute properly, check the JavaScript Console for any error messages.

HTML Editor

Much like the JavaScript Shell, the HTML Editor has a window with two sections. In the upper section you enter your HTML code, and in the bottom, as you are working, you will see the rendered results of the HTML.

This small tool supports clipboard copy and paste, letting you easily move HTML code into and out of the HTML Editor. (This is important because there is no file Open, Save, or Close command.)

Figure 16.7 shows the HTML Editor with a small piece of HTML that was lifted from my cooking web page.

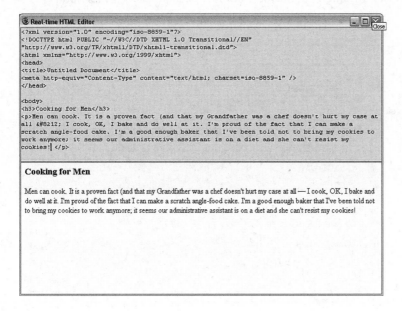

FIGURE 16.7

This HTML was created completely in the Real-time HTML Editor. If you are a guy and think you can't cook, think again.

The Real-time HTML Editor gives you immediate feedback by showing what the HTML code will look like in a browser window.

XUL Editor

When you find that JavaScript won't do everything you want (and JavaScript is limited, intentionally), the next avenue to greater functionality is XUL. XUL allows for easy development of platform-independent user interfaces, although Java and JavaScript must still be relied on for much of the underlying functionality.

In Firefox, click Edit in the menu for an example of a menu using XUL. It is not a part of Windows. Firefox doesn't use the Windows GUI interface except for client output. Everything you see in the Firefox window—the menu, the toolbar(s), the status bar, and so on—is a creation of Firefox. Most Windows applications use Windows to display titles, menus, toolbars, and the like. That is fine for those applications, but Firefox was designed to be platform independent.

Someday most applications will use XUL—a victory for developers who don't want to be tied down to a specific operating system. The XUL Editor is shown in Figure 16.8. This code example is a bit more complex than our previous JavaScript examples, but it does more. Though not obvious, our XUL example uses JavaScript.

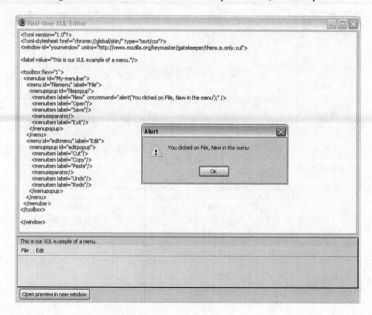

FIGURE 16.8

XUL frees you from the operating system, just like the operating system frees you from the hardware.

To be more readable, this simple bit of XUL code is shown in Listing 16.1. In this code, several items are highlighted in bold; these are areas that deserve closer inspection.

LISTING 16.1 THE SAMPLE XUL CODE FROM FIGURE 16.8

```xml
<?xml version="1.0"?>
<?xml-stylesheet href="chrome://global/skin/" type="text/css"?>
<window id="yourwindow" xmlns="http://www.mozilla.org/keymaster/
➥gatekeeper/there.is.only.xul">

<label value="This is our XUL example of a menu."/>

<toolbox flex="1">
  <menubar id="My-menubar">
    <menu id="filemenu" label="File">
      <menupopup id="filepopup">
        <menuitem label="New"  oncommand="alert('You clicked on File,
        ➥New in the menu');" />
        <menuitem label="Open"/>
        <menuitem label="Save"/>
        <menuseparator/>
        <menuitem label="Exit"/>
      </menupopup>
    </menu>
    <menu id="editmenu" label="Edit">
      <menupopup id="editpopup">
        <menuitem label="Cut"/>
        <menuitem label="Copy"/>
        <menuitem label="Paste"/>
        <menuseparator/>
        <menuitem label="Undo"/>
        <menuitem label="Redo"/>
      </menupopup>
    </menu>
  </menubar>
</toolbox>

</window>
```

In Listing 16.1, we have added code to the file menu's New command. Added is an oncommand attribute. The data assigned to the oncommand attribute is what will happen when the user selects (clicks) this item. In this example, `"alert('You clicked on File, New in the menu');"` is JavaScript code. I enclosed the entire item in double quotation marks. Usually, a text literal passed to the JavaScript alert() function is enclosed in double quotation marks, but because this entire item is in double quotation marks, I instead used single quotation marks for the alert()'s parameter.

After you get used to using XUL, you will find it easy to create user interface functionality using a combination of XUL and JavaScript.

Reload All Chrome

Chrome is the look and feel of an application's user interface. Colors, button shapes, fonts, sizes, and so on are all specified as parts of chrome. Chrome is always affected by themes and, to a lesser extent, by extensions. This lesser extent is typically parts of chrome that are directly part of the extension's functionality (such as added dialog boxes, menu items, and so forth).

When Firefox loads, it loads the chrome. From then until Firefox closes, Firefox does not change the chrome. When a new theme is selected, Firefox implements the theme when it restarts. The same is true in regard to extensions—extensions are loaded and configured at startup, not during the normal operation of Firefox.

The Extension Developer extension forces Firefox to reload the chrome without a restart. The concept is that this makes developing extensions (and themes) much faster. At least that is the idea.

My experience has been that developing extensions can be a risky process. Not only can you load the extension you are developing and have Firefox crash, but you also can damage the profile. In fact, it is too painfully easy to corrupt a profile when developing extensions.

If you are willing to take the risk that a reloading of the chrome might not resolve some problems your extension has caused but that you might not realize have occurred), you should try the Reload All Chrome option.

NOTE

Both `stdout` and `stderr` are from pre-Windows days. Back when we used command prompts, characters, terminals, and graphics were what we put on the wall and called art. Ah, the good old command prompt days....

It was common to redirect either (or both) to files, but in today's Windows GUI environments, we don't have a console or any way to easily grab this valuable information. The Firefox Console solves this problem in a crude but usable way.

Debugging Consoles

Two consoles are available to extension developers. The first console is the Firefox Console, which receives messages relating to errors in Firefox. The second console, the JavaScript Console, specifically displays errors relating to JavaScript. Both are vital to creating extensions.

The Firefox Console

The Firefox Console is a separate window started when the Firefox command contains the switch –`console`.

The Firefox Console displays the streams `stdout` and `stderr` in a simple, display-only window (refer to Figure 16.2). Both `stdout` (which is short for *standard output*) and `stderr` (which is short for *standard error*) are terms that are inherited from the C and Unix days.

stdout is the nonerror output from a number of I/O statements. stderr is error output, either specifically written to stderr by the program or from runtime functionality's error trapping routines.

The JavaScript Console

The JavaScript Console serves a function very similar to that of the Firefox Console. The JavaScript Console receives error message information from JavaScript about errors and other problems that occur in JavaScript code.

Unlike the Firefox Console, though, the JavaScript Console has some management tools. There are controls to restrict how much information is displayed (All, Errors, and Warnings and Messages) and a Clear button. Plus, the JavaScript Console allows copying information about an error to the Windows clipboard so it can be pasted into other applications if necessary.

The JavaScript Console can be displayed in a Firefox sidebar (see http://www. digitalmediaminute.com/article/1348/updated-open-firefox-javascript-console-in-a-sidebar), as a separate window (select JavaScript Console in the Tools menu), or in a tab (by creating a new tab and entering the following URI in the Location bar):

```
chrome://global/content/console.xul
```

Figure 16.9 shows the JavaScript Console displayed as a separate window (go to the Tools menu and click JavaScript Console).

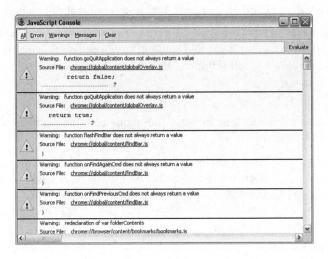

FIGURE 16.9

The JavaScript Console; no matter how it's displayed, it always looks the same.

TIP

Programmers love to indent their code using tab characters. (Indenting is vital to creating readable code.) I'm going to suggest that you not put tabs in any files you use when creating your extensions. Instead, use spaces to indent. Many of the error-reporting tools display a pointer to the exact place in the file where the error occurred. This pointer might not reflect the correct position if there are tabs in the source line.

At the top of the screen are the buttons that limit the display to either a severity level or all messages and a Clear button to clear the console's display. Below these buttons is a small text area in which you can type a JavaScript statement and have it evaluated by either clicking the Evaluate button or pressing the Enter key.

Another powerful advantage of the JavaScript Console is that it provides information about errors in a consistent format. Each error has a severity level symbol (Error, Warning, or Message), an error description, an error source (usually a file), along with optional error-specific information.

The filename for the error is a link to that file. Click the filename, and the file is opened in a browser window.

Multiple Instances of Firefox

When developing extensions and themes, it can be useful to have several copies of Firefox running at the same time.

However, if you attempt to run a second copy of Firefox, all that typically happens is that you are switched to the currently running copy—not what you want in this situation.

Mozilla has taken care of this problem. There is a way to force Firefox to open a second independent copy of itself on demand. And, this small feat of magic is easy to do.

Multiple instances of Firefox are allowed when the environment variable MOZ_NO_REMOTE exists and is set to a value of 1. You can do this in one of two ways. One way is to create a batch script file with the following two lines:

```
Set MOZ_NO_REMOTE=1
Firefox %1 %2 %3 %4 %5
```

Save this file as `firefox2.bat` (or any other name you find suitable, as long as you use `.bat` for the extension).

NOTE

You can't run two copies of Firefox using the same profile. Plan ahead and create a clone of your profile, so you won't have to reinstall extensions and themes when using these techniques.

Next, run this batch file in a command prompt window (go to the Start menu and select All Programs, Accessories, Command Prompt). Or, from the Windows run command box (go to the Start menu and select Run), you can enter the following command:

```
Firefox2 -p my_second_profile
```

where `my_second_profile` is the name of a profile different from the profile the other copy of Firefox is running. If you fail to specify a profile that is not in use, Firefox might prompt for one.

The second method is to set a permanent user environment variable, as the following steps show:

1. Open the Windows Control panel.

2. Double-click System.

3. Click the Environment Variables button at the bottom (just above the OK button).

4. In the top section, labeled User Variables for, click New (see Figure 16.10).

5. In the Variable Name box, type **MOZ_NO_REMOTE**.

6. In the Variable Value box, type **1**.

7. Click OK to save this variable; then click OK to close the Environment Variables window.

8. Click OK to close the System window, and close the Windows Control panel.

FIGURE 16.10

Make sure the variable name is in uppercase and that the value is the number 1.

After you finish adding the new environment variable, all that is necessary to start another copy of Firefox is to click the Firefox icon!

Understanding XML User Interface Language

Firefox makes extensive use of XUL. In the previous section, "Extension Developer," the effect of a simple XUL fragment was shown. Of course, that example is not a full application, but it does show what XUL can do.

XUL Syntax

XML User Interface Language (XUL), which is based on XML, has a syntax that at first glance seems similar to HTML. This syntax is made up of events, widgets, tags, and data. There are some rules that are global and must be followed. Four basic rules are

- Events and attributes must be in lowercase only. No mixed case, except for quoted strings, is allowed.

- Strings must be double quoted.

- Widgets must have close tags. Valid close tags are `<tag>`, `</tag>`, and `<tag/>`.

- Attributes, when specified, must be assigned a value.

Comments

Comments in XUL and XML are begun with the characters `<!--` and end with `-->`. The number of hyphens in a beginning or ending comment must be exactly two—no more, no less. Comments must not contain any double hyphens. A sample comment is shown here:

```
<!-- This is a valid comment -->
```

Processing Instructions

Processing instructions are lines that contain instructions for the application that is processing the XUL or XML. An example of a processing instruction is

```
<$xml version="1.0"$>
```

This instruction tells the application that the version of XML is 1.0.

XUL Example

Earlier in "XUL Editor," you created a simple window with a menu. The code was shown previously in Listing 16.1. Now let's take a closer look at this code, on a line-by-line basis:

```
<?xml version="1.0"?>
```

This is an application directive specifying the XML version.

```
<?xml-stylesheet href="chrome://global/skin/" type="text/css"?>
```

This is another application directive specifying the stylesheet used.

```
<window id="yourwindow" xmlns="http://www.mozilla.org/keymaster/
gatekeeper/there.is.only.xul">
```

This creates the window and gives it the ID `"yourwindow"`. The XML name space (`xmlns`) is also specified.

```
<label value="This is our XUL example of a menu."/>
```

This creates a label at the top of the window. We specify the text in double quotation marks.

```
<toolbox flex="1">
```

Next, we create a toolbox that holds one or more toolbar widgets. The `flex="1"` part describes how unused space is divided between children.

```
<menubar id="My-menubar">
```

This creates a container that will hold menu items.

```
    <menu id="filemenu" label="File">
```

This line creates a top-level menu item labeled File.

```
        <menupopup id="filepopup">
```

Next, we create a pop-up menu (one that drops down, actually) that is displayed whenever the user clicks the top-level menu item, Files.

```
            <menuitem label="New"  oncommand="alert('You clicked on File,
            ➥New in the menu');" />
```

Our first pop-up menu item is labeled New and has an action that takes place when the user clicks it. The action is a JavaScript `alert()` box displaying the text specified.

```
            <menuitem label="Open"/>
            <menuitem label="Save"/>
```

These are the two additional pop-up menu items. Neither has an action that will take place when it is clicked. Eventually, however, it will be necessary to write the handlers.

```
            <menuseparator/>
```

A menu separator draws a line between pop-up menu items.

```
            <menuitem label="Exit"/>
```

This is the last pop-up menu item.

```
        </menupopup>
```

This line closes the pop-up menu.

```
    </menu>
```

And this line closes the File menu.

```
    <menu id="editmenu" label="Edit">
```

Next, we create a second top-level menu item named Edit.

```
        <menupopup id="editpopup">
            <menuitem label="Cut"/>
            <menuitem label="Copy"/>
            <menuitem label="Paste"/>
            <menuseparator/>
            <menuitem label="Undo"/>
            <menuitem label="Redo"/>
        </menupopup>
```

This adds a pop-up menu to our Edit menu. None of these items have any actions written for them yet.

```
</menu>
```

This ends the Edit menu.

```
</menubar>
```

And this ends the menu bar.

```
</toolbox>
```

Now we end the toolbox.

```
</window>
```

And finally we end the window definition. (A copy of this script is available on the book's website at http://www.quepublishing.com/title/0789734583.)

The best source of reference information for XUL is http://www.xulplanet.com.

Working with JavaScript

Java or JavaScript? And, what's the difference?

Java is a programming language developed and controlled by Sun Microsystems. It is proprietary, licensed, and readily available on a number of platforms.

JavaScript was developed by Netscape as a scripting language for its browsers.

The difference between Java and JavaScript is roughly the same as the difference between C/C++ and Java (or C/C++ and JavaScript). There are similar syntax requirements, and some of the names are the same (or sufficiently similar that it is easy to figure out what's what). For many years, C and C++ have been the programming languages of choice for many applications and systems. Unix, Linux, and Windows contain extensive C and C++ code. Even Firefox has thousands of C and C++ source files.

JavaScript Reference

I'm including a simple JavaScript reference here. For a more complete reference, try http://wp.netscape.com/eng/mozilla/3.0/handbook/javascript/, which contains tutorial and reference sections. JavaScript supports operations (assignments, math, and so on), conditionals (if, loop, and so forth), objects, and functions. JavaScript statements are

- break—This immediately ends a while or for loop.
- comment—This inserts a comment into the JavaScript code.

- `continue`—This ends the current iteration of a loop and begins a new iteration. Essentially, it skips following statements.

- `for`—This is a basic looping structure in which the start, condition, and increment can be specified.

- `for...in`—This iterates the variable for all properties in an object.

- `function`—This creates a function that can be called from multiple locations. Optionally, it returns a value.

- `if...else`—This is the basic conditional test block.

- `new`—This creates a new array, Boolean, date, functions, math, number, or string object.

- `return`—This returns from a function, optionally passing back a return value.

- `this`—This is a reference to the current object.

- `var`—This declares and initializes a variable. It is not an error to initialize a variable, but it is bad programming practice.

- `while`—This creates a conditional loop structure that is executed as long as the condition is true.

- `with`—This allows you to specify a default object for a collection of statements.

The Firefox `window` Object

The Firefox `window` object is used to create all windows in Firefox. They can be manipulated as a whole (such as applying a theme) or individually (adding a menu item or button to one window), as the developer desires.

Take a look at Firefox's main window. It has a title bar, a menu bar, toolbars, scrollbars, status bars, and other features. When a window is created, its feature can be specified. Features are classified into three broad categories:

- **Position and size**—Enable the specification of a window's size and position.

- **Toolbars and chrome**—Control which features (as mentioned previously) the window will have.

- **Window functionalities**—Used to describe how the window will behave. These include resizing, scrollbars, and other similar functions.

A good reference on the windows object is at http://www.mozilla.org/docs/dom/domref/dom_window_ref.html.

Creating a Unique GUID

Each extension is ultimately identified by a complex number called a globally unique identifier (GUID). Any extension you write will need its own GUID, and it is best to not make one up. The reasons to have GUIDs are found in the history of software development and how components such as software interact with each other and the operating system.

As computers have become more complex, the use of names to describe unique content, features, and functionalities has become problematic. Names created by independent parties who were developing these features often were identical to names from other developers. Usually, this similarity was unintended, but the results were that Windows (and applications) often got confused as to which object was being referred to because two items had the same name.

As a solution, Microsoft created a methodology to ensure that every component had a unique name that would never be duplicated under normal circumstances. These identifiers were first used with Object Linking and Embedding (OLE) to allow objects to be embedded into documents. Each object needed a global identifier that never changed for that object (even between two computers) and was unique. Enter the GUID, a system that was initially set up by Microsoft and adopted by many others along the way.

A GUID is a 16-byte (128-bit) number. In reality, a GUID is divided into groups of 8 hexadecimal digits, 4 hexadecimal digits, 4 hexadecimal digits, 4 hexadecimal digits, and 12 hexadecimal digits. Neither the value nor the position of any part of the GUID is significant—nor is there any meaning for the groupings.

A GUID is generated, under optimal conditions, by taking the generating computer's Ethernet or Token Ring hardware address (the NIC MAC address, a value that in itself is unique to this one computer), the current time, and a pseudorandom number. All three are mixed together with a bit of programming magic to create a GUID. We are guaranteed that no two computers will have the same NIC MAC address. Even if there were to be two identical MAC addresses, it is very unlikely that both would try to generate a GUID at the same time or that the pseudo number portion would be the same. This makes GUIDs sufficiently unique so that we will never have duplicate GUIDs. There are GUID generators that do not use the NIC's MAC address; therefore, these GUIDs cannot be guaranteed to be unique. However, the likelihood of duplication is remote at best.

For example, Firefox's GUID is {ec8030f7-c20a-464f-9b0e-13a3a9e97384}. Usually an application does not change GUIDs unless it changes sufficiently that compatibility issues would result from it being confused with earlier versions of the same application.

GUID generators are available online. The website at http://www.hoskinson.net/webservices/guidgeneratorclient.aspx creates all the GUIDs you might ever want. However, should you not trust an outside source to generate your GUIDs, you can get your own GUID generator from Microsoft (GUIDGEN.EXE is part of Visual Basic 6's tools pack).

For the sample extension, GUIDGEN.EXE is used. Figure 16.11 shows the results of generating the GUID.

FIGURE 16.11

GUIDGEN can create GUIDs in four formats; we want ours in Registry Format.

The GUID shown is the one used in this chapter's example.

Firefox Command Options for Developers

Firefox offers a few command-line options. Some are useful for developers, and having shortcuts for these options can make the process of developing an extension much easier.

The following table lists Firefox startup options.

Option	Description
`-console`	Runs Firefox using the debugging console. The console provides error message output.
`-contentLocale <locale>`	Forces the locale to be the one specified in `<locale>`.
`-CreateProfile <profile>`	Creates a profile named `<profile>`.
`-h` or `-help`	Displays a list of Firefox command options.
`-height <value>`	Makes Firefox's window height equal to `<value>`. Also see `-width`.

Option	Description
`-install-global-extension </path/to/extension>`	Tells Firefox to install the extension pointed to by `</path/to/extension>` as a global (available to all users) extension.
`-install-global-theme </path/to/theme>`	Tells Firefox to install the theme pointed to by `</path/to/theme>` as a global (available to all users) theme.
`-p <profile name>`	Starts Firefox with the specified profile.
`-profile <path/to/profile>`	Starts Firefox with the profile pointed to by `<path/to/profile>`.
`-ProfileManager`	Starts Firefox with the Profile Manager.
`-ProfileWizard`	Starts Firefox with the Profile Wizard.
`-safe-mode`	Starts Firefox with all extensions disabled. This is used to recover from an extension that keeps Firefox from starting.
`-SelectProfile`	Starts Firefox, first displaying the Profile Select dialog box.
`-UILocale <locale>`	Forces the Firefox user interface to be the one for the specified locale.
`url`	Starts Firefox and displays the URL provided. This option does not use a dash prefix.
`-v or -version`	Prints the Firefox version.
`-width <value>`	Makes Firefox's window width equal to `<value>`. Also see `-height`.

Working Through an Extension Development Example

With the introduction of Firefox version 1.5, extension development has been made a bit easier. The `contents.rdf` files are gone, replaced by an easier-to-understand `chrome.manifest` file.

In the following paragraphs, you will build a simple extension that works with most versions of Firefox below version 1.5 and a second extension for Firefox version 1.5 and later. The basic functions of these two extensions are identical: You add a menu item and a call to a relatively trivial JavaScript piece of code. These examples have been kept as simple as possible, with the intention that they be easy to learn and implement. After you gain more experience, you can either add to these examples or create your own from scratch.

First, we will describe items that are common to all versions of Firefox. Following this, we will discuss the version-specific bits and pieces.

You will need a few helper batch files. One batch file will package your extension, creating your JavaScript Archive (JAR) contents file and the extension's XPI installation file. This batch file will then call another batch file that will clear Firefox's profile, restoring it to a known starting point. For extensions, the best starting point is with no extensions or themes installed.

Development Profile Save and Restore

First, start Firefox with the -profilemanager command-line option. This starts the Profile Manager. In the Profile Manager, create a new profile, naming it **Testing Profile**.

Next, set your development preferences as described previously in the section "Preferences for Extension Developers." If you want to set a home page, do so now. After your preferences (and home page, if desired) are set, exit Firefox. Some developers might want to also load the Extension Developer extension; if you do, do this before exiting Firefox. Restart Firefox and ensure that your setup is what you want and that any necessary extensions are loaded (and functional). Then exit Firefox again.

Now you will create a backup copy of your profile.

The easiest way to back up your profile is to open a Windows Explorer window and navigate to Firefox's profiles folder (for example, in Windows XP, it's Documents and Settings\user-id\Application Data\Mozilla\Firefox\Profiles). Right-click the profile you created—there should be only one profile at this point if you have started with a clean Firefox installation and deleted any preexisting profiles. Next, drop it in the same folder and select Copy Here from the pop-up context menu Windows Explorer displays. You will then have a second copy of the profile with an additional extension of .bak added to the profile's name. Make a note of this backup copy's name. Now repeat the copy again and save the third copy with the extension .backup. This third copy is your emergency recovery copy.

Next, you need to configure a development folder.

The Development Folders

You must create a folder to hold your new extension. Although you probably will develop your extension by using an existing extension as a foundation to build upon, let's take a look at what the folder structure for this sample extension looks like.

Chapter 16 | Writing an Extension

NOTE

There is nothing to say that your extension can not have more folders than those described here. However, most extensions have these two subfolders as a minimum. As well, none of the folder names are absolute—you can use other names if you want. The names given here are simply those used by many developers of Firefox extensions.

CAUTION

Windows programmers are used to having filenames and folder names that are not case specific. So, for a Windows programmer, MyExtension is the same as myExtension and myextension. However, Firefox might not always be so forgiving. A good rule of thumb is to be case conscious when working with Firefox extensions.

MyExtension's Root Folder

Your new extension needs a name. I've picked the name MyExtension as the name for the extension. After you have a name for the extension picked out, the extension will need a home. The name for this top-level folder is not critical. Other subfolder names will be significant, but the topmost level folder can have any convenient name, usually the same name as your extension.

In My Documents, I created my MyExtension folder. In this folder we need two subfolders. The first is named content, and the second is called chrome. We now have these folders:

- MyExtension
- MyExtension\content
- MyExtension\chrome

Contained in the root folder will be two or three project files: the install.rdf file, the extension's .xpi file, and (for Firefox 1.5 and later) the chrome.manifest file.

content

The content folder is where you will put your working copies of the extension's files.

In MyExtension the three files in the contents folder are

- contents.rdf (for versions of Firefox before 1.5)
- myextension-Overlay.xul
- myextensionOverlay.js

More complex extensions will have more files in the contents folder.

chrome

The chrome folder will hold the extension's JAR file. Most extension developers use the chrome folder only to hold the JAR file, and nothing else. However, this name is significant to Firefox, so you should not put your JAR file anywhere else.

Extension Files

With the folders created, next you need a few files. Your extension is rather simple, so you only have a few files that must be created for it.

`extension.XPI`, the Extension Distribution File

All extensions are distributed using XPI files. The definition of an XPI file is that it is a Mozilla extension distribution file, although that tells little of what it really is.

XPI files are, for all intents and purposes, simply renamed Zip files. You can create them in several ways. My method uses the WinZip command-line interface driven by a batch file. (I will go more into depth regarding this batch file later in this chapter.)

Contained in the XPI file will be a minimum of two files:

- The `install.rdf` file that describes to Firefox the extension
- The extension's JAR (JavaScript Archive) file
- For versions of Firefox from 1.5 onward, the `chrome.manifest` file

More complex extensions might have other files that are used as part of the installation process. An example is the Google Bar extension that also has `install.js` and `googlebar.js`.

All the root files in the XPI file are used for the extension's installation. The extension's actual functionality is always contained within the JAR file.

The following paragraphs cover the contents of the XPI file for this chapter's extension project (see Figure 16.12).

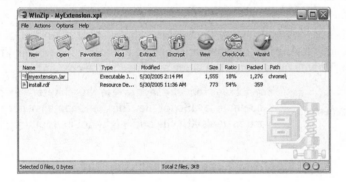

FIGURE 16.12

This extension has only `install.rdf` *and the extension's JAR file for contents.*

`extension.jar`, the Extension's JAR File

Contained within the extension's JAR file are all the files that make up the extension. Some of the files often found in a JAR file include XUL, RDF, JavaScript, and various image files.

The files contained in this extension's JAR file are shown in Figure 16.13.

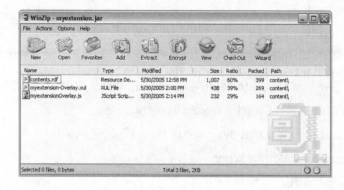

FIGURE 16.13

The JAR file contains the actual extension's working code.

There will be two or three files in the JAR:

- contents.rdf—This file contains information about the extension. This file is required, with this name. Contained in the contents.rdf file is an extension description and the extension's internal name. This file also contains information regarding the extension's XUL file. This file should be found only in extensions for Firefox versions 1.0.x and earlier.

- myextension-Overlay.xul—Contained in the myextension-Overlay.xul file are instructions telling Firefox what functionality the extension will modify or enhance. This file's name must match the name specified in the contents.rdf file.

- myextensionOverlay.js—In this chapter's extension, there is a simple JavaScript file. This file's name is specified in the extension's XUL file and might not be found in every extension.

> **NOTE**
>
> The makexpi.bat file depends on WinZip and the command-line interface. Both are available at the WinZip website (http://www.winzip.com). By default, WinZip and the command-line interface, wzzip.exe, are installed in C:\program files\winzip. If you want to use another Zip-type program, such as TUGZip, makexpi.bat must be modified accordingly.

Other Files for Extension Developers

A few other files can be used to streamline the extension packaging process. If you want to use it, the Extension Developer extension also provides this functionality.

The first supporting file is named makexpi.bat (see Listing 16.2). This is a command batch file that calls the command-line version of WinZip to create both the JAR file and the XPI file. Optionally, this batch file can do other cleanup tasks as well. Comments have been added to this file to make its function clearer.

LISTING 16.2 THE makexpi.bat FILE

```
@echo off

If X%1 == Xhelp (
Echo makexpi [firefox]
Echo where specifying firefox builds for Firefox 1.1.x and later.
Echo if no parameter is specified this will build
Echo a Firefox version 1.0.x and earlier
Echo extension.
goto end
)

REM the debug.txt file holds the output from all the commands.
REM This keeps execution cleaner.
time /T >debug.txt

REM - Create the JAR file first. WinZip will add or create as
➥necessary.

echo Refreshing the JAR file! >>debug.txt
REM This line is for versions of Firefox 1.0.x and earlier.

If X%1 == Xfirefox (
    "%programfiles%\WinZip\wzzip" -a -r -P chrome\myextension.jar
➥content\myextensionOverlay.js
➥content\myextension-Overlay.xul >>debug.txt
) else (
    "%programfiles%\WinZip\wzzip" -a -r -P
➥chrome\myextension.jar content >>debug.txt
)

REM - Build the XPI file
echo Refreshing the XPI file! >>debug.txt

If X%1 == Xfirefox (
"%programfiles%\WinZip\wzzip" -a -r -P MyExtension.xpi
➥chrome\myextension.jar chrome.manifest
➥install.rdf >>debug.txt
) else (
"%programfiles%\WinZip\wzzip" -a -r -P MyExtension.xpi
➥chrome\myextension.jar install.rdf >>debug.txt
)

REM - Tell when this build was made

echo Desplaying the timestamp! >>debug.txt
Echo Generate time was
```

LISTING 16.2   CONTINUED

```
type time.txt

REM - Restore profile to clean version

echo Refreshing the Firefox profile! >>debug.txt

call clearprofile.bat

Rem bailout on help and errors label
:end
```

In Listing 16.3, you must change the parts in **bold** to whatever filenames you want for your extension.

LISTING 16.3   THE clearprofile.bat FILE

```
@echo off

Rem you *must* fix the profile name below (in bold) to match your
➥profile name!

RD /s /q "%appdata%\Mozilla\Firefox\Profiles\jvaofcos.Testing Profile"
MD ""%appdata%\Mozilla\Firefox\Profiles\jvaofcos.Testing Profile"
xcopy /s /y ""%appdata%\Mozilla\Firefox\Profiles\jvaofcos.Testing
➥Profile.bak"
➥"%appdata%\Mozilla\Firefox\Profiles\jvaofcos.Testing Profile"
>>debug.txt
```

In Listing 16.3, you must change jvaofcos.Testing Profile to reflect the name of the Firefox profile you created for testing and debugging purposes.

An Extension for Firefox 1.0.x

Firefox 1.0.x represents versions of Firefox before 1.5. Some users have not switched to Firefox 1.5 due to concerns that their favorite extensions and themes will not be compatible with the newer version.

Firefox 1.0.x does not support the chrome.manifest format (we'll talk about chrome.manifest later). Thus, any extension for these platforms require the more complex contents.rdf file. This makes these extensions slightly more complex.

First, for your extension, you will create some folders. The first folder will be the extension's root folder. In the extension root folder, you will create two additional folders, chrome and content.

In this example, you have to create or modify four files: `install.rdf`, `contents.rdf`, `myextension-Overlay.xul`, and `myextensionOverlay.js`. I've listed each of these files in the following sections, showing the parts that are relatively generic and those areas that you'd rewrite or enhance for your extension.

install.rdf

The `install.rdf` file is the file Firefox uses to install the extension (see Listing 16.4). This file describes the extension and provides Firefox with the name and location for the extension's JAR file.

LISTING 16.4   install.rdf

```
<?xml version="1.0"?>

<RDF xmlns="http://www.w3.org/1999/02/22-rdf-syntax-ns#"
     xmlns:em="http://www.mozilla.org/2004/em-rdf#">

  <Description about="urn:mozilla:install-manifest">
    <em:id>{71536D06-A8BD-411a-BC0C-15C1FDB7DF2A}</em:id>
    <em:version>0.1.05</em:version>
    <em:targetApplication>
      <Description>
        <em:id>{ec8030f7-c20a-464f-9b0e-13a3a9e97384}</em:id>
        <em:minVersion>0.9</em:minVersion>
        <em:maxVersion>1.0</em:maxVersion>
      </Description>
    </em:targetApplication>
    <em:name>My Extension</em:name>
    <em:file>
      <Description about="urn:mozilla:extension:file:myextension.jar">
        <em:package>content/</em:package>
      </Description>
    </em:file>
  </Description>
</RDF>
```

In the `install.rdf` file, you must provide a new GUID for your extension. My GUID was `71536D06-A8BD-411a-BC0C-15C1FDB7DF2A`, and it is in bold in the listing. Please don't just change a few numbers trying to make your own GUID; use a generator as described previously to make a new GUID.

The `minVersion` and `maxVersion` need to be changed to reflect for which versions of Firefox your extension is designed. The defaults in Listing 16.4 are what you should use for versions of Firefox before 1.5.

MOZILLA VERSION NUMBERS

Mozilla uses a multipart version number. The version number has four parts, followed by an optional plus sign. Extension and theme developers frequently need to specify which versions of Firefox their extension or theme will work with. The version number format is

WW[.XX[.YY[.ZZ]]][+]

Each part has a meaning:

- **WW**—The major release number. For Firefox, the major release is 1.

- **XX**—The optional minor release number.

- **YY**—The optional release number.

- **ZZ**—The optional build number.

- **+**—From the development period between releases.

Each of these must be a number; no alphabetic characters are allowed in the version number. Only the major release number is required—all other parts are optional. If a part is missing, no attempt is made to match that part.

The plus sign signifies that the extension is from the development period between releases of Firefox.

The name My Extension should be changed to the name of your extension. Spaces are acceptable, and no quotation marks are needed.

The JAR filename, myextension, must be the same as the JAR file created by makexpi.bat.

Everything else in install.rdf should remain the same.

contents.rdf

The contents.rdf file needs some modifications, as shown in Listing 16.5.

LISTING 16.5   contents.rdf

```
<?xml version="1.0"?>
<RDF:RDF xmlns:RDF="http://www.w3.org/1999/02/22-rdf-syntax-ns#"
     xmlns:chrome="http://www.mozilla.org/rdf/chrome#">

  <RDF:Seq about="urn:mozilla:package:root">
    <RDF:li resource="urn:mozilla:package:myextension"/>
```

LISTING 16.5   CONTINUED

```
    </RDF:Seq>

    <RDF:Description about="urn:mozilla:package:myextension"
      chrome:displayName="My Extension"
      chrome:author="Peter D. Hipson"
      chrome:authorURL="http://www.hipson.net"
      chrome:name="myextension"
      chrome:extension="true"
      chrome:settingsURL="chrome://myextension/content/settings/
    ➥settings.xul"
      chrome:description="Add a menu item to Files in Firefox.">
    </RDF:Description>


    <RDF:Seq about="urn:mozilla:overlays">
      <RDF:li resource="chrome://browser/content/browser.xul"/>
    </RDF:Seq>

    <!-- overlay information for Mozilla Firebird-->
    <RDF:Seq about="chrome://browser/content/browser.xul">
      <RDF:li>chrome://myextension/content/
    ➥myextension-Overlay.xul</RDF:li>
    </RDF:Seq>
</RDF:RDF>
```

In Listing 16.5, the lines starting with chrome: should be changed as appropriate. The chrome:name value should match the name in chrome:settingsURL and in the chrome://myextension line.

The myextension-Overlay name should match the name of your extension's XUL file. Mozilla conventions say that overlay should be part of the name.

myextension-Overlay.xul

You need to modify the myextension-Overlay.xul file as shown in Listing 16.6. This filename needs to match the name in the contents.rdf file (refer to Listing 16.5). This file is identical for all versions of Firefox.

LISTING 16.6   myextension-Overlay.xul

```
<?xml version="1.0"?>

<overlay id="MyExtensionOverlay"

xmlns="http://www.mozilla.org/keymaster/gatekeeper/there.is.only.xul">
```

LISTING 16.6 CONTINUED

```
// Include the Javascript

<script type="application/x-javascript"
src="chrome://myextension/content/myextensionOverlay.js">
</script>

<menupopup id="menu_FilePopup">
  <menuitem label="My Extension" position="1" oncommand=
  ➥"myextensionmessage();" />
</menupopup>
</overlay>
```

In the myextension-Overlay.xul file, you must give the overlay a name. Change MyExtensionOverlay to a name that suits your extension's name.

In the chrome: line, the myextension should be changed to match the chrome:name in the contents.rdf file.

The menuitem line needs to reflect whatever chrome changes your extension is doing. I'm adding a menu item, but you might be doing something different. The myextensionmessage() call to JavaScript must match your JavaScript functions, if you use JavaScript, or whatever way you choose to add functionality to the menu item.

myextensionOverlay.js

The myextension.js file contains the JavaScript code to give my extension its functionality (see Listing 16.7). In the listing, you would rename it to match the name in the myextension.xul file. This extension is trivial—it just displays a message box using the JavaScript alert() function call. This file is the same for all versions of myextension.

LISTING 16.7 myextension.js

```
// An example of some JavaScript functionality.
// You could code virtually any functionalty that
// JavaScript supports here:

function myextensionmessage() {

    alert("        ...and, it worked!        ");

}
```

If you decide to use JavaScript in your extension, you could use this file to hold your JavaScript functionality. As extensions grow more complex, additional JavaScript source files might need to be added.

An Extension for Firefox 1.5

Firefox 1.5 and later versions are compatible with extensions written for earlier versions of Firefox. However, it is best to adhere to the new extension conventions as described here.

In this sample extension, both `myextension.js` and `myextension-Overlay.xul` won't change based on versions of Firefox. For the contents of these two files, refer to the previous section.

In addition to these two files, two other files exist in the Firefox 1.5 version of this sample extension. One file (`install.rdf`) will be modified, whereas the other (`chrome.manifest`) will be added to your extension. The file `contents.rdf` is no longer used. If Firefox finds a `contents.rdf` file and does not find `chrome.manifest` (for example, an old extension written for earlier versions of Firefox), a `chrome.manifest` file is created from the `contents.rdf` file.

install.rdf

Because some of the changes to `install.rdf` will be new even to experienced extension writers, let's cover them in detail. First, Listing 16.8 shows the new `install.rdf` file.

Most of the changes in `install.rdf` involve the addition of lines and some minor rearranging of content.

LISTING 16.8 install.rdf

```
<?xml version="1.0"?>

<RDF xmlns="http://www.w3.org/1999/02/22-rdf-syntax-ns#"
     xmlns:em="http://www.mozilla.org/2004/em-rdf#">

  <Description about="urn:mozilla:install-manifest">
    <em:id>{71536D06-A8BD-411a-BC0C-15C1FDB7DF2A}</em:id>
    <em:version>0.1.05</em:version>
    <em:targetApplication>
      <Description>
        <em:id>{ec8030f7-c20a-464f-9b0e-13a3a9e97384}</em:id>
        <em:minVersion>1.0</em:minVersion>
        <em:maxVersion>1.5+</em:maxVersion>
      </Description>
    </em:targetApplication>
```

Listing 16.8 Continued

```
<!-- Front End MetaData -->
<em:name>My Extension</em:name>
<em:creator>Peter D. Hipson</em:creator>
<em:description>Add a menu item to Files in Firefox.
➥</em:description>
<em:homepageURL>http://www.hipson.net</em:homepageURL>
<em:updateURL>http://www.hipson.net</em:updateURL>

<em:file>
   <Description about="urn:mozilla:extension:file:myextension.jar">
      <em:package>content/</em:package>
   </Description>
</em:file>
   </Description>
</RDF>
```

In addition to the name and GUID changes outlined in Listing 16.8, in versions of Firefox earlier than 1.5, you need to make the following changes to your install.rdf file.

You should create a new section, preceded by the following comment line:

```
<!-- Front End MetaData -->
```

This comment indicates that data for your extension follows. Next, add four lines that take data that was in your contents.rdf file and place them in install.rdf. The format of the lines will change—we are only interested in the extension-specific data that has been highlighted in the listing.

The <em:name>My Extension</em:name> remains the same as the previous example:

```
<em:creator>Peter D. Hipson</em:creator>
```

The em:creator line takes the data that was in the contents.rdf file's chrome:author line. No quotes are needed for this field:

```
<em:description>Add a menu item to Files in Firefox.
➥</em:description>
```

The em:description line takes the description that was in the chrome:description line in the contents.rdf file:

```
<em:homepageURL>http://www.hipson.net</em:homepageURL>
```

The data in em:homepageURL is the chrome:authorURL data from contents.rdf:

```
<em:updateURL>http://www.hipson.net</em:updateURL>
```

The `em:updateURL` data was not present in the sample `contents.rdf` file and simply specifies where to look for updates to this extension.

chrome.manifest

The `chrome.manifest` file is new to Firefox 1.5 (see Listing 16.9). It is intended to replace the complex and often problematic `contents.rdf` file with something that's easier to work with.

This file, in this example, has just two lines, making it considerably shorter than `contents.rdf`. The file is a simple text format, created with Notepad or your favorite text editor.

LISTING 16.9 chrome.manifest

```
overlay chrome://browser/content/browser.xul chrome://myextension/
➥content/myextension-Overlay.xul
content myextension jar:chrome/myextension.jar!/content/
```

A `chrome.manifest` file has, at a minimum, the lines shown in Listing 16.9. Some additional lines might be present in a more complex extension's `chrome.manifest` file.

These potential lines are listed in the following, along with a description. Compare these specification lines with the lines in Listing 16.9 to see how the parameters would change. Items in bold would change to match your extension.

The content package line describes the extension (`packagename`) and the location of the extension's JAR (or other content) file:

```
content packagename path/to/files
```

In the `chrome.manifest` file, the `path/to/files` was `jar:chrome/myextension.jar!/content/`. The exclamation point after the JAR file's extension is required, so don't forget it.

The locale package line specifies the locale name and the path to that locale's files. This line is required in `chrome.manifest`:

```
locale packagename localename path/to/files
```

An example of this line is `locale myextension en-US jar:en-US.jar!/locale/en-US/myextension`. In this example, `en-US` is the locale identifier for English in the United States. The `en-US.jar` file is the JAR file containing elements specific to the locale and the location in that JAR file of the necessary content. This file is optional in `chrome.manifest`.

The skin package line specifies the extension's skin (think theme) location. Again, it includes the package name and a path to files that would be similar to that in the previous examples:

```
skin packagename skinname path/to/files
```

The XUL overlay package line specifies the extension's XUL overlay's location. There is a path to the chrome for this extension:

```
overlay chrome://file-to-overlay chrome://overlay-file
```

An example of this line from `chrome.manifest` is

```
overlay chrome://browser/content/browser.xul chrome://myextension/
➥content/myextension-Overlay.xul
```

This code gives the information provided in the `contents.rdf` file's overlay section.

Many extensions modify the Cascading Style Sheets (CSS) used by Firefox. The style overlay line provides this information in a format similar to the previous overlay line:

```
style chrome://file-to-style chrome://stylesheet-file
```

Firefox is a multiplatform product, meaning it will run on Windows, Linux, and Mac OS/X. If your extension is specific to one of these platforms, add the keyword `platform` at the end of the `content` lines.

More complex extensions have multiple occurrences of these lines in `chrome.manifest`. If you want to learn more about `chrome.manifest`, go to http://www.mozilla.org/xpfe/ConfigChromeSpec.html.

Extension Writing Secrets for Power Users

Here are a few ideas from the experts:

- To prepare for extension developing, it is important to set up the development environment. A clean (new) installation of Firefox, with a clean (never used) profile, can make debugging much easier.

- Some preferences make extension development much easier. These, used in conjunction with Firefox command-line options, make testing easier.

- A number of extensions have been created just to help others create their extensions. One notable extension is the Extension Developer extension.

- Firefox has a debugging console that is displayed when Firefox is started with the `-console` option.

- Developers can set an environment variable to allow multiple instances of Firefox to run. Normally, Firefox runs only one instance (copy) at a time.

- Programs and objects are uniquely identified using a GUID. There are programs to create GUIDs and websites that will create GUIDs online.

- Understanding Firefox command options is important for developers. Having shortcut icons on the desktop preconfigured for these options lets you easily launch Firefox with an option.

- Extensions have a basic arrangement and names for the extension's folders. Following these conventions makes an extension's development easier.

- The `chrome.manifest` file is new to Firefox 1.5. This file is designed to replace the `contents.rdf` file with a file that is easier to work with.

The Way of Mozilla for Programmers

The Mozilla suite includes a number of tools developers can use to create their own builds of Firefox and Thunderbird. Because they're open-source applications, any programmer can work with the code, report bugs, and get involved with the overall Mozilla organization.

Find out more about these tools and what's due in future versions of Firefox and Thunderbird in three bonus chapters on our website: http://www.quepublishing.com/title/0789734583. On this page you can also download a glossary of new terms used throughout the book.

Part V

INDEX